Drama and the South African state

CULTURAL POLITICS

All available from Manchester University Press

Drama and the South African state

Martin Orkin

MANCHESTER UNIVERSITY PRESS
MANCHESTER and NEW YORK

WITWATERSRAND UNIVERSITY PRESS
JOHANNESBURG

distributed in the USA and Canada by ST. MARTIN'S PRESS, New York

Published by Manchester University Press
Oxford Road, Manchester M13 9PL, UK
and Room 400, 175 Fifth Avenue,
New York, NY 10010, USA
and in the Republic of South Africa
by Witwatersrand University Press,
1 Jan Smuts Avenue, Johannesburg 2001, South Africa

Distributed exclusively in the USA and Canada
by St. Martin's Press, Inc.,
175 Fifth Avenue, New York, NY 10010, USA

British Library cataloguing in publication data
Orkin, Martin
    Drama and the South African state. – (Cultural politics).
    1. South Africa. Theatre. Political aspects
    I. Title II. Series
    792.0968

Library of Congress cataloging in publication data
Orkin, Martin.
        Drama and the South African State / Martin Orkin.
            p. cm. – (Cultural politics)
        Includes index.
        ISBN 0-7190-2576-1. – ISBN 0-7190-2577-X (pbk.)
            1. South African drama (English) – History and criticism.
        2. South African drama – History and criticism. 3. Literature and
        state – South Africa. 4. Theatre and state – South Africa.
        I. Title. II. Series.
        PR8361.2.O75   1991
        822 – dc20   90-6556   70930 / PR
                                                    9361.2
                                                    .O75
                                                    1991
ISBN 0 7190 2576 1 hardback
      0 7190 2577 X paperback

South African ISBN: 1 86814 194 2 paperback

Typeset in Joanna
by Koinonia Limited, Manchester
Printed in Great Britain
by Bell & Bain Limited, Glasgow

Contents

Acknowledgements

I should like to thank Athol Fugard, Matsemela Manaka, Maishe Maponya, Julius Mtsaka and Mbongeni Ngema for their generosity with their time in discussing their work with me. Martin Chanock and Isobel Hofmeyr read parts of the manuscript and I thank them for their astute and generous criticism. I also thank the Reader at Manchester University Press for the care with which the whole manuscript was read and for the immensely useful advice I received. I thank the University of the Witwatersrand for granting me a year's sabbatical to prepare for this book. The financial assistance of the Institute for Research and Development of the Human Sciences Research Council towards this research is also hereby acknowledged. Opinions expressed in this publication and conclusions arrived at, are those of the author and are not necessarily to be attributed to the Institute for Research Development or the Human Sciences Research Council. I thank too David Kramer and Taliep Peterson, Matsemela Manaka, Maishe Maponya and Mbongeni Ngema for providing me with copies of unpublished scripts. Tim Couzens and Ian Steadman have given me continuing support and encouragement. I owe a debt of gratitude also to Jonathan Dollimore and Alan Sinfield for first encouraging me to write this book, for their kindness and for the continuing example and stimulation their work provides. And I am indebted to John Banks for his inestimably warm support, assistance and encouragement. Finally I thank my beloved parents Jenny and Morris Orkin as always. This book is dedicated to the three people who help me most.

again to Joan, to Chloë and to Mikhail

INTRODUCTION

Theatre of the suppressed

When on 19 May 1988, in the South African Houses of Parliament, the then Minister of Home Affairs turned his attention to those people who in his estimation 'under the banner of art and literary merits wanted to bypass the Publications Act', a major instrument of censorship in South Africa,[1] *The Star* newspaper reported his comments as follows:

This was an attack on the interests which the Act was intended to protect, namely the morality, religion and dignity of South Africans and the safety of the State. In certain communities, spontaneous theatre was used to agitate the audience. He said: 'When the show ends, the audience is so emotionally charged that they will not calm down before everything in the vicinity, from buildings to cars and even other people, have been attacked.' It was impossible to control this form of theatre. Mr Botha added: 'It should never be doubted that it is a matter of great importance for the State to protect the spiritual and moral welfare of the community, and to maintain the necessary equilibrium between the freedom of the individual and the interests of the community.' He said the State would not interfere with the moral function of parents, educationists and the Church – but it would defend and protect proper Christian norms acknowledged by all population and religious groups.[2]

The Minister spoke as South Africa was about to enter the third year of a national emergency. The government was grappling to assert its authority and to control a social order that for several years – rather than months – was experiencing contestation and struggle on a scale that exceeded even that initiated a decade or so earlier by the 1976 Uprising. Furthermore, his threats were, potentially, not without substance. Theatre practitioners in the apartheid state, especially in the last three decades, have been subject to a variety of pressures including not only intimidation and banning but detention and worse. Perhaps the most notorious and tragic example of this involves a play called *Shanti*. Its author, Mthuli Shezi was elected Vice President of the Black Peoples Convention in July 1972, but died in December of the same year. He was pushed in front of an oncoming train at the Germiston station during a scuffle with Germiston railway policemen. The play was banned and when Sadacque Variava, Solly Ismael and Nomsisi

Kraai, members of the group that produced his play, were arrested and charged under the Terrorism Act in 1975, *Shanti* was appended to the charge sheet as an example of an 'anti-white, racialistic, subversive and/or revolutionary' drama.[3]

The attempt to engage with the social order, the presentation of the subject within the South African space on stage, has never been easy. Overt government and ruling class interference in dramatic practice in South Africa is only one of several factors that have worked right until the end of the 1980s towards its suppression. Plays have been and still are performed in the context of relentless processes of industrialisation and capitalism coupled with the steady determination on the part of ruling classes and groups to obfuscate and marginalise awareness not only of relations of domination and subordination, but of material conditions, the very existence of the subordinate classes. Government control of television and radio broadcasting, control of newspapers by the ruling classes and widespread legislation on censorship, has been and remains extensive and pervasive.[4] Drama practitioners have often to struggle against and to contest, not only the communications media, but those discourses which, privileged by the apartheid state and the ruling classes, flow powerfully through cultural, educational and social institutions. The ruling settler classes in South Africa have always comprised many more members than, as was the case elsewhere in Africa, a more uniform colonial presence (predominantly British, French, Belgian or German). They include Afrikaners, the British, non-British Europeans, North Americans and East Europeans. But the importance, in the dominant institutions of the country, of British cultural influence – as the century unfolds second only to the impact of Afrikaner Nationalism – results not only from British conquests of the South African terrain at crucial moments in its history, but from the subsequent enormous and continuing investment of British capital in South Africa. The growth of South African drama entails too, therefore, a continuing struggle against the dominance of a British colonial and imperial centre, compounded in the post-colonial period by the powerful influence of the emergent North American metropolis.

Such factors collude in the processes of suppression, providing obstacles to the production of plays as well as their publication, while attendant academic neglect of the study of indigenous plays has begun to be challenged only recently. I will deal with each of these problems in turn.

I Drama and the discourses of the apartheid state

The title of this book mentions 'drama' rather than 'theatre' because it deals mostly with those South African plays, in variants of English, that have been published. Some of these plays, particularly before the 1960s, were written as much to be read as for performance. They are always plays that are located within the South African social formation and understood, in the attempt to constitute or achieve meaning, in different ways to mirror or represent past or present history, interrogate or explore it, in fictive or other terms. The concerns such plays address, will be, as in any drama, always varied; but these concerns have in common the fact that they are located in or engaged in some way with the South African process. Whether this is an engagement with past events in South African history, or a representational or fictive version of current experience in the South African context, what a play chooses to focus on, what it attempts to understand through dramatic discourse, may be seen as, always, an activity located within history.

Inevitably, such plays often come into conflict with prevailing discourse within the South African state; those discourses privileged by the ruling classes. The human being is regarded in this book as in part at least the subject of discourse as well as familial and social practice or, again, material conditions. I do not intend to imply by this, however, that the subject can ever be unified, for each subject may be thought to be itself a composite of multiple, intersecting, often conflicting or contradictory and changing subjectivities. When this book refers to the construction of the subject in particular plays, then, it attempts to single out particularly dominant emphases in the presentation of those subjects on stage, but this should never be taken as implying that the subject has lost manifold complexities.

'Discourse', we may recall, has been defined as 'a linguistic unity or group of statements which constitutes and delimits a particular area of concern, governed by its own rules of formation and its own modes of distinguishing truth from reality'.[5] Accordingly, we may also note,

the discourse within which we make an utterance determines to a large extent the nature of the connections we can make between ideas; it determines, for example, what can stand as the cause of an effect, and what can be claimed to be the effect of a given cause. *Thus it determines what can be said within it, about, for example, what it is to be human or the nature of social experience*(my emphasis).[6]

As he utters his threats to theatre practitioners, the Minister of Home Affairs posits something unchanging and universal, something naturalised and exclusive, about the particular moral and religious discourses towards which he gestures. But he speaks a language that indicates or reveals the underlying hegemonic project of his government, one that works to legitimate and naturalise those discourses privileged by the ruling classes and to marginalise and render peripheral all other discourses that might challenge it. His language needs to be perceived, like everything else in twentieth-century South Africa and earlier, within the context of 'the lived relations of paternalism which bound black and white together' and which have always 'presented white supremacy as part of the natural order of things in its (im)moral universe'.[7] Although he condemns that theatre which, according to him, endeavouring to engage with the South African social formation attacks 'morality' and 'religion','the dignity of South Africans', and 'the safety of the state', the particular discourses he has in mind include versions of Afrikaner Calvinism and nationalism, within which are imbricated racist investment in white supremacy. And it is in the name of such discourses, often the discourses of erstwhile colonisers as well as the present rulers of South Africa, that he presents himself as guardian of the 'spiritual and moral welfare of the community', preserver of the 'necessary equilibrium between the freedom of the individual and the interests of the community' and defender of 'the proper Christian norms acknowledged by all populations and religious groups'.

Implicit in the Minister's language is a claim to an absolutist and universal knowledge of 'truth', 'reality' and 'order' to which everyone in the state should 'naturally' be subject. But work on discourse decades before his outburst has long since argued that there are no completely authoritative unchanging qualities to be found either in people or in the social order. On the contrary, often 'the qualities that human beings express are ... culturally constructed, and furthermore are constructed within language'.[8] Vološinov, early in the twentieth century, stressing that 'utterance ... is constructed between two socially organised persons', that the 'word is oriented toward an addressee' and that 'there can be no such thing as an abstract addressee, a man (sic) unto himself, so to speak ... with such a person, we would indeed have no language in common, literally and figuratively',[9] argues that in our use of language we presuppose a certain typical and stabilised *social purview* toward which the ideological creativity of our own social group and time is oriented, i.e., we assume as our addressee a contemporary of our literature, our science, our moral and legal codes. (pp. 85-6)

In terms of this, social groups, social groups within institutions, or the institutions to which people belong will often share the same social purview or operate within the same discourse. Discourse may often be identified, consequently, by the 'institutions to which it relates and by the position from which it comes and which it marks out for the speaker'.[10] Thus, if we reiterate that in twentieth-century South Africa the social formation has been notoriously segregationist, in terms of this view of language and discourse we may also argue that those discourses which have prevailed within governmental, educational and other official institutions, have constructed not only the human being, but, for instance, versions of the body, the land or the social order in particular ways.

But as Macdonell amongst others observes, the position marked out by any particular discourse 'does not exist by itself...indeed, it may be understood as a standpoint taken up by the discourse through its relation to another, ultimately an opposing discourse...any discourse concerns itself with certain objects and puts forward certain concepts at the expense of others' (p. 3). Inevitably, in the South African social order, as elsewhere, the dominance of certain discourses within state institutions and dominant social groups works against other discourses which endeavour to construct different versions of reality. Especially when people occupy different positions within relations of power they are not often likely to share the same social purview. Because of the dialogic nature of drama, much South African drama inevitably presents or raises that which the Minister of Home Affairs in the apartheid state most fears, sites of conflict between different discourses where agents of the state endeavour to legislate for, prescribe and demand, often threateningly, uniformity, and conformity to the discourses of apartheid only. Moreover, in South African theatre, which entails at the least acts of utterance devised by dramatic practitioners and performed within spaces populated by audiences, the participants are also often multi-positioned within the relations of power in the social order and so themselves draw upon different discourses. Discursive struggle of one kind or another will almost always therefore be part of the theatrical endeavour.

No doubt it is this that drew the Minister's ire in his warning to drama practitioners, but it is worth noting that he delivered it during 1988, in a context in which, as a result of a continuing and brutal police presence in South African townships, township theatre had been largely disabled. Moreover his sudden concern over the activities of theatre practitioners could hardly have included those occurring in the, by then, well-established and always peaceful Market Theatre Complex, patronised and supported, often predominantly, by members of the affluent ruling classes and situated at the heart of the mostly empty-by-night metropolitan Johannesburg. A certain opportunity in over-statement was here clearly being seized upon by this agent of the apartheid state in order to further the state's hegemonic thrust. But it is true that if the subversive tendencies of theatre can often be contained, as they arguably were at the time of the Minister's speech, theatre remains always potentially potent. The subversive power of theatre has perhaps been most overtly evident in South African theatrical history in the period immediately preceding the 1976 uprising. Nevertheless, the production by the Minister of an allegedly active subversive theatrical element at the time of his speaking when theatre, particularly in the townships, was no longer operating as it had done a decade or so earlier, may be seen as part of well-established ruling class practice in the 1980s and before in South Africa – one that actively creates, in the name of its preferred discourses, difference and subversion in order to justify a continuing state of emergency and the often ferocious modes of repression accompanying it.

II Early South African drama as means of control: The light

Andrew Geddes Bain's *Kaatje Kekkelbek, or life among the Hottentots* was performed in 1838 by the Graham's Town Amateur Company and is perhaps one of the earliest known plays produced in South Africa attempting to locate itself within the periphery.[11] Kaatje Kekkelbek is a Hottentot who speaks a creolised language that incorporates English, Dutch and indigenous languages and in his work Bains also attempts a measure of social satire. Again, in the early decades of the twentieth century, Stephen Black, encouraged by Rudyard Kipling, dramatised and satirised Cape social behaviour and referred to current social and political issues in a series of plays which were extremely popular.[12] Black attempted too to reflect the mixed language usage of early twentieth-century South Africa. But none of these plays was published at the time of performance, and they remained in manuscript form to be rediscovered by a present-day scholar, some of them eventually only belatedly appearing in published form. Potentially important early attempts at the displacement of the colonial centre, they had little or no practical influence beyond perhaps encouraging those who had participated in productions to continue with work in theatre.

In the early twentieth century, a more influential beginning, albeit perhaps inadvertent, of an awareness of the need for an effective relationship between self and place within the periphery rather than in relation to the colonial centre, may be traced to the missionary use of drama in education. To propagate their beliefs missionaries utilised not only staged versions of biblical teaching but didactic plays which they located within a South African place. At Marianhill in the 1920s, Father Bernard Huss had argued that religious and moral instruction, crucial in the socialisation of those individuals subject to missionary influence, could be aided by suitable theatre: 'Drama of high character provides an excellent and instructive recreation'.[13] He encouraged and participated in the production of – as well as religious plays – comedies and dramatisations of Zulu narratives. But such work, although it was sometimes located within the periphery, continued to communicate or reproduce colonial discourse which often presented the South African ruling classes, and particularly their preferred religious discourses, as the bringers of civilisation and order to an otherwise barbaric people.

A significant example of this use of theatre may be found in one of the earliest published plays in English located in the Southern African context, The light, by Mary Waters. She was a young woman of missionary stock who studied at St Andrews in Scotland and who then spent most of her life in education in South Africa. The light, her first play, was published in 1924.[14] According to James Henderson, who wrote the Preface, it resulted from the attraction of many missionaries 'to the idea of teaching religious history and Christian ethics by means of stage-plays, as, they remember, was a method of the early Church in Europe' (preface; no pagination). But where Waters's play is concerned, the history in question is black history rather than religious history, although the play attempts to mystify and spiritualise the conquest of the black inhabitants of South Africa by white invaders. As Henderson has it:

This 'Drama of the Light' embodies the story of the incoming of Christianity and of Christian civilisation among the southern Bantu, presenting their tribal struggles, after the manner of Greek tragedy, as the outcome of an omnipotent purpose directing human destinies to its own end; and it is written in the spirit of one who understands Native feeling sympathetically and can interpret their aspirations (preface).

In this, The light may be said to privilege essentialist and idealist discourse. Essentialism involves the notion that the essence of the human being is 'presocial', 'invested with quasi-spiritual autonomy' and, transcending history and society, to be found in religion.[15] In idealism, we may note, ideas are supposed to be fundamental whether these 'are the divine or universal Idea or Ideas, or the constitutive ideas of human consciousness'.[16] But the play suggests discursive struggle as well because, in its didactic thrust, it appears actively to direct itself against certain discourses and events current within the social order at the time of its appearance. It was published in the aftermath of industrial and political ferment in South Africa which had included a passive resistance campaign against certain pass laws and the strike of men who removed night soil in 1918, strikes at the Cape Town docks, riots in schools in 1920, and a strike on the gold mines involving 40,000 to 70,000 black workers. It included, too, shootings in Port Elizabeth after the detention of a labour leader that left twenty-one dead and many injured, in 1921 the shooting and killing of 190 protestors at Bulhoek near Queenstown[17] and a struggle between the Chamber of Mines and white workers over the ratio of white to black labour which culminated in the Great Strike and Red Revolt of 1922. White workers resisted, in this, any advances for blacks.[18] At the same time, one of the most significant of organisations for black workers, the Industrial and Commercial Union, was beginning, especially after 1923, to grow rapidly.

The light's concern and effects, in this context, may be said also to be with discouraging the manifestation at any level from the subordinate classes of the impulse to resistance. Thus the play presents a string of brief scenes which, despite the reference in the preface to tribal wars, actually enact the clash between colonial invaders and the African population. Throughout, a figure called 'Civilisation' provides commentary on what is happening which, predictably takes a firm missionary line. Various of the peoples of South Africa are shown in turn starting with the Xhosa and in each case, addressed by Civilisation as 'my children'; they are faced with what is presented as the inevitable advance of the light of civilisation that will come with the white man (pp. 3, 6, 19). The violence that is to accompany this process is deemed entirely necessary:

I see war, war, much bloodshed. Many of these present will fall in the struggle, but none can stay the hand of fate. The light must break, and these are but victims in the struggle...This is the last struggle, and now light will break sure and certain in a sea of blood in the east. (pp. 10, 19).

If such colonialist discourse, privileged through use of the redemptive metaphor of approaching light, encourages the acceptance of white rule, the play's utilisation of the frontier image actively helps to discourage any concern with the possibility of present-day resistance. When in the play the impulse to resist on the part of frontier blacks is voiced through the rhetorical image of driving the whites into the sea, it is an impulse that significantly, in terms of the conditions of material struggle and existence in the industrialising South Africa contemporary to the writing of the play, has at best only figurative value indicating dislike. Indeed, the play's location in a frontier society long since vanished may be said to contribute to the disablement of any potential understanding of current material conditions in the third decade of the twentieth century, while the image of the light to communicate spiritual promise may be said similarly to encourage non-worldly acceptance of material exploitation and deprivation.

Notwithstanding the proclaimed concern in the preface to The light with teaching religious history and Christian ethics then, the play's use of the frontier image and the way in which it ignores current unease in the social order even as it appears to argue directly to its audiences for particular political responses should not be sidestepped. And the way in which the writer of the introduction to the play, Henderson, sees its function is significant. He appears clearly aware of the likely political effect of The light, in its presentation of past, present and future South Africa upon the children of the oppressed classes:

To the people too in their present phase of gloom and discontent it offers timeous encouragement, for it strikes notes of hope and courage, and gives ground to them for faith in the future. (preface)

Even if that faith in the future, presumably strongly mediated by representatives of the play's speaker 'Civilisation', were to include the notion of liberation – highly unlikely in the context of the thinking of the time – the postponed millennium, in the essentialist and idealist argument of the play is to be brought about through providential intervention: no hint of human agency that might address 'the present phase of gloom and discontent' or interrogate white tutelage is permitted. Disturbingly, Henderson is only too eager to apply this spiritually focused but historically biased lesson wherever he can. He calls on the help of whatever governmental institutions prove to be willing:

I would bespeak for it not only a cordial reception among all those interested in Native affairs generally, but also (for without this it will fail of its main objective) the consideration of the Departments of Education, and of the heads of the higher Native schools and institutions. (preface)

The light, then, concerned to propagate an essentially spiritual view of the human subject, coloniser and colonised, on the South African terrain, does so in ways that not only provide a particular reading of the past it is concerned to represent, but, in what appears to be a continuing potentially unstable situation, in ways that were perceived to be useful to those concerned with maintaining existing relations of domination and subordination.

Agents of the ruling classes, in the arguments of certain historians, it is worth noting, have repeatedly consciously appropriated certain discourses in South Africa in a variety of cultural and educational contexts for their own purposes. Thus James Dexter Taylor commented in 1926 on the function of the Gamma Sigma Club, formed to attract young black school graduates working on the mines, in offices and in commercial firms:

Some...were political extremists. Racial feeling ran high and there was little respect for the church...Gradually many of the most radical of its members have been led to more sober views and to a spirit of inter-racial co-operation. A voluntary Bible Class has been well attended and religious and moral matters have been discussed with as much avidity as political and economic subjects.[19]

Nevertheless, Mary Waters's work in locating itself within South Africa not only in The light, but in her next play, U-Nongqause, remains significant. Despite The light's transmission of colonialist and ruling class forms of discourse, its location, like that of U-Nongqause, within the periphery inadvertently helped to initiate the search in drama for a more authentic South African place, against the hegemony of the colonial centre. As chapter 1 will show, a performance of U-Nongqause was likely to have inspired the young Herbert Dhlomo to undertake the first really significant attempt in South African dramatic history to recover such an authenticity.

Evidence of other early attempts in South African drama to challenge the privileging of the colonial centre remains scanty and needs further research. Peter Larlham has provided information about various kinds of performance in traditional Zulu Rites and ceremonies, Zionist rituals, Festivals of the Nazareth Baptist Church and Contemporary Folk Dance.[20] These include narrative forms of folk tale and the praise poem, but, he also observes, there are 'no dramatic performances of the kind associated with the Western theatrical tradition with fixed, formal spoken dialogue between costumed actors who impersonate characters' (p.61). There is too a paucity of information about what at present must be the putative existence of early twentieth-century popular or working-class theatre. Possibly related activities have been traced in a study of the growth of a branch of the Industrial and Commercial Union (ICU) in the late 1920s in Durban which argues that 'local political economy, patterns of exploitation, domination and dispossession, as well as popular idioms of and traditions of resistance, served to create a peculiar local form of culture'.[21] Cultural alternatives to everyday coercion and control included the formation of *amaleita* gangs (pp. 9-10), *isihabahaba*, 'groups of workers who developed patterns of homosexual behaviour and styles of female dress'(p. 11) and the development of *ngoma* dance (p.12). Again, although it is argued that often the consciousness of workers was not 'overtly political', it was, it is also argued, 'infused with notions anchored in pre-capitalist ideologies, and at times recreated imagined rights enjoyed in a collective historical past' (p.12), positing 'military symbols and rituals' from that 'pre-industrialised past' (p.30). In this context, the ICU participated in the development of more overtly political awareness, the development of 'alternative popular institutions which became pivotal in mobilising a worker constituency' (p. 28), using the dance hall as 'a central mechanism in the creation of a common sense of identity amongst racially-oppressed workers' (p. 28). And some of the songs emerging in this context were clearly used 'to express collective experiences and an explicitly political frame of reference' (p. 28). Such research suggests the possible existence of early working-class attempts through drama to resist the dominance of the colonial centre but if these occurred to any marked extent they remain as yet largely undiscovered.

III Drama and colonialist and post-colonialist hegemony

Such early dramatic attempts to locate an authenticity within the South
African place, as well as those that follow – indeed almost until the
present time – have always taken place against the prevailing colonialist
and then post-colonial fixation, within establishment institutions,
upon the colonial/North American metropolis. Thus, describing the
growth of interest in theatre from the turn of the century, one
commentator observes:

from the 1890s on show business habits and audiences swelled out of all
recognition – from occasional amateur shows in barracks and drill halls, the
odd appearance of an overseas touring musical company and a scratch music-
hall presentation, to an institutionalised business with its own theatres,
regular bills and the whole apparatus of reviews, advertisements, first nights
and entrepreneurial pizzaz. It was a sound investment for a manager like
Luscombe Searelle to import an entire prefabricated theatre, complete with
fixtures and fittings...the spreading entrenchment of British cultural mores
throughout the subcontinent produced empires of newspapers and showbiz
as extensive and as remunerative as the British Empire enterprise itself.[22]

And another commentator, as recently as 1986, notes the tenacity of
colonialist, Eurocentric and North American dominated attitudes to
culture. The sense that South Africa is a country on the periphery of
a metropolis destined always to be situated six thousand miles or more
away and the cultural denigration attendant on this, the belief that
'anything imported is somehow of superior inherent quality, and
anything locally generated inferior', persists:[23]

if one turns to the entertainment pages of any edition of Johannesburg's Citizen
or the Cape Times or the Natal Mercury, one finds little overt evidence of either
the range or the social immediacy of much contemporary South African
theatre. What one does find are theatre and cabaret listings which uncannily
resemble those in London's Sunday Telegraph or the New York Times – fewer offerings, certainly, but much the same sort of thing: The Little Shop of Horrors, an
Alan Ayckbourn or Neil Simon comedy, an Agatha Christie revival, and a
Performing Arts Council production of Aida or The School for Scandal.The impression given is that urban South Africa is culturally little more than a far-
flung suburb of London or New York, a Sevenoaks or Scarsdale in the veld.[24]

Such attitudes also pervaded much of the South African academy,
at least until a decade or so ago. Despite Henderson's excitement about
The light, those critical discourses that traverse secondary and tertiary

education in South Africa have hardly responded to South African drama – most of which does not, like Waters's simple morality, encourage submission. The colonial perspectives of members of the English establishment in schools and universities up to the establishment of the Republic in 1961 and long after often meant the absence of any impulse to 'literary nationalism' – 'almost all their reading', according to one trying to move beyond their horizons, came 'from across the water'.[25] Strong focus upon feeling and the moral core of the individual, as F. R. Leavis particularly encouraged it, further dominated attitudes in the establishment, the sense not only that, as a contributor to the inaugural number of *English studies in Africa*, argued, universities are 'centres of intelligence and perceptiveness', that 'great literature...by its very beauty leads the reader into new and important perceptions', and that the 'essence of literature is its impact...unless it has a notable and enriching effect it can hardly be said to exist at all as literature' but also that any tendency 'to subordinate what is valuable in literature to the (still of course important) facts of its historical background or of its linguistic significance' ought to be resisted.[26]

Such attitudes entailed too an obsession with interiority of a particular kind. In the same number of *English studies in Africa*, another contributor declares that 'the basis and indeed the whole *raison d'être* of the theatre is the portrayal of character in action'.[27] While the presentation of interiority may, inevitably, draw in different cases upon different discourses, in the South African academy the concern with interiority usually practised, and the one sometimes evident in literary and dramatic works draws on certain reductive and simplified versions of essentialist and idealist discourse. It may be argued that in the apartheid state this has helped to erase recognition that interiority may in part at least be a result of social and material conditions or the dominance of certain discourses within the social order.

It is primarily in this South African context then that any predilection for such a reductionist focus upon interiority discovered in one or other play in this book should be understood. We may recall here what Catherine Belsey in another context identifies as the humanist assumption that ' "man" is the origin and source of meaning, of action and of history' (*humanism*)', that 'our concepts and our knowledge are held to be the product of experience (*empiricism*)', that 'this experience is preceded and interpreted by the mind, reason or thought, the property of a transcendent human nature whose essence is the attribute of each individual (*idealism*)', and that 'literature reflects the *reality* of experience as it is perceived by one (especially gifted) individual, who *expresses* it in a discourse which enables other individuals to recognise it as true'.[28] From the perspective of Jameson, such 'ethical criticism' 'projects as permanent features of human "experience", and thus as a kind of "wisdom" about personal life and interpersonal relations, what are in reality the historical and institutional specifics of a determinate type of group solidarity or class cohesion'.[29]

Against the dominant thrust within departments of English literature, interest in the study of South African literature grew amongst a small group of practitioners and researchers, particularly in the 1970s. For the study of drama this shift, taking place largely outside Departments of English literature, has resulted in the appearance in the 1980s of several studies including Robert Kavanagh's *Theatre and cultural struggle in South Africa* which endeavours to provide a brief materialist context for South African theatre and examines two plays from the late 1950s and two plays produced in the early 1970s.[30] Tim Couzens's seminal study of the life of Herbert Dhlomo was published in 1985 and Ian Steadman's extensive research into black drama on the Witwatersrand was completed in 1985.[31] As well as these works other recent studies include David Coplan's *In township tonight!* which, although largely a study of music, includes chapters providing brief surveys of drama in the townships, and Peter Larlham's *Black theatre dance and ritual in South Africa* which, primarily concerned with traditional rites and ceremonies as well as religious drama, also provides a brief survey of theatre.[32]

However, the fact that this work has appeared only within the last five years testifies to those antipathetic attitudes which for many decades inhibited the study of South African literature and so discouraged interest in the drama. Indeed, as late as 1970 many members of the South African literary establishment were still fiercely resisting the suggestion that such literature be taken seriously in institutions of education. 'Can we', asked one Professor of English at a Conference held at the University of the Witwatersrand in that year,

find time to study books which (chosen not mainly because of their literary value but for some foreground interest of local subject or setting) will make it necessary to drop out of our course a play of Ben Jonson's, a novel of Jane Austen's, a major work of modern criticism or poetry? Certainly the local flavour may be very exciting, and it is delightful to recognise a familiar landscape in a work, or to see 'ourselves' in a well-drawn social situation; and no one can deny that enjoying this flavour may encourage wider reading. But what if, when its taste fades from our memory, we are left with little or nothing comparable to what remains in our minds after reading a great work of literature, no permanent disturbance of the spirit, no unforgettable intensity of art?[33]

The 'political turn'[34] which this practice of criticism by the South African English literary establishment in the schools and universities has entailed at least up to the time that these comments were made (and in some Departments of English until the present day still entails) the almost complete suppression of any study of South African drama as literary object worth either their own or their students' concern. These attitudes complemented nicely the government banning of numbers of plays over the decades.

IV South African drama and discursive struggle

Such factors produce problems for any study of theatre in South Africa. For one thing the paucity of research and evidence makes the study of purely subordinate or working-class dramatic activity of one or other kind extremely difficult. A recent paper, making a rare attempt to explore 'the affinities between popular and working-class culture, between performance and cultural formations, between defensive combinations, social structure and grassroots creativity',[35] notes that prior to 1983, 'trade union meetings were not devoid of performance-genres':

A typical meeting would involve the chairperson leading crowds into prayers, militant and defiant songs, call and response chants and depending on the individual's symbolic capital, through poetic reveries. In total control s/he would rhythmically indicate that the 'defiant' mode was over and workers would settle down for the discussions and resolutions. At crucial moments again in the midst of speaking, the chairperson would energise proceedings with more chants, slogans and songs. Finally, beyond the relationship between call and response between the foreground and the crowd, a choir might add some religious or traditional harmonies, or a dancing group would emerge and entertain the participants. The process of participation reconfirmed most of the time the dominance of Zulu (in Natal)-based performance languages. Whereas discussion usually was conducted in both English and Zulu. (pp. 3-4)

The performance of poetry was and remains particularly significant at such meetings:

a worker able to master the craft of the izibongo (praise song) and who stands in front of a gathering, pouring-out aggregative and additive metaphors in the requisite fury will get a response and will elicit participation in pre-coded ways: after the initial roar of approval, the end of every stanza would bring forth the stock responses of encouragement and appreciation. The better able poet will elicit more than stock responses and send the crowd in a flurry of exclamations and phrases, impromptu power-dances and ululations. Such a process of interaction makes the praise-poem a fertile symbolic resource for the affirmation of identities and comradeships...but the praise poem is only one 'poetic' strategy: propaganda poems in English punctuated with chants, toyi-toyi sequences with quasi-poetic call and response vocalisings, struggle songs all serve to create solidarities and to strike defiant chords.

More recently, as part of the 'festive or more "carnivalesque" mode' at such gatherings in Natal, 'where people (and in this case workers) are asked to "enjoy" performances that assert strictly speaking the performance vitality of popular culture' (p. 4), worker leaders began to introduce plays as part of their agendas. Chapter 7 briefly examines this phenomenon, but beyond that, because of continuing lack of research and evidence, this book is not able to investigate whether or how the subject has been constructed by working classes and groups in drama with either minimal or no intervention from dissidents or others attached to the petit-bourgeois or to the ruling classes. That map of purely working-class constructions within drama, if these too to any extensive degree exist, still awaits, in view of the brevity and incompleteness of the forays so far made, its main cartographer.

Again, although Kavanagh has examined the conditions of production of the four plays he studies in his book – the publication of some of these, partly a result of his own intervention – more extensive research than the present book is able to undertake into the conditions of production and the constitution of audiences in South African theatre over the decades remains an imperative if we are to acquire a better understanding of the nature of intersecting contributions and their effects over periods of time. Participants in theatre are often multi-positioned with differing class and group allegiances and affiliations and, consequently, multiple contradictions have become the rule rather than the exception in theatrical endeavour in South Africa. Again, relatively little is known about much popular theatre in the townships in the twentieth century, particularly in the last three decades, because often no script or record of performance was transmitted to the published page. Scripts usually have to be submitted to township authorities before performances and, needless to say, likelihood of permission for a performance being granted is frequently slight. Often, even of plays which have been published, much that might have been said or enacted in performance is eliminated from the written page version. Although such unscripted theatre-in-performance must perforce lie beyond the parameters of this book its contestatory nature may be assumed from some of the plays that are discussed here.

From these points of view the present study may be understood as an exploratory attempt to map part of a territory that, some of it, remains still to be explored. It endeavours to examine mainly published plays, both from dissident ruling-class practitioners and from the oppressed classes, which have also for the most part been performed in city theatres or township venues or both. In the matter of production or often in the conditions of publication, these plays are often produced, as I have just remarked, as a result of the endeavours of a variety of people from intersecting classes and groups including sometimes in one or other way members of the dominant as well as the subordinate classes. And many of these plays, in their attempt to situate themselves within the South African landscape reveal, to different degrees, understandings that are only partial, sometimes obfuscatory, perceptions not always fully grasped, aspects of the relations of domination and subordination within the social order approached tangentially or not at all. As this chapter attempts to recognise, such dramatic ventures are and have been in the past fraught with difficulty precisely because theatre has always been threatened by the state, and by the powerful and enduring hegemonic processes that work for selective awareness of South African history and the South African present. And colonial and post-colonial theatre establishments as well as publishers, largely in control of the material conditions of production and publication always have restrained, marginalised and suppressed their emergence – often continue to do so. Moreover it should always be remembered that over the decades even until the present day, oppressed class participation in theatre has often been after-hours and only after full time non-theatrical employment. The problems attendant on this alone – for rehearsal, the energy and strength of the participants, their ability to travel and their availability – have in themselves drastically inhibited the growth of theatre.

I do not attempt to provide a complete history of modern South African drama here, but examine how, over the past five decades or so, at the significant moments of South African dramatic activity, the subject, the land, the body and culture, amongst other concepts, have been imagined or presented on stage and in playtext. It will be clear that I am particularly concerned to observe the ways in which plays contest prevailing apartheid discourse and the moments when such plays become subversive, entailing sometimes the exploration and assertion of alternative discourses – although some of the plays I discuss, as in the case of The light, consolidate existing relations. Certain of Pêcheux's terms have been useful for this aspect of this study.[36] At the most obvious level, the interrogation of, say, segregationist or apartheid discourses entails simple inversion, the demonstration, for example, that what offers itself as justice is in fact an instance of injustice, what claims to be law is criminality. Pêcheux calls such attempts to contest prevailing discourse through simple inversion counteridentification. In the struggle to contest prevailing discourse, the attempt to go beyond simple inversion or counteridentification entails the use of alternative discourses, discourses that might, say, argue directly for resistance or that entail a view of the social order or construct the human subject in ways different from those to be found in prevailing discourse. These discourses threaten the dominance of those ideological discursive formations compatible with the continuing power of the ruling classes[37] and do not, in Pêcheux's terms merely counteridentify with prevailing discourse, but disidentify with it. Inevitably, particularly these plays are threatened with suppression by a dominant order anxious to secure its own position.

It should be recognised that attempts at counteridentification or disidentification do not account for the extent to which a play may still include evidence of dominant ideological discursive formations that have been naturalised or rendered opaque so that they remain unchallenged. The language of the Minister of Home Affairs, with which this chapter opened, provides an instance, as I remarked, of the presentation of particular discourse as naturalised incontestable fact.

Such naturalisation of ideologically situated language and position, furthermore, means, as Fairclough notes, that often 'subjects are typically unaware of the ideological dimensions of the subject positions they occupy'.[38] Accordingly, 'it is quite possible for a social subject to occupy institutional subject positions which are ideologically incompatible, or to occupy a subject position incompatible with his or her overt political or social beliefs and affiliations, without being aware of any contradiction' (p. 753). For this as well as for other reasons, just as in the social formation any attempt or struggle to resist prevailing discourse may only partly succeed, so the presence in plays of discursive contestation should not necessarily imply that any point of clear resolution or closure will always be reached. Indeed most texts present discursive struggle, and this may not necessarily be resolved; even when disidentification is consciously sought, strands of prevailing discourse may survive. Furthermore, the extent to which prevailing discourse continues to work to suppress all other voices always remains a complicating and inhibiting factor.

Whether theatre in South Africa has often approached, if ever, the status of a revolutionary force, is debatable. But awareness of that discourse which emphasises the social nature of language helps students of South African drama to address that which prevailing discourse in South Africa continues to evade: not only the social nature of theatre, but the extent to which language in the South African social formation is inescapably bound up with the operation of power. From this point of view South African theatre at the very least reflects something of the often frightening, vicious and murderous battles, that have been and continue to be waged throughout the country, particularly in the twentieth century, not only over land, the actions of interested power groups, the constitution of the subject, but over language as well. This book was begun during a state of emergency, when the struggle for liberation entered a new phase of courage as well as hardship and repression. Its publication takes place on the brink of what might be a new period entailing subtler forms of oppression in South Africa as certain of the less essential mechanisms of the apartheid machine are jettisoned. It may lead to this, indeed, just as easily as it may herald any quick road to a freer South Africa. In either event, and may it be, we fervently hope, the latter, it is as well to note, as point of departure for this study of South African drama – against the thrust of prevailing apartheid discourse – those directions evident in the South African Freedom Charter, adopted at the Congress of the People in 1955:

The government shall discover, develop and encourage national talent for the enhancement of our cultural life;

All cultural treasures...shall be open to all, by free exchange of books, ideas and contact with other lands;

The aim of education shall be to teach the youth to love their people and their culture, to honour human brotherhood (sic), liberty and peace;

Education shall be free, compulsory, universal and equal for all children;

Higher education and technical training shall be opened to all by means of state allowances and scholarships awarded on the basis of merit;

Adult illiteracy shall be ended by a mass state education plan;

Teachers shall have all the rights of other citizens;

The colour bar in cultural life, in sport and in education shall be abolished.[39]

Notes

1 See, for example, Akerman, Anthony, ' "Prejudicial to the safety of the state": censorship and the theatre in South Africa', *Theatre quarterly*, VII, 28, 1977-78, p. 56; Horn, Andrew, 'South African theatre: ideology and rebellion', *Research in African literatures*, XVII, 2, 1986, p. 220; van Rooyen, J. C. W., *Censorship in South Africa*, Cape Town: Juta, 1987, p. 7.

2 Reported in *The Star*, 19 May 1988.

3 Kavanagh, Robert Mshengu ed., *South African people's plays*, London: Heinemann, 1981.

4 See Tomaselli, Keyan, Tomaselli, Ruth and Muller, Johan, *Narrating the crisis: hegemony and the South African press*, Johannesburg: Richard Lyon, 1987.

5 Weeks, Jeffrey, 'Foucault for historians', cited in Cairns, David and Richards, Shaun, *Writing Ireland*, Manchester: Manchester University Press, 1988, p. 1.

6 Barrell, John, *Poetry, language and politics*, Manchester: Manchester University Press, 1988, p. 8.

7 Dubow, Saul, 'Race, civilisation and culture: the elaboration of segregationist discourse in the inter-war years', in Marks, Shula, and Trapido, Stanley, *The politics of race, class and nationalism in twentieth century South Africa*, London: Longman, 1987, p. 75.

8 Barrell, *Poetry*, p. 8.

9 Vološinov, V. N., *Marxism and the philosophy of language*, trans. Matejka, L. and Titunik, I. R., London: Harvard University Press, 1986, p. 85.

10 Macdonell, Diane, *Theories of discourse*, Oxford: Blackwell, 1986, p. 3.

11 Gray, Stephen, *Southern African literature: an introduction*, Cape Town: David Philip,1979, pp. 53-8.

12 Black, Stephen, *Three plays*, ed. Gray, Stephen, Johannesburg: Donker, 1984, pp. 7-41.

13 Peterson, Bhekisizwe, ' "All work and no play makes civilisation unattractive to the masses": The emergent formations of theatre amongst Africans from Fr. Bernard Huss to the Bantu Dramatic Society', Paper presented to the Division of African Literature 'Work in Progress Seminar', Witwatersrand University, 18 October 1989, p. 11.

14 Waters, Mary, *The light – ukukanya*, Lovedale, South Africa: Lovedale Institution Press, 1925. References to all plays will be to the text first cited in the notes, unless otherwise indicated. I am indebted to Professor F. G. Butler for this information about Waters.

15 See Dollimore, Jonathan, *Radical tragedy*, Brighton: Harvester, 1984, esp. Ch. 16, p. 250.

16 Williams, Raymond, *Keywords*, Glasgow: Fontana, 1976, p. 125.

17 Hirson, Baruch, 'Tuskegee, the joint councils and the all African convention', *Collected seminar papers on the societies of Southern Africa in the nineteenth and twentieth centuries, October 1978-June 1979*, Institute of Commonwealth Studies, University of London, 1978 p. 68.

18 See Roux, Eddie, *Time longer than rope*, Madison: University of Wisconsin Press, 1964, pp. 153ff.

19 Cited in Hirson, *Tuskegee*, p. 68.

20 Larlham, Peter, *Black theatre, dance and ritual in South Africa*, Ann Arbor, Michigan: UMI Research Press, 1985.

21 la Hausse, P., 'The message of the warriors: the ICU, the labouring poor and the making

of a popular political culture in Durban', Paper presented at the University of the Witwatersrand Workshop, 'The Making of Class', 9-14 February 1987.

22 Gray, Stephen, ed., *Stephen Black, three plays*, pp. 18-19.

23 Gray, Stephen, 'South African drama: bedevilling categories', *The English academy review*, II, 1984, p. 122.

24 Horn, Andrew, 'South African theatre: ideology and rebellion', *Research in African literatures*, 17:2, 1986, p. 211.

25 Butler, Guy, ed., *A book of South African verse*, Oxford: Oxford University Press, 1959, 1963, p. xix.

26 Gardner, C.O.,'The English School at Oxford', *English studies in Africa*, I, 1, March 1958, pp. 39-40.

27 Inskip, D, 'Drama in the university', *English studies in Africa*, I, 1, March 1958, p. 56.

28 Belsey, Catherine, *Critical practice*, London: Methuen, 1980, p. 7.

29 Jameson, Frederic, *The political unconscious*, London: Methuen, 1981, p. 59.

30 Kavanagh, Robert Mshengu, *Theatre and cultural struggle in South Africa*, London: Zed, 1985.

31 Couzens, Tim, *The new African: A study of the life and work of H. I. E. Dhlomo*, Johannesburg: Ravan, 1985; Steadman, Ian Patrick, 'Drama and social consciousness: themes in black theatre on the Witwatersrand until 1984', unpublished thesis for the degree of PhD, University of the Witwatersrand, 1985.

32 Coplan, David B., *In township tonight!*, Johannesburg: Ravan, 1985. See also Banning, Yvonne, 'English language usage in South African theatre since 1976', unpublished MA dissertation, University of the Witwatersrand, 1989.

33 Segal, Philip, 'The place of South African writing in the university', *English studies in Africa*, XIII, 1, 1970, pp. 177-8.

34 Cf. Donoghue, Dennis, 'The political turn in criticism', *Salmagundi*, 81, Winter 1989, pp. 105-22.

35 Sitas, Ari, 'The voice and gesture in South Africa's revolution: a study of worker gatherings and performance-genres in Natal', Paper delivered at the History Workshop, University of the Witwatersrand, February 1990, p. 2.

36 See Pêcheux, Michel, *Language, semantics and ideology*, London: Macmillan, 1982.

37 See Fairclough, Norman L., 'Critical and descriptive goals in discourse analysis', *Journal of pragmatics*, IX, 1985, pp. 739-63, p. 751.

38 Fairclough, 'Goals in discourse analysis', p. 753.

39 Cited in Cronin, Jeremy, and Suttner, Raymond, *30 years of the freedom charter*, Johannesburg: Ravan, 1986, p. 265.

1

The white savage beneath

The dramatic projects which Herbert Dhlomo undertook in the 1930s and 1940s in South Africa may be said to mark the first significant attempt in drama to challenge the dominance of the imperial and colonialist centre as well as to contest aspects of prevailing ruling class discourse emanating from the white-settler culture. The first dramatist to attempt the construction of a South African place in a way different from that presented in colonialist and imperialist discourse, Dhlomo also attempts the appropriation of certain colonialist forms of discourse in his attempt to contest the move towards segregation then intensifying in South Africa.

I The conflicting search for identity in early modern theatre

Dhlomo's plays emerged in a period during which a variety of conflicting pressures and tendencies in the production of art and culture was evident. Drama was being used on the one hand by members of the ruling classes and by an educated elite from the subordinate classes as a means of strengthening affiliation with the colonial centre. As the best means to counter discrimination and exploitation, mission-educated and petit-bourgeois blacks tended to advocate progressive westernisation and assimilation. Art and literature were in this sometimes privileged: 'A nation that has no arts of peace and no abstract thought is barbarous' wrote E. Makofane in 1936.[1] The predilection for American jazz and the popularity of American cinema no doubt further enhanced interest in performance and the potential of theatre. More specifically, too, awareness of drama was encouraged amongst mission-educated blacks, because of their frequent encounters with Shakespeare in school, including in Natal in the 1930s performances of versions of *The merchant of Venice* and *Julius Caesar*. 'Everybody thought he was great when he could quote a word or two from Shakespeare', commented Dan Twala.[2] In Zululand 'nativity' tableaux were performed annually. There, and elsewhere, dramatic performances were a feature of school concerts and such interest was fed too by the Eisteddfodau and by enacted scenes in minstrelsy and public concerts.

On the other hand, differently positioned members of the subordinate classes were becoming aware, not only of the need to appropriate ruling class forms of culture for non-oppressive ends, but of the need to identify their own place as well as the conditions of struggle within it. It is possible that the dramatised animal satires of Job Moteame and Azariele M. Sekese in Lesotho in the 1880s, dramatic sketches at Mariannhill in the 1920s and Guybon Sinxo's Imfene ka Debeza, a Xhosa play published in 1925, were early factors contributing to interest. in a drama located within the South African terrain.[3] Proponents of 'progressive' views in this period were stressing the importance of social awareness – 'the duty of Bantu writers and journalists', wrote R. V. Selope Thema in 1929, 'is to call the attention of the leaders to things that are detrimental to the interests and welfare of the people'.[4] The composer Reuben Caluza sought, amongst other goals, to provide in his work a basis for a national music and a national culture – although men such as he disapproved of the achievement of what they considered to be non-African tendencies in jazz or the overtly traditional or rural aspects of the marabi dance. Nevertheless, performance arts were becoming increasingly popular in the 1920s and 1930s as a form of working-class entertainment. Coplan describes a range of activities which included the singing and dancing of marabi and famo (lengthy recitative songs performed by women) in slumyard and shebeen culture, dance and social clubs.[5] According to Coplan, working-class cultural practice often manifested the impulse to address urgent issues within the social order, to identify aspects of exploitation and to affirm a sense of community and the importance of values retained from rural life. Such tendencies may be found in proletarian forms of song, music and dance including not only the famo but the lifela or male likoata's praise songs,[6] as well as, again, many of the songs sung at and made popular in the Eisteddfodau. All of these activities in location, township or city in one or other way 'helped to develop social rules and relationships and provided cultural expression of common social aspirations'.[7]

Perhaps due to these as well as to other factors, several ambitious dramatic ventures were undertaken in the late 1920s and early 1930s. In 1929 Esau Mthethwe formed a group called the Mthethwe Lucky Stars. They 'based their drama on totally indigenous themes of rural life and customs', performing their most popular plays Umthakathi (The

Sorcerer) and Ukuqomisa (Lovemaking) in many parts of the country.[8]
Unlike the Bantu Dramatic Society which played to largely petit
bourgeois or middle-class audiences, including some liberal whites,
their appeal in the 1930s was popular in township and slumyard as
well as petit bourgeois context. They had a great success at the Empire
Exhibition in Johannesburg in 1936. The Bantu Dramatic Society,
formed in 1932, was more self-consciously engaged in the search for
a new cultural formation. According to a British Drama League
Pamphlet published in 1934 it had asserted

Although the Society will present European plays from time to time, the aim
of the Bantu Dramatic Society is to encourage Bantu Playwrights, and to
develop African dramatic and operatic art. Bantu life is full of great and
glorious incidents and figures that would form the basis for first-class drama.[9]

The league itself had begun an African drama section, 'both a symptom
and a cause of the spread of interest [shown] in drama throughout
Africa.'[10] Another society called the Bantu People's Players was also
formed in the early 1930s (putting on O'Neil's *The hairy ape*), while
evidence exists of some theatrical ventures undertaken in the same
period in Cape Town by a group of Trotskyites.[11] In 1934 at the 'Great
National Thanksgiving Celebrations' a play by R. R. Dhlomo and
produced by his brother Herbert, was performed, in one description,
by 'children and adults, who made the past live by their realistic
performance of the suffering of American Negroes on the slave market,
in the cotton fields, and at home, until the joyful news of liberation'.[12]
If, as Couzens remarks, one of the interesting aspects of this event is
its concern with the metropolis (American and not South African
slavery) this only serves to accentuate the importance of the attempts
by Dhlomo, in his plays, as well as the reported attempts of a few others
like him, to displace the imperial centre.

Many of these ventures occurred, as I have already noted in the
introductory chapter, in one way or another with at least some
involvement on the part of liberal or sympathetic whites, interested in
some cases in fostering indigenous art, or in others, intensifying the
processes of affiliation to and assimilation with the imperial centre.
Belgian socialist André van Gyseghem came out to direct The Bantu
People's Players. The Bantu Dramatic Society received a visit and
support from Dame Sybil Thorndike. Their programme for their
opening productions lists as patrons, as well as Dame Sybil Thorndike
and Lewis Casson, a number of other dignitaries attached to the ruling

classes including the Hon. Mr Justice Solomon, Professor R. Kirby and the Rev. R. E. Philips. This followed the pattern of liberal involvement in organisations such as the Joint Councils and various clubs including the Bantu Men's Social Centre where the Bantu Dramatic Society was founded and met. The Mthwethwe Lucky Stars were 'discovered' by the white showwoman Bertha Slosberg who had turned their performance into a music and dance show primarily intended for white consumption, and who tried to arrange an overseas tour for them – the first of many attempts of this kind.

It is important to note too that such endeavours to promote dramatic activity by members of the subordinate classes together with some support from liberal or sympathetic whites, occurred in a social order in which the dominant classes in theatre were pursuing or practising segregation. A number of theatres had been built or opened in the late nineteenth and early twentieth centuries in South Africa. In these traditional segregationist practice largely applied. The choice of *She stoops to conquer* as first production by the Bantu Dramatic Society, bespeaks a desire for affiliation with and assimilation to the colonial centre, but it was made also partly because it had recently been played by an overseas company at His Majesty's Theatre in Johannesburg, 'unique among South African places of entertainment in that it admitted black spectators to the gallery.'[13] Van Gyseghem had enormous problems in finding a suitable hall for performances of *The hairy ape* by the Bantu People's Players.[14] Even in the cinema some films were often given an age limit, censored or banned for blacks where they were shown without restriction to white audiences.

Moreover the dominant classes were themselves still relatively uninterested in theatre. With the advent of cinema most theatres were converted to movie houses and the relative decline in theatrical activity amongst the ruling classes, despite a few exceptions, lasted until the 1940s.[15] Dhlomo's concern to write plays from the 1930s on, in contrast to the relative indifference of the ruling classes, and, as well, despite the lack of appropriate venues for oppressed class audiences, may be set against the attitudes of the few members of the ruling classes who remained interested in theatre in the 1930s. These had no impulse to seek identity within the periphery, as the following paragraph in the Hoffman history of the Johannesburg Repertory Players clearly indicates:

Avalanche by Beverley Nichols followed from 24-26 November 1934 at the

Jewish Guild, following which came a wonderful presentation of *Queen's Majesty* by Lucy Bowditch. It played from 9-11 March 1935. This historical play was written by an active member whose profound knowledge of Elizabethan England made her qualified to write on this subject. The production was the most sumptuous costume play staged by the Johannesburg Repertory Players up to that time. Alice Barnett as Queen Elizabeth magnificently headed an enormous cast of players well versed in the mannerisms of the time. As recent arrivals from Cape Town, this was our introduction to the Reps. We were invited to see *Queen's Majesty* by director Muriel Alexander, and then and there we made up our minds to become Reps members.[16]

II Land and assimilationism in *U-Nongqause*

Herbert Dhlomo himself was born in 1903, one of five children whose father worked in a lift manufacturing or installing company and then tended minor wounds in the dressing stations of various mines.[17] His mother worked as a laundry woman collecting and returning washing from whites in Johannesburg. Herbert went to the American Board Mission School in Doornfontein and to the Amanzimtoti Training Institute (later Adams College). He became a teacher and then a principal, was active as a journalist and, a gifted musician, participated in Eisteddfodau and recorded gramophone records. He has been described as one of the 'new Africans', member of a petit bourgeoisie which, from the perspective of materialist and Marxist critics, believed in 'social advancement, individualism, belief in a neutral state above classes'[18] and he has been characterised on the basis of his first play *The girl who killed to save*, as a dramatist unable to do more than reproduce the prevailing ideological discursive formations of his time.[19]

But such a reading does not take into account the extent to which Dhlomo dramatises an authentic pre-colonial world on the periphery that at least interrogates colonialist versions of traditional societies, and the extent to which his play attempts to a degree to engage with prevailing ruling class discourse about contemporary conditions of material struggle. To understand the nature of Dhlomo's project in drama it is useful firstly to consider the ways in which *The girl who killed to save*, the first play by a black writer, in English, to be published (in 1936, by the Lovedale Missionary Press) is likely to have been a direct response to Mary Waters's *U-Nongqause*. Waters's play was performed at the launching of the Bantu Dramatic Society at the Bantu Men's Social

Centre in 1933, and Dhlomo, who appeared in the parallel play performed to celebrate the opening, She stoops to conquer, must have seen it and been inspired by it to write his own play on the same theme.[20]

Waters's play, like Dhlomo's after it, presents the South African place primarily as land over which the colonial power and indigenous inhabitants struggle. The question of land, with which both plays are concerned, has always been crucial in South African history. Amongst the ruling classes and groups the population of South Africa by the twentieth century included, as I have already indicated, the Afrikaners, who were descendants of the original Dutch settlers, and the British colonists together with, after the discovery of gold and diamonds, a continuing influx of Europeans and North Americans.[21] The subordinate classes included SeSotho and SeTswana speaking peoples together with the AmaPondo, descendants of the AmaXhosa, with whom the land hungry settlers of the original expanding Cape Colony fought nine frontier wars in the hundred years after 1777, and the Zulus. The Mfecane or unification of many clans into the Zulu military state had produced as well as a united Zulu nation, a 'tremendous upheaval and scattering of...tribes'.[22] The Zulus resisted the advance of the Afrikaner trekkers from the Cape Colony, but were defeated at the Battle of Blood River in 1838. Their kingdom was finally destroyed in 1879. The subordinate classes also included migrant workers coming into the country in increasing numbers, inhabitants of mixed descent, referred to as 'coloureds', and descendants of workers originally brought from India to populate the Natal sugar cane farms. When the Union of South Africa was formed in 1910, the Afrikaner republics joined with the insistence that no extension of black rights be made, despite the fact that in the Cape Colony the black voters were on the common voters roll. This could only be changed by a two-thirds vote of members of both Houses of Parliament. The organisation that was to be the forerunner of the African National Congress was formed in Bloemfontein in 1912 to contest the impending Land Act passed in 1913. This exploitative act was to deprive blacks of the right to own anything of over nine-tenths of the land mass of South Africa. And Prime Minister Hertzog, who had formed the National Party in 1914, first introduced a number of bills in the 1920s which attempted to remove blacks from the voters' roll in the Cape. These acts also promised slightly to increase, as alleged compensation, the approximately 7.5 per cent of the land permitted blacks in the whole of the Union of South Africa by the Native Land Act of 1913, to 12 per cent.

And they included the establishment of a Native Council to consult with the (white) Minister of Native Affairs. Despite continuing black hostility to these Bills over the years, Hertzog published a new version of them which was passed in 1936.

In its treatment of the South African place, Mary Waters's play draws on the colonialist discourse of assimilationism. An extract from a nineteenth-century study by the Reverend William C. Holden, which the *South African bibliography* describes as 'one of the standard works on South African natives', suggests the ways in which this discourse traversed the concerns of many British colonists of the nineteenth century and subsequently members of the ruling classes and groups in the early twentieth century.[23] Holden published his study of the relations between colonists and blacks on the frontier in 1866 having spent twenty-six years in the Cape and Natal colonies and having 'numbered amongst my personal friends many ministers and colonists of long experience' (p. iv.). Amongst his reasons for writing the book he gives the need to be fair to the black inhabitants of the country and 'to arouse interest in the minds of the Christian public on behalf of one of the most interesting barbarous nations in the world' (p. vii). Towards its conclusion Holden discusses the role of the British power towards its black subjects. He quotes one of the most famous missionaries in South Africa, Dr Philip, who argues that Cape governors should encourage 'every tribe to know its limits, to be content with its own, to respect its neighbours, and to drink with eagerness from the fountains of our religion, civil policy, and science' (p. 459). And Holden, on the periphery of the empire, constructs an idealised view of the social conscience of the British government in its own island (pp. 459-500) – with which Dickens for one did not concur – in order to declare that the spirit and polity of Great Britain has at last been 'impregnated with the spirit and principles of true humanity' and that 'whilst it is the province of the minister of religion to visit the sick, the poor, and the ignorant; it is the province of the minister of state to apply those remedial measures by which the ignorant may be instructed and the fallen raised' (pp. 460-1). This leads him to assert:

What is thus acknowledged to be the duty of the state to her abject white population we claim on behalf of the ignorant coloured barbarian of this land. Why should the colour of the skin interfere? why should distance from the heart of empire thrust into the shade? why should the evil unseen fail to affect the eye, hand, and heart of the state? nay, rather strike at the root of the evil, stanch (sic) vice in its fountain, penetrate the depths of heathen darkness, barbarism, and sin; enlighten, raise, purify; and the God of nations shall smile, and say, "Well done". (p. 461)

This view of the ruling class presence in South Africa is shared by Mary Waters, not only in The light as the introductory chapter of this book suggests, but in U-Nongqause, published in 1924, and also likely to have been written, like The light, for use in missionary secondary school education.[24] Little else is known about performances of this play apart from one given by the Bantu Dramatic Society in 1933.

The cattle killing episode on which U-Nongqause draws occurred in the nineteenth century during the period of frontier wars in the expanding eastern Cape Colony – since 1806 the British had replaced the Dutch as the permanent rulers of the Cape Colony. The prophesying medium Nongqause, together with the seer Umhlakaza predicted the resurrection of the dead and the expulsion of the white colonial oppressors provided that the AmaXhosa slew all their cattle and destroyed their grain. But on the appointed day, when the sun was supposed to turn in its path in the sky and produce a storm that would drive the white man into the sea, nothing happened. Widespread suffering followed in which 20,000 people are thought to have died, while 15,000 cattle perished.[25]

U-Nongqause displays no interest in those frontier complexities which, some historians have argued, suggest mutual acculturation and no single source of legitimate authority[26] but as in Waters's earlier work, manifests instead the paternalist vision of frontier relations established by white settler historiography. A missionary is thus the most important presence in the play – his repeated commentary on the action contributes to an overall impression that the cattle killing incident in actuality formed part of a divine plan to redeem errant blacks from their unnecessarily rebellious ways. His continuing presence suggests moreover the observing masterful eye of the colonial order – the fact that the missionary might be an agent of the civil authority is something of which the text is not ashamed. The close relationship between the two is emphasised when the first scene, which gives examples of and extols the work of the colonialist presence, ends with 'family devotions' – a reading of an extended passage from the Bible by the missionary in the presence of his wife and the governor, Sir George Grey. Here, the images of family, civil power and Christianity are interwoven to set the seal on the legitimacy of the dominant order – an assertion repeated at the play's end (p. 20).

The play also works to discourage all forms of resistance to its proselytising thrust, representing Mhlakaza the 'witchdoctor', stereotypically as a figure muttering dissent, literally stirring a pot of mischief and describing white men as completely destructive:

They come to the area like fish to water, they roar like lions, they go around attacking people, they stab brave warriors…they put a spear into the hearts of their enemies. (p. 4)

This language, in Pêcheux's terms, simply inverts prevailing colonialist and missionary discourse presenting the civil and religious authority. In terms of the previous scene, Waters's text has shown the dominant order to be acting on the frontier in ways that are the opposite of this language, which in consequence, is rendered impotent even as it is uttered. Thus, although the play purports to dramatise a black attempt at counteridentification it does this in a deliberately trivialised way; the Xhosas would do well to remember, the text accordingly implies, that they need the system which Mhlakaza talks of resisting. The play also repeats the formulation said to have been uttered during the actual cattle killing, that a storm will 'sweep the whites into the sea', several times[27] but here, too, the attempt at resistance is trivialised. For the audience watching U-Nongqause or studying it, the impotence of this formulation, in contemporary terms, would be all too evident while the play itself dramatises an attempt at resistance that operates within the audience's knowledge not only of the failure of the cattle killing but also of the fact that Xhosa power has since been subdued. The inevitable presence of the dominant class is thus entailed in the very positing of its absence. Again, the specific consequence of resistance is asserted in the play to be savagism – 'women eat their children, men die at the side of the road' while even the impulse to resist is defined as a sign of immaturity: the wavering chief Sandile is told 'Remember you are not a child, pray to the Christian God' (p.14), and a magistrate observes that 'these people are like children' (p. 20).

Inevitably, too, the culture across the frontier, is presented, in accordance with colonialist and assimilationist discourse, in terms of absence – apart from, as in The light, a token praise song, no attempt is made to invest the non-colonised world with any authenticity. And in the first scene the governor, after extolling the colonial presence, opines that although the Xhosa have great promise, laziness, ignorance and the continuation of ancestor worship undermine their potential (pp. 1-2).

U-Nongqause, by means of the frontier metaphor, in these ways invites its audiences or students in 1924 and after to produce relationships between dominant and subordinate classes. To notice the 'vicious' – including the 'immature' predilection to resistance – as well as the 'virtuous' qualities of the colonised is both to recognise the potentially deviant desires that may be harboured in the body politic[28] and to identify any possible alternatives to the virtue of submission in terms only of savagism and absence. And the text's ability to admit the fact of dissent – as we have seen to allow brief moments of counter-identification which are at the same time trivialised – is itself further evidence of the watchful eye of the civil power. Even as it recognises something contestatory and ineradicable in the subordinate classes, it actively encodes such impulses in stereotypical ways, in terms of prevailing discourse – to render them inoperable, the marks of a savagism that lie beyond what is posited as the only possible order. The image of colonial/frontier society is used in ways that enable such simple juxtapositions: civilisation v. destruction; the presence of the civil authority and its absence, submission or savagism.

In terms of this reading, it is significant, too that Waters chooses to write her play in Xhosa. In his preface to The light I noted in my Introduction that Henderson congratulates the dramatist for being one who 'understands the native feeling sympathetically and can interpret their aspirations', skills which may be set against the 'mobile sensibility' and capacity 'to transform given materials into one's own scenario', the 'Europeans'' ability again and again to insinuate themselves into the pre-existing political, religious, even psychic structures of the natives and to turn these structures to their advantage' – described in another context by Stephen Greenblatt.[29] It is important to remember, moreover, that the proselytising thrust in Waters's play came at a time when there was not only continuing black discontent, and the Rand Strike which took place to assert white paternalism and maintain job reservation, but at a time when the rural policies of the state, which the play argues to be benign and a mark of civilisation was producing for the subordinate classes to whom these arguments were directed, the exact opposite, further exploitation and increasing poverty.[30] In view of the implication in U-Nongqause that (rural) waste and deprivation attends resistance to the dominant classes who otherwise ensure spiritual and material well-being, and in view of the sustained struggle over land in South African history, we may set the following reading of the dominant order's role in engineering the decline of surplus producing peasantry. One of the aims of the Land Act of 1913 was, in terms of this reading, the provision of an adequate cheap labour supply for mining and agricultural capital:

this Act was not a simple device of legislative dispossession. By retaining the reserves system and (now restricted) individual access to land while simultaneously controlling the influx of Africans into urban areas (through legislation and the pass system) it sought to provide and control a supply of cheap labour through the maintenance of pre-capitalist relations of produc- tion in the Reserves. Yet, by effectively restricting peasant production, it increasingly produced conditions which undermined these relations. By 1920 the once large peasant surpluses had dried up as the productive capacity and ability of the Reserves to support their increasing populations rapidly declined. Impoverishment and landlessness accelerated. With monotonous regularity reports and commissions after 1920 attested to 'the creation of desert conditions in the Native areas', 'warned of appalling poverty', and raised the spectre of mass starvation.[31]

From these perspectives, the frontier image in the play, as used by Waters, and the processes which it entails and enables, help to mask or obfuscate conditions in the South African social formation in 1924 and after. And such processes in U-Nongqause, seen in this light, may be understood too, in the discourse of anti-colonialism, in terms of Fanon's well-known observation:

Colonialism is not satisfied merely with holding a people in its grip and emptying the native's brain of all form and content. By a kind of perverted logic, it turns to the past of the oppressed people, and distorts, disfigures and destroys it...the total result looked for by colonial domination was indeed to convince the natives that colonialism came to lighten their darkness. The effect consciously sought by colonialism was to drive into the natives' heads the idea that if the settlers were to leave, they would at once fall back into barbarism, degradation and bestiality.[32]

III Contestation and the search for authenticity in The girl who killed to save

Dhlomo's The girl who killed to save continually evidences attempts to contest the colonialist discourses everywhere evident in U-Nongqause. It is true that in its final three scenes, Dhlomo's The girl who killed to save reproduces the arguments to be found in U-Nongqause that the cattle killing was part of a divine pattern to lead the Xhosas to a more enlightened world (see pp. 18-19, p. 25).[33] But unlike U-Nongqause which is concerned to emphasise the limitations of the pre-colonial ancestors of the subordinate classes, the text's concern is partly to assert, especially at its ending, the *acceptability* of completely assimilated, converted and totally devout blacks. This was an attempt to appropriate the discourse of assimilationism in a way that would encourage the desire for liberation rather than insist on submission.

Dhlomo's faith in missionary/Christian discourse reflects a view, prevalent at the time he wrote, that the cause of oppression lay in the abuse rather than in the practice of Christianity. In this Dhlomo was one step away from a more subversive position – in which, indeed, most committed adherents of Christianity in South Africa repeatedly find themselves. Implicit in the final stage image of a harmonious family of practising Christians from the oppressed classes is criticism of a social order that despite its Christian pretensions, fails in practice to realise them. Indeed, one of the typical kinds of counteridentification current at the time of Dhlomo's play does more than simply reject the image of the subordinate classes as pagan. It reverses the claim in prevailing discourse that the dominant classes are Christian. An appropriate instance of this is to be found in an extract from the presidential address at the All African Convention, with recent events in Ethiopia in mind, quoted in an article by M. L. Kabane published in *The South African Outlook* on 1 August 1936:

All Africans as well as other non-White races of the world have been staggered by the cynical rape by Italy of the last independent State belonging to indigenous Africans. After hearing a great deal for twenty years about the rights of small nations, self-determination, Christian ideals, the inviolability of treaties, humane warfare, the sacredness of one's plighted word, the glory of European civilisation, and so forth, the brief history of the last eight months has scratched this European veneer and revealed the white savage hidden beneath.[34]

We may recall the trivialised version of counteridentification apparent in Mhlakaza's language in *U-Nongqause*. This time however a different voice speaks. Kabane reports further:

After pointing out the failure of organised Christianity to curb the animal propensities of rapacity and selfishness in the hearts of men who rule empires, and the abandonment of Christianity as a working proposition in politics, the speaker ascribed the 'thirty pieces of colour bar legislation against us' to the guiding philosophy of self-preservation which the Union Premier in a recent speech extolled above all Christian principles. (p. 187)

These comments relate to that segregationist legislation which Hertzog – in the 1930s Prime Minister and head of the new United Party – was bringing to successful conclusion.

The first two scenes of The girl who killed to save suggest an even more vigorous process of contestation. For one thing, the text evokes an hierarchy, order and system of conventions that will give the lie to the savagism and absence that the language of assimilationism entails and that colonialist discourse postulates as residing in the 'other' – that which lies beyond the periphery of the colonial power's influence. The stage directions at the beginning of scene 1 (pp. 4-5) work to create the impression of productivity while much of the procedure in scene 2 suggests an enactment of the delicate relations between the chief and his people to be found in John Henderson Soga's description published in 1931:

The principal safeguard against an abuse of power by the chief is the existence of the Court of Councillors. This is ever in session, for matters affecting tribal and private life are daily brought before the chief for decision. The chief is head of the council, but he dare not veto a decision of this court except at the peril of his reputation and authority in the tribe. The decision or finding of the councillors becomes his finding, and when announced by the appointed spokesman of the court, is given in the name of the chief.[35]

If such versions of the past, evoked in Dhlomo's play as well as in Soga's account, in the argument of certain historians, may not necessarily have been possible in the actuality of the fragmenting nineteenth-century frontier world, they may nevertheless be seen as an attempt to construct a vision of the oppressed subject that contested the assertions of savagism and absence accompanying assimilationist forms of discourse. The girl who killed to save also includes discussion of love and lobola (bride-price), while unlike the thrust in U-Nongqause, there is no denigration of ancestor worship.

The play's attitude to resistance is also manifestly different from that evident in Waters's work. Whereas in the earlier play Nongqause is merely a mechanism, The girl who killed to save presents her as a young woman who cares above all for the future of her people, and one who is torn between her need to be of use and her fear that she may be mistaken:

I did hear strange sounds…near the river. Father and the Elephant assured me, after using the bones and medicine, the sounds were the voices of our ancestors. But are their interpretations correct? Why did not the spirits speak to me in the language I understand? (p. 10)

Her scepticism, shared by the young man whom she loves and who implores her to abandon the struggle is balanced against her reason for persevering which, unlike the reductive trivialisation 'to drive the white man into the sea' is because she believes 'we shall get new cattle and grain...and...the dead shall rise' (p. 10). This presentation of Nongqause, as well as demonstrating sensitivity to her private conflicts, posits the cattle killing as a tragically mistaken tactic rather than as immature futility. And her commitment, despite her scepticism, foregrounds the need for resistance even as it identifies an error in strategy. An impulse towards resistance in the play may be detected too in several moments of ambiguity which, even in scenes 3, 4 and 5, interrogate the momentum towards submission. Hugh Thompson's argument that 'both the missionary and the Administrator have long been trying to civilise the black man, turn him into a regular efficient worker, and into a peaceful citizen' (p. 17) comes shortly after the praise singer's salute to Kreli in scene 2 as 'hater of the white thieves' (p. 12). His comment introduces a sequence of dramatised incidents of submission which is interrupted by the appearance of a snake, 'the bodily form the ancestors must often take', and usually a warning or a reminder of sacred custom and tradition,[36] and followed by an exchange between Ngesi and Brownlee in which the hint of exploitation runs close to the surface of the language:

Ngesi: Sir the draft reached the place safely. *The men were given over to their various employers. They told me they were happy to find help and work, and they promised to be honest, industrious servants...*

(*Ngesi goes to the door and shouts at the men to come in. They pack together sitting on their legs.*) Brownlee: I'm glad to hear you prefer to go and work for the European than to remain in Xhosaland and kill yourselves by destroying cattle. You are brave and wise. The white man is just. *But remember you must be honest, obedient, loyal servants. I shall find you good employers.* (my emphasis; pp. 17-18).

In the fourth scene Nomaliso, who discovers the snake in the previous scene responds to the Missionary's assertion of the importance to people of knowledge and salvation, 'No, they thirst for water – food. People can only think about salvation when their stomachs are not empty. First give the people food and then talk of salvation' (p. 24), while in the final scene the Missionary and his doctor friend whisper to one another about the other occupants of the room in a way that seems for an instant to introduce acknowledgement of at least an element of manipulation. The most powerful mood of resistance in the

play is, however, engendered at the conclusion to scene 2, when, after
a careful discussion of the pros and cons of resistance, word comes to
the Xhosas that a raid in the Gonubie and another on the Kobongo
Church Mission Station have both been successful. At this point the
sound of approaching warriors is heard; when they enter in full war
dress, Kreli delivers an oration to them supporting the Cattle Killing
but ending 'Kreli will triumph over the European. Kreli will rule over
all the country. Go!' (p. 15). The aim of resistance, although the
method is mistaken, is clear enough. Again, the stage directions help
us to see the effect worked for in the text:

Kreli stands with legs apart, right hand clasping spear and left hand pointing
out in front. The soldiers burst into the warrior's song. The seer sprinkles the
warriors with medicine. The Chief's Bard repeats the praises of Kreli – music,
poetical phrases and medicinal treatment all done together, giving grandeur
and emotion to the scene. (p. 15)

This climax brings the play closest to an alternative discourse – one
that might lead to dissatisfaction with those aspects of assimilationism
and the arguments for submission with which it does take issue. But
instead of the development of a discourse more directly appropriate
to the concerns of members of the oppressed classes who formed the
play's first audiences, this image on stage of the militancy of the black
subject is deflected again in the last three acts. The text's attempt to
separate a vision of Christian discourse and the glimpse of a just future
which it entails from the practice and abuse of Christian discourse
manifest in the dominant classes, and its struggle to assert a stance of
resistance is finally contained, particularly in the dying Daba's vision
of Nongqause surrounded by the host of those who perished in the
great famine:

there is triumph in death; there is finding in death; there is beauty in death.
Nongqause laughs as she tells them that she was really in earnest but was
ignorant. They laugh and sing. They call her their Liberator from Superstition
and from the rule of Ignorance. These people are dressed not in karosses and
blankets as we are, but in Light. (p. 29)

The redefinition of liberty not as the militant search for appropriate
resistance but, in terms of assimilationist and colonialist discourse, as
freedom from superstition and ignorance, is exactly what agents of the
dominant classes, as many commentators argue, in different ways
worked for and desired.

IV Segregationism and *Cetshwayo*

Cetshwayo comes at a moment in South African history when a significant attempt was made, in Eddie Roux's estimation, to put 'the clock back'.[37] Ruling class and subordinate subjects, until then predominantly constructed in terms of colonialist and assimilationist discourses, were, especially with the passing of General Hertzog's Native Bills, re-situated in terms primarily of the discourse of segregationism. The emergence of segregationist discourse, through which relations between the dominant and subordinate classes in South Africa have in the twentieth century most predominantly operated, has been traced by Saul Dubow, to the demise in Europe of cherished nineteenth-century liberal ideals about the 'equality of man' and the 'doctrine of inevitable progress'.[38] He cites the development of racist discourse preoccupied with evolution and eugenics in Europe and North America together with 'growing pessimism and collectivism' (p. 73) in late nineteenth-century British thought. In South Africa, during the decade after the First World War the full implications of industrialisation had become clear in, as I have already partly noted, 'the declining agricultural capacity of the reserves, the rapid dissolution of the tribal system, nascent working-class radicalism and the growth of urban slums'. (p. 79). And in the context of 'transition from a mercantile to an industrial economy' (p. 79), the segregationist policy that was 'elaborated by liberal theorists in the first decade of the twentieth century' was 'essentially conceived as a conservative policy of social containment' (p. 88).

In their abandonment of assimilationist reasoning, segregationists focused upon notions of 'culture', 'differentiation' and 'racial groups' (p. 80). Thus anthropologically determined concepts of culture, striving to explore and expound the 'complexity' of African culture and its distinctive nature, enabled the emergence of arguments for the differentiation of African from European culture. Such arguments about 'culture' inevitably pleased segregationists whose notions of culture substituted the word 'civilisation' for 'culture' and also situated culture 'along the barbarian/civilisation continuum' (p. 83), asserting, of course, the supremacy of 'white' culture. These associations, coupled with the notion of the African race as one at a lower level of development, allowed for what Dubow calls the 'ubiquitous' flexibility of versions of the black as a member of the African 'child' race (a concept sometimes not absent, as we have seen, in the paternalist aspects of assimilationist discourse):

The usefulness of this concept was its essential ambiguity; as 'children' it could be expected that Africans would in time attain the maturity of white civilisation. On the other hand, however, it could also be implied that on account of their essential differences, Africans would remain children, perhaps for ever. (p. 86)

Dubow points out that even certain liberals, believing that African culture might be 'protected' by means of segregation, began to draw on segregationist arguments. R. F. Alfred Hoernle, head of the Department of Philosophy at the University of the Witwatersrand and a well-known liberal, observed in 1939 in a series of lectures at the University of Cape Town that 'for the Native peoples of the Union, at any rate, it should be clear that there is *no escape from white domination by way of Parallelism or Assimilation, but only by way of Total Separation*...the one way of freeing Whites and Blacks from an entanglement with each other which is bad for both but worst for the non-Whites'.[39]

But someone such as Selope Thema, however, was able to see clearly one of the many important implications in the shift from assimilationism to segregationist views, arguing that segregationists were

not in favour of a segregation policy that will free the Bantu people from European control...They want a segregation which will protect the Europeans against Bantu competition in the labour market and in the fields of industry and commerce...the white man must control the lines along which the Bantu people are asked to develop.[40]

Government ideologues such as George Heaton Nicholls were quite forthright about those aims in segregationism men such as Thema recognised:

An adaptationist policy demands as its primary concept the maintenance of chieftaindom without which tribal society cannot exist...It assumes some measure of territorial segregation. It assumes what is in effect the growth of a national consciousness amongst the Bantu themselves which will either become inimical to the interests of the Europeans or form a harmonious part of our complex society. *The opposite policy of assimilation substitutes class for race, and if continued on its present basis, must lead to the evolution of a native proletariat, inspired by the usual antagonisms of class war.* (my emphasis)[41]

If white fears of African proletarianisation and the black influx into the cities intensified this use of the notion of an 'African system' and 'culture' for political ends, numerous others in the 1920s and 1930s were well aware of the motives that underlay segregationist attempts to define the oppressed subject differently. Dhlomo wrote in 1932 in a newspaper article:

Tribalism was encouraged. But it was a new type of tribalism. It gave peace, encouraged non-progressive institutions among the people, and it made the government the supreme chief and dictator. As the aftermath of this form of tribalism we have the Native Administration Act and the recently promulgated Natal Code Amendment, both of which seek to perpetuate and extend retrogressive tribalism.[42]

Reactions to developing segregation included not only the responses of the representatives of a weakened African National Congress but, far more important at the time, the formation of the All African Convention to resist the process, in 1935. The Chairperson, Professor D. D. T. Jabavu in his opening address gave voice to the current outrage:

There are Black men today fully capable of sitting and representing their people in the House of Assembly. Why are they not allowed to sit there?...The Bantu people know what justice is by nature and tradition without having to be taught...the object of these Bills is to shunt the Natives from all civilised spheres back to tribal life and to a purely agricultural economy, because the Native is an apple of discord in European politics...the Black race must be regarded as a child race, and as such should be ruled under a system of trusteeship. It is therefore manifest that these Bills were framed on the assumed basis that the Black race is a race of children who will continue to be children for all time.[43]

Cetshwayo is likely to have been written by Dhlomo shortly after *The girl who killed to save* in late 1936/early 1937.[44] He was not the first to attempt to address directly the problem of land in South Africa by means of art or literature. Solomon Plaatje had raised some of the problems, which Dhlomo's plays explore in the 1930s, as early as 1917, in the novel Mhudi, eventually published in 1932. Indeed Plaatje's most famous work was his direct attack upon the Natives Land Act of 1913 in his book Native life in South Africa.[45] He was much admired, particularly amongst petit-bourgeois intellectuals and, like many others, Dhlomo recalled him with great respect. Mhudi anticipates many of the concerns evident in Dhlomo's work. It argues implicitly for unity against oppressive rulers. Plaatje also portrays the struggle over land, endeavours to construct a positive vision of traditional African life – preferable to that which replaced it – and presents the white presence as one, in the end, duplicitous factor in a larger battle amongst conflicting interests for dominance.[46] Concern over the question of land distribution had also obsessed poets and musicians of the period – a well-known example of which may be found in the composer Reuben Caluza's song, 'iLand Act'.[47]

Cetshwayo, like *The girl who killed to save*, uses the frontier image, but in order to engage directly with the intensification of the segregationist movement in South Africa.[48] It opens during the final years of the reign of the son of Dingaan, Mpande, just after Cetshwayo, one of Mpande's sons, in the struggle for the succession has defeated his brother Mbuyazi in battle. The first half explores episodes in Cetshwayo's rise set against the developing threat of a clash between the colonial power, represented amongst others by Shepstone, governor of the Cape, and the black inhabitants beyond the frontier. The subsequent attack by the colonial power, temporarily halted by the famous black military victory over the British at Isandhlwana, and the British recovery, provide the setting for the second half of the play. This leads, by the end, to Cetshwayo's defeat and death.

Tim Couzens describes *Cetshwayo* as 'the play of the All-African Convention'[49] and cites J. R. Sullivan 'who wrote in 1928 that Hertzog's policies were logical and just successors to those of Shepstone's' (p. 135) to demonstrate that the play was written not only to probe a narrative which was not and remains not 'household knowledge in a country where some of the most important historical events have been so distorted or ignored that whole facets of the story have often disappeared from view' (p. 126) but also to contest the policies which had culminated in Hertzog's Bills of 1936.

The play's anti-segregationist thrust is most crucially to be found in the confrontation in scene 5 between Shepstone and his clerk Park. But this is prepared for by several scenes which depict the conflicting perspectives, differences, and colonial exploitation of these differences that that are to lead both to war and to Cetshwayo's defeat. Thus scene 2 presents the differently positioned participants in the struggle to retain or assert influence on the frontier. The understanding of Mpande, the ailing King, of the shaky balance of power is juxtaposed against the comments of John Dunn, a totally expedient adventurer, while at the conclusion of the scene, Shepstone speaks for the colonial presence itself, the soldiers of the Queen who 'like waves... roar and charge, fall back, press on, ever toil, never die, can never be exterminated' (p. 125). If the scene thus acknowledges that what is at issue is a struggle for power between a variety of forces with in each case very different positions and allegiances, its detailed business emphasises the crucial but also ambiguous nature of language and action in a situation fraught with conflicting interest, and suggests manipulative tendencies in both settler and colonialist presence. This manipulative behaviour is dramatised more fully in the following scene which shows Dunn exploiting differences amongst black chiefs, the self-interest of the farmers as well as the proselytising ardour of the missionaries, in order to check Cetshwayo's increasing power. His desires accord with that of the colonial government whose motives are spelt out in the fifth scene of the play by Shepstone himself when he asserts that Cetshwayo

wants to unite the various tribes into one strong nation that will be a menace to us... If civilisation and white supremacy are to be maintained in this country, the Natives must be demilitarised. It is not a question of ethics. It is one of arms and government. He who has power rules and dictates. (p. 146)

This language reflects the fear of increasing black power which historians argue obsessed Shepstone. Any measures leading to the general extension of black participation in the franchise, would in his opinion, as Sullivan pointed out lead to 'an ultimate transfer of government to the black races'.[50] Black unity especially offered a threat which the policy of segregationism and the encouragement of what in effect would be the divisive policy of tribalism would help to diminish. Such views were shared by Hertzog who in his speeches on segregation 'invariably warned of the vulnerability of white civilisation in the face of the numerical preponderance of Africans, and... frequently equated political rights for Africans with "swamping"'.[51]

The drama in Cetshwayo turns partly on the ways in which this discourse is contested. A central argument in this is advocacy of the importance to the oppressed subject of black unity in the face of Hertzog's thrust, a unity that by implication, as Couzens has argued, is to be led by the 'new Africans' of the All African Convention. The play repeatedly stresses the power of and need for militant black unity, climaxing with the dying prime minister's appeal:

Black man! Black man! Trust yourself. Serve yourself. Know yourself... Black man you are your own enemy! You are your own oppressor...My people!...Get out and fight. Our Soul lives. The battle still rages. (p. 174)

This is followed by another speaker's emphasis that 'the fight is not between those here today;/ The battle stands between those yet to be' (p. 175), and by Cetshwayo's dying assertion addressed directly to

Dhlomo's contemporary audience:

We shall be free!
Each race its lord and clime.
And Africa for Africans remains. (p. 176)

Cetshwayo also develops counteridentification of the claim to Christianity, made by the dominant order in prevailing discourse, present mainly by implication in *The girl who killed to save*. Thus when Bishop Colenso, in contrast to the missionaries who have decided to join Dunn, disapproves of the betrayal of Christian values in current policies, and accuses Shepstone of waging an unjust war, Shepstone's response is to advise him, 'The Church should keep out of politics' (p. 156), a remark which Couzens takes as a 'clear echo of Hertzog's statement in Parliament in 1936: "I do not understand at all what you mean by Christian principles. Christian principles count for very much, but there is a principle of self-preservation for a nation, the principle which causes everybody to sacrifice his life in time of war...I place that principle still higher. It is the only principle, that of self-preservation, self-defence, by which humanity itself and Christianity itself will ever be able to protect itself".'[52] Earlier, Dunn, in what is almost an example of Brechtian alienation comments on his manoeuvring to the audience,

My ambition to overthrow Shepstone?... There is nothing immoral and unusual in that. It is the Western game and way of life. Are we not Europeans, playing our dirty sweet, old game of gain, greed and power? No, conscience, the true tragedy is to cheat these poor savages who are blind and gullible, not to rob the European who himself stands to rob. Ah! One of my race of deceivers and liberators, of ruthless conquerors and just administrators, of callous exploiters and Christian gentlemen! (p. 133)

The text also resists the claim of altruism on the part of the dominant classes and, in so doing, moves towards a measure of disidentification by stressing the economic basis of the colonialist push for domination. Thus the farmers ask Dunn:

Why should niggers own land? What do they know about land purchase, boundaries, tillages and values? We want more land but cannot get it owing to the hostile attitude of Cetshwayo and his hordes. (p. 133)

and Shepstone himself justifies the segregationist impulse and the need to break black power by explaining:

The defeat of Cetshwayo and the control of the Native population would mean a great source of wealth by means of taxation; would provide an unfailing reservoir of labour, appease the Transvaal Volksraad, pacify and win over the Boers, and settle once and for all the boundary disputes between black and white. Her Majesty's Government refuses to give us more loans and subsidies, the Transvaal Boers are unable to raise money or pay enough taxes to run their Republic efficiently. (p. 146)

As Couzens shows, the replies which Shepstone's senior clerk, Park, gives to the colonial administrator in scene 5, are a clear statement of the inadequacies of Shepstone's policies in language that points to Hertzog's segregationism as well. And resistance to this process in the play is developed too in counteridentification of the alleged salutary effects of their presence upon South Africa claimed by the ruling classes as well as in the use in *Cetshwayo* − as in *The girl who killed to save* − of an idealised vision of the black past.

V Towards an epic theatre

Dhlomo endeavoured, on the margins not only of the imperial centre, but of the ruling classes within South Africa, to recover or to construct an authenticity within the periphery which these centres worked continually to erase. Nevertheless, his search to discover or construct a past non-colonised essence was balanced by a compelling awareness of the importance of current conditions of struggle. Thus he argued for 'African playwrights who will dramatise and expound a philosophy of our history', but he also called for 'dramatic representations of African Oppression, Emancipation, and Evolution' and he stressed that 'the African dramatist cannot delve into the past unless he has grasped the present…African art must deal with the things that are vital and near to the African today'.[53] In all of this Dhlomo was contesting prevailing ruling class indifference to the development of a South African theatre, contesting in his own plays, as this chapter argues, the ineffectiveness of many versions of assimilationist discourse and, even more fiercely, the segregationist discourse designed to position the black in history as well as in her or his contemporary world, as I have tried to show, in positions suggesting savagism and absence, childishness, inferiority, and subjugation.

Against dominant attitudes towards theatre amongst the ruling classes, Dhlomo's sense that traditional drama in Africa 'was national' and 'treated matters that concerned the people as a whole'[54] and his concern to write of 'great heroes whose activities are near enough to be of interest and meaning, but remote enough to form subjects of great, dispassionately passionate creative literature'[55] prompted him to write, as well as *Cetshwayo*, two other plays, on Shaka and Dingane, aimed at 'the cultural regeneration of his people through the creation of a national (partly tragic) epic'.[56] These impulses led him, too, in theatrical practice to go beyond the emphasis described, for instance, by Boal[57] in what he calls bourgeois theatre where the character on stage ceases to be an 'object' within a larger process but becomes instead the 'subject of dramatic action' (p. 63). Boal notes Hegel's insistence that in dramatic poetry, 'the event does not appear to proceed from external conditions, but rather from personal volition and character' to observe that in such theatre:

The denouement arises out of the dramatic conflict...It is the repose that comes after the tumult of human passions and actions. In order for this to occur, the characters must necessarily be 'free'; that is, it is necessary for the internal movements of their spirit to be freely exteriorised without limits or restraints. In short, the character is the absolute *subject* of his actions. (p. 88)

Accordingly, in this theatre the concern is predominantly with interiority: 'the soul is the subject that determines all external action...the drama shows the external collision of forces originating internally' (p. 87).

In contrast to such foregrounding of issues exclusively within character, and despite his own concern to portray black heroes, Dhlomo's dramatisation of history in both the plays I have discussed always locates its central figures within larger processes in ways that dislodge this kind of privileging of interiority. Thus, while Dhlomo manifests an interest in Nongqause's interiority, *The girl who killed to save* explores this in the context of the culture and needs of her people, as well as in its interrogation of the significance of the assimilationist forces ranged against them. And Dhlomo's presentation of Cetshwayo dramatises to a remarkable degree the extent to which the king himself exists within a process involving not only the vitality of his own culture but one that involves also the operation of material forces and conflicting interests in the colonialist push for power, shown in the play to combine in an unholy alliance that defeats him. It involves also interrogation of the segregationist thrust operating within the social order concerning audience as well as actors and dramatic characters. This is not to suggest that there is no concern with interiority in the play, which is explored both in scene 4, when Cetshwayo's love for

Basikele together with his overriding sense of destiny and ambition, are examined, and in the final scene when he reacts to his defeat. But what might by contrast be identified as a primary concern with interiority in Boal's terms is gone. Dhlomo's treatment of his dramatic characters here recalls Plaatje's interest in the developing relationship between Ra-Thaga and Mhudi in Mhudi, a relationship at the same time always set within and affected by larger processes with their own momentum.

VI Appropriating the language of the coloniser

If in this way Dhlomo challenged some of the assumptions in traditionalist bourgeois theatre, he also struggled against those prevailing discourses within the educative processes privileged by the colonial and ruling class centres. He, and indeed most of the writers of his generation were the products of a particular system of education based in part at least upon the vision of those British or British-trained administrators and educators who made their way to South Africa in the nineteenth and twentieth century. As Eagleton has remarked, from the perspective of Marxist discourse, this tradition operated on the assumptions that

literature should convey timeless truths, thus distracting the masses from their immediate commitments, nurturing in them a spirit of tolerance and generosity, and so ensuring the survival of private property...the pill of middle-class ideology was to be sweetened by the sugar of literature.[58]

Eagleton also notes studies of 'the importance of the admission of English literature to the Civil Service examinations in the Victorian period' to argue that, 'armed with this conveniently packaged version of their own cultural treasures, the servants of British imperialism could sally forth overseas secure in a sense of their national identity and able to display that cultural superiority to their envying colonial peoples.' (pp. 28-9) This process was exacerbated after the Great War, Eagleton maintains, for 'an English ruling class whose sense of identity had been profoundly shaken, whose psyche was ineradicably scarred by the horrors it had endured' so that literature would become 'at once solace and reaffirmation, a familiar ground on which Englishmen could regroup both to explore, and to find some alternative to, the nightmare of history' (p. 30).

The 'nightmare' Eagleton identifies, for English colonial educationists, no doubt seemed to intensify on the South African terrain. Certainly, exclusive obsession with the literature of the metropolis, about an entirely different landscape from the South African veld, and an attendant predilection for Romantic and Victorian literature, operating from the late nineteenth century on, endured well into the mid-twentieth century and beyond in the use of literature in South African education. Romantic preoccupations with self, transcendentalism, and pantheism, from these perspectives could only serve to intensify this tendency to use literature as a means of intellectual withdrawal into the 'timeless' and away from the fluctuations and unpredictabilities of material struggle.

Together with many of the poets of his generation, Dhlomo, as a result of his own missionary education, manifested a strong predilection for Romantic and Victorian rhythms, a trait generally considered to be a defect in his work.[59] The criticism was levelled too against Plaatje's style in Mhudi. But Couzens argues in the case of Plaatje that such objections fail to account not only for the difficulties such writers faced but also ignores the subtleties and strengths in Plaatje's prose that often led to the disappearance of 'Victorian' elements at moments of climax.[60] It is, similarly, possible to argue that – as in the case of the work of many other poets too – the use to which Dhlomo puts this style ran counter to the assumptions underlying the presence of Romantic and Victorian literature in the education syllabus and, especially, contested the stress upon the timeless and transcendental import of such literature probable in the teaching of it. Furthermore, his use of language sometimes provides illuminations despite the stylistic hegemony of his time. For instance Dhlomo's interest in the ambiguity of power and the shifting perspectives that comes with the changing positions occupied by different subjects within the social order, is paralleled by what are often circular statements in the detail of the language that tend to illustrate exactly that point. Thus, when two warriors confront one another, at the beginning of scene 2, the second warrior mocks the first's request for proof and he replies 'Prove proof wrong – and fight if you dare!' (p. 126). After the fight when the superiority of the first warrior has emerged he tells the dying second warrior: 'proof is proven'. (p. 127) Similarly in the first scene, during the account of the battle between Cetshwayo and his brother, the warrior describes how many of the defeated warriors 'felt unfeeling pain' and again the sense of the same word signifying

differently for each individual according to the position each occupies
in the relationships of power pertaining between them complements
the awareness of precisely this in the larger contestation for power
between groups dramatised in the play. This is pointedly evident in
the detail of the language in the climax to what is the deliberately
contorted speech about his ambition which Dunn utters in scene 3. He
uses the word 'Rest' to indicate the fulfilment of his dreams:

Ah! perfect Rest that craves no rest from Rest!
The Rest that lives, conceives, creates, wields power! (p. 130)

In the repetition, lastly, to describe the role of the people, of the
formulation 'We, the lowly, remain remaining' (p. 119), whereas the
first verb asserts a position of subordination within the prevailing
hierarchy, the participle adjusts the perspective somewhat to assert
within the perspective of time, qualities of endurance and strength.

Dhlomo's style of writing is likely also to have been influenced by
the techniques of the morality play evident in Waters's work.
Concerned as he was to 'teach, by drama, lessons that cannot be taught
in the pulpit or the classroom'.[61] Dhlomo seems to work, particularly
in the direct assertion to the audience of black militancy and identity,
for an inspirational and didactic effect that, in its communal directness,
evokes the morality play genre. But in the case of Dhlomo's use of the
frontier image, also likely to have derived from Waters's work, the
results can be equivocal. It may be argued that especially in The girl who
killed to save, the inspirational thrust in the play towards the assertion
of oppressed-class militant identity is undermined because of its
presentation, as in Waters's work, in the context of a frontier world
that has limited applicability within a world undergoing rapid
industrialisation. But while this may be partly true the choice is
certainly not as disabling in Cetshwayo where the frontier metaphor is
used as a means of addressing the segregationist push currently under
way in Dhlomo's own world. Nevertheless it is interesting that, in the
late 1930s and 1940s Dhlomo turned more directly to the task of
dramatising or presenting the fabric of social and political experiences
in his own time and space on stage. Ruby and Frank was an attempt to
provide a musical representation of current life for the oppressed, and
in its subject matter contrasted with his earlier endeavour in Moeshoeshoe
to construct with both music and dance a great episode from past
history. Two of his plays in the 1940s, although written simply in the
form of a report or dramatised case study of current moments in

history, were similarly unique, initiating and anticipating the concern to displace the colonial and ruling class centres and to endeavour instead within the marginalised sites of exploitation and oppression, to discover sustaining and enabling means of self-definition. *The pass* portrays the arrest of a black journalist for failing to carry a pass at night entitling him to be in an urban area inhabited by whites, the night he spends in prison and, on his release, his resolution to campaign against pass legislation.[62] *The workers* portrays working-class conditions and the need to develop proper unions as well as tactics for strike action.[63] And its language, whilst still subject to the mannerisms of his earlier style, itself struggles towards a more contemporary idiom. In *The workers*, the Manager, faced with resistance from his labourers, responds in a way that may briefly indicate the change in approach:

The machines must not stop or slow down even if men die out like flies... men are easily produced every and anywhere – in slums, streets and gutters ... machines... bring wealth, power, progress and happiness. Civilisation is machines. We no longer believe in the myth of the soul and dignity of man ... Men are tools, brawn and dust; machines are money, brains and life. (p. 216)

Unlike the earlier attempts in Dhlomo's texts to postulate an ideal alternative construction of the oppressed subject, this language recognises the way in which the subject is actually constructed as an expendable labour mechanism within her or his contemporary world.

VII Dhlomo and hegemony

The significance of Dhlomo's plays lies in their remarkable endeavour to engage with their own world. They were texts that emerged too at an important moment in the intensification of segregation in the history of South Africa. The texts are impressive, moreover, because of the fact that they were written at all (and sometimes performed), in a world in which, in almost every way, prevailing discourse worked to inhibit their appearance. It is worth glancing here at the recollections of Tom Thomas, who, a dissident in England, established the Hackney People's Players in the 1920s:

I spent many hours in the library of the British Drama League searching for plays which dealt with the realities of the lives of the working class in Britain, and which analysed or dissected the social system which had failed to prevent the war, had completely failed to deliver the 'homes for heroes'...it was clear that if the People's Players was to fulfil its aim of exposing the evils of the capitalist system, and the oppression of the people, then the plays had to be written. By whom? At that juncture there was only one answer – by me. And by anyone else whom I could persuade to attempt the task.[64]

Dhlomo was up against similar but infinitely greater odds. Bizarrely, but also prophetically, his importance is also to be found, given the extent of his achievement, in the story of what has been in practice, in effect, his suppression. He died in 1956 at the age of fifty-three. His editors tell us that as well as short stories, poems, essays and countless published journalistic articles, he wrote twenty-four plays.[65] Nine of these plays are known to have survived in reasonably complete form. But only two of Dhlomo's works were published in his lifetime: *The girl who killed to save* and a long poem entitled *Valley of a thousand hills*.

Furthermore, scant evidence about the performance of Dhlomo's plays survives. It is known for certain that a performance of *Moshoeshoe* took place in 1938, and that another of *The girl who killed to save* also took place before 1935. But, although it is certain that other plays, despite Dhlomo's apparent belief that he was developing a form of literary drama, were also produced, little of this is yet fully established. Indeed, it was only as a result of the research of two scholars working at the University of the Witwatersrand and the University of Cape Town, Tim Couzens and Nick Visser, in the early 1970s, that many of his manuscripts were recovered – found still hidden away in a cupboard of the University of Natal Durban Library canteen although presented by members of Dhlomo's family to the library on his death. And it was only in 1985 that a volume of his collected works, including these nine plays, was published. Whereas study of *Cetshwayo* alone confirms Dhlomo as the first modern South African dramatist of stature, and in his ideas as well as his practice probably the (unknown) father of much that is significant in present-day South African drama, the fact that he has been for so long neglected, is equally important. What, we may speculate, might have been the nature of the subsequent development of South African drama if it had been easier for him to publish or produce his work? And, in view of the richness of the issues his plays raise both in terms of the aesthetics of drama and history, as well as in terms of the culture he strives to dramatise and that within which he works, his continuing absence for the most part in tertiary as well as secondary education provides eloquent testimony to the process of suppression in present-day South Africa. This applies currently even in institutions asserting commitment to the promotion of a post-apartheid culture. In terms of current methodological and pedagogic practice in tertiary institutions, for example, whilst he researched Dhlomo's work Couzens was situated in the Witwatersrand University English Department. He fought a largely lonely and futile battle to win some recognition for non-British African literature as a respectable area for teaching and study. The student body in this department numbers in any year well over 1000, thus making it an influential contributor to attitudes amongst future teachers and educated members of the social order. In the end Couzens left it for a full time research position in the African Studies Institute where he still does some teaching, but only to very small numbers of students in any one year.

This process of suppression began early in South African dramatic history, as I have already remarked. Although *The girl who killed to save*, a far less powerful play than *Cetshwayo*, was published by Lovedale Press, when Dhlomo submitted a collection of plays to the editor of the Press, the Reverend R. H. Shepherd, in 1938 entitled *This is Africa* and likely to have included *Cetshwayo*, the response was negative. Couzens is careful to point out that Lovedale was wary as 2000 copies of *The girl who killed to save* had been published on 22 October 1936, and only 336 sold by 1938, when sales appeared to be dormant.[66] But Shepherd explained that although the plays submitted showed 'considerable talent' (p. 177), he thought they were not, on the whole up to publication standard. His response may further be understood in the light of the research he undertook into black literature, for which he was three years later awarded a DLitt by the University of the Witwatersrand.[67] Many of the comments he makes in his dissertation suggests often identified paternalist and patronising attitudes to be found in many South African educators. Thus, recalling the missionaries who first encountered blacks he observes:

It deserves to be noted that from...the first...respect for their intellectual qualities was engendered...though...they are entirely destitute of education, and of every species of learning, yet their minds are neither blunt nor dwarfish...as early as 1823 the missionaries at Chumie reported that the Bantu were a fine race of people and that nothing but religion and civilisation were wanting to exalt them in the scale of being – to raise them to the true dignity of human nature. (pp. 4-5)

This belief in European versions of knowledge as a prerequisite for the elevation of blacks to 'the true dignity of human nature', may be set against another of Shepherd's observations in his view of the 'development' of blacks:

They are at the adolescent period, a period which, as in the life of individuals, is difficult for any people. It is difficult and trying not only for themselves but for those who are in any sense their guardians or their guides. A people at this stage is strong enough to feel its own strength, but sometimes not wise enough to be completely independent. Emotion is often more powerful than reason, and such emotion may find expression at times in strange and startling forms. The guardian or helper must be prepared for disappointments and must exercise tact mingled with kindness. Over-firmness leads to estrangement but over-indulgence...leads to separation. (pp. 84-5)

Such a view could not have taken kindly to the presentation of colonisers and settlers, the role of many if not all of the missionaries, and that of the farmers, in Cetshwayo. It would have been even less pleased with the advocacy of resistance and black militancy and victory in the play. Moreover, the importance of such attitudes is intensified when we realise that they come not from the more actively segregationist agents of the ruling classes, but, indeed, in the case of Waters as well as Shepherd, from relatively well-intentioned educators who believed they were furthering a moral (assimilationist) cause and who dedicated, often, the major portion of their lives to this cause.

Notes

1 Couzens, The new African, pp. 51-2. I am indebted to the work of Couzens throughout this chapter.
2 Couzens, The new African, p. 51.
3 Kavanagh, Theatre and cultural struggle, pp. 45-6.
4 Cited in Plaatje, Sol T., Mhudi, ed Couzens, Tim, 'Introduction' to Plaatje, Sol T., Mhudi, Johannesburg: Quagga Press, 1975, p. 14.
5 Coplan, In township tonight!, pp. 90-142.
6 Coplan, In township tonight!, p. 98.
7 Coplan, In township tonight!, p. 75.
8 Steadman, 'Drama and social consciousness', p. 84.
9 Steadman,'Drama and social consciousness', pp. 61-2.
10 Couzens, The new African, p.174.
11 See Roux, Time longer than rope, p. 312.
12 Cited by Couzens, The new African, p. 99.
13 Steadman, 'Drama and social consciousness', p. 64.
14 Couzens, The new African, p. 176.
15 See Vandenbroucke, Russel, 'A brief chronology of the theatre in South Africa', Theatre quarterly, VII, 28, 1977-78, pp. 44-6; Kavanagh, Theatre and cultural struggle, pp. 43-8.
16 Hoffman, Arthur and Hoffman, Anna Romain, They built a theatre, Johannesburg: Donker, 1980, pp. 42-3.
17 For this and what follows see Couzens, The new African, esp. chapter 2.
18 Sole, Kelwyn, 'Class, continuity and change in black South African literature 1948-60', in Bozzoli, Belinda, comp., Labour, townships and protest, Johannesburg: Ravan, 1979, p. 145; Couzens, The new African, pp. 6-7, 16-17.

19 See Kavanagh, *Theatre and cultual struggle*, pp. 46-7.

20 A copy of the programme accompanying the performances of these two plays is held by the Africana Library, University of the Witwatersrand.

21 For what follows see, as well as Roux, Couzens, *The new African*, esp. ch. 4; Le May, G. H. L., *Black and white in South Africa*, London: British Commonwealth and American Heritage Press, 1971.

22 Couzens, 'Introduction', p. 6.

23 Holden, Reverend William C., *The past and future of the Kaffir races*, Cape Town: Struik, 1963, Introduction (no pagination).

24 Mrs B.Mokgata has very kindly translated Waters, Mary, *U-Nongqause*, Cape Town: Maskew Miller, 1924, for me.

25 A brief account of the incident is supplied in Visser Nick, and Couzens, Tim, ed., H. I. E. Dhlomo, *collected works*, pp. 3-4. See also Soga, J.Henderson, *The south-eastern Bantu*, Johannesburg: Witwatersrand University Press, 1930, pp. 241-7, (Soga appears to have based part of his account on Waters's play); Wilson, Monica and Thompson, Leonard eds., *The Oxford history of South Africa*, I, Oxford: Clarendon Press, 1975, pp. 256-60.

26 See Wilson and Thompson, eds., *History*, I, pp. 252, 256, 260-3; Legassick, Martin Chatfield 'The Griqua, the Sotho-Tswana, and the missionaries, 1780-1840: the politics of a frontier zone', PhD dissertation submitted to the University of California, Los Angeles, 1969, pp.17-18.

27 See Wilson and Thompson, eds., *History*, p. 257.

28 See Brown, Paul, ' "This thing of darkness I acknowledge mine": *The tempest* and the discourse of colonialism', in Dollimore, Jonathan, and Sinfield, Alan, eds., *Political Shakespeare*, Manchester: Manchester University Press, 1985, pp. 48-71.

29 Greenblatt, Stephen, *Renaissance self fashioning*, Chicago: University of Chicago Press, 1980, pp. 224-7.

30 See Simons, H. J. and R. E., *Class and colour in South Africa 1850-1950*, Harmondsworth: Penguin, 1969; Bonner, Philip, 'The Transvaal native congress: 1917-1920', in Marks, S., and Rathbone, R., *Industrialisation and social change in South Africa*, London: Longman, 1982, and 'The 1920 black mineworkers' strike: a preliminary account' in Bozzoli, *Labour, townships and protest*, Hirson, 'Tuskegee'.

31 D. O'Meara, 'The 1946 African mine workers' strike and the political economy of South Africa', *Journal of commonwealth and comparative politics*, XIII, 2, July 1975, p. 149.

32 Fanon, Frantz, *The wretched of the earth*, Harmondsworth: Pelican, 1983, p. 169.

33 See Dhlomo, Herbert, *The girl who killed to save*, in Visser and Couzens, *Dhlomo, collected works*.

34 *The South African Outlook*, 1 August 1936, p. 187.

35 Soga, John Henderson, *The Ama-Xosa: life and customs*, Lovedale: Lovedale Press, 1931, pp. 28-9.

36 Couzens, *The new African*, pp. 127-8.

37 Roux, *Time longer than rope*, pp. 286-301.

38 Dubow, Saul, 'Race, civilisation and culture: the elaboration of segregationist discourse in the inter-war years', in Marks, Shula and Trapido, Stanley, *The politics of race, class and nationalism in twentieth century South Africa*, London: Longman, 1987, p. 71-4.

39 Hoernle, R. F. Alfred, *South African native policy and the liberal spirit*, Cape Town: University of Cape Town, 1939, pp. 182-3.

40 Cited in Couzens, *The new African*, pp. 137, 134-41.

41 Cited in Dubow, 'Race, civilisation and culture', p. 86.

42 cited in Couzens, *The new African*, p. 139.

43 cited in Couzens, *The new African*, p. 140.

44 Couzens, *The new African*, pp. 125-6.

45 Plaatje, Sol T., *Native life in South Africa* (first published London: P. S. King and Son, 1916), Johannesburg: Ravan, 1982.

46 Couzens, 'Introduction' to Mhudi, pp. 1-15.
47 Coplan, In township tonight!, p. 73.
48 Dhlomo, Herbert, Cetshwayo, in Visser and Couzens, Collected works, pp. 115-77.
49 Couzens,The new African, pp. 142-3.
50 Cited in Couzens, The new African, p. 136.
51 Dubow, Race, civilisation and culture, p. 76.
52 Couzens, The new African, p. 149.
53 Dhlomo,Herbert, 'Drama and the African', The South African Outlook, 66, 1 October 1936,
    p. 234.
54 Dhlomo,Herbert, 'Drama and the African', p. 233.
55 Dhlomo, Herbert, 'Why study tribal dramatic forms?', reprinted in English in Africa, 4:2,
    1977, p. 41.
56 Couzens, The new African, p. 150.
57 Boal, Augusto, Theatre of the oppressed, London: Pluto, 1979.
58 Eagleton, Terry, Literary theory, Oxford: Blackwell, 1983, p. 26.
59 See Visser and Couzens, Dhlomo, collected works, p. xiii.
60 Couzens, 'Introduction' to Mhudi, pp. 10-11.
61 Dhlomo, 'Drama and the African', p. 234.
62 Dhlomo, The pass in Collected works, pp. 189-209.
63 Dhlomo, The workers in Collected works, pp. 211-27.
64 Samuel, R., MacColl, E., and Cosgrove, S., Theatres of the left 1880-1935, London:
    Routledge and Kegan Paul, 1985, pp. 81-2.
65 Visser and Couzens, Dhlomo, collected works, p. xii.
66 Couzens, The new African, p. 177.
67 R. H. W. Shepherd, 'Lovedale and literature for the Bantu', unpublished thesis
    submitted to the University of the Witwatersrand, 1941.

2

Families live in limited spaces

Several plays in the 1950s attempt to find a measure of self-definition within the South African periphery. These come, on the one hand, from a privileged descendant of the white settler ruling classes, and, on the other, from individuals connected in one or other way with Union Artists, a dramatic organisation which flourished in the 1950s and which had a membership drawn from both ruling and subordinate classes and groups, reflecting the intersection of a variety of interests. Some of these plays attempt as Dhlomo had done, to dramatise or represent South African subjects and their relationship to the land but all attempt as well, for the first time, to acknowledge or represent urban township space on stage.

I Theatre and the colonial centre in the 1940s and 1950s

Theatre historians record continuing interest in theatre and perform-ance in the 1940s and 1950s amongst the oppressed classes which again suggests conflicting impulses, on the one hand, towards authentication of life at the periphery whilst, again, abrogating or displacing the colonial and imperial centre, and, on the other hand, towards affiliation with that centre. At the end of the 1930s, Bartholemew Pashe and his Self Help Club Revue had, as well as producing a play called *The girl friend*, adapted a Sepedi story to the stage.[1] By 1940 there was an Orlando Boy's Club dramatic society and Griffiths Motsiela had presented 'Africa', a revel pageant at the Communal Hall, Western Native Township, in which the impresario Bertha Slosberg was also involved (p. 186). Drama was introduced more widely in youth clubs while schools too continued to promote theatrical performances – activities often organised with support from whites.[2] In 1945 Es'kia Mphahlele as a teacher at Orlando High School – encouraged by Norah Taylor who continued to lend her support to his and similar projects – arranged several dramatic performances of Shakespeare and dramatisations of other English writers such as Dickens. Again, the Jan Hofmeyr School of Social Work offered teacher

training courses in theatre direction which were run from 1941 by
Teda de Moor.[3] She 'produced African dance dramas acted by
students...and made honest attempts to have rural, migrant and urban
African culture portrayed authentically' (p. 205). However, despite the
efforts of a small westernised elite to encourage theatre based on
written 'literary' drama, 'most urban Africans held the traditional
preference for verbal expression linked to music, dance and dramatic
action' (p. 149). In the 1940s an eclectic performance culture was
developing in the townships and particularly in Sophiatown shebeens
– drinking houses such as Aunt Babe's, The House on Telegraph Hill
and The Back of the Moon – which drew upon American, English and
African cultural traditions and involved comic sketches and acting as
well as jazz, singing and dancing. Again, radio plays and films explored
the clash between 'traditional values and institutions with Western
culture' (p. 203) and the transitions involved in the move from
country to town, sometimes tending as well to present 'urban Africans
as simple-hearted, dogged and irrepressible in the face of hardship' (p.
168). But the new radio service for blacks in various African languages,
run initially by King Edward Masinga, was under strict government
control and therefore unable to address the social order in any convincing way. It was attacked as offering a 'back-to-the-kraal apartheid and
never-never-land' service in a 'develop-along-your-own-lines pattern'
(p. 161). Nevertheless, Coplan argues that endeavours such as *Izinkwa*
(bread) do contain implicit indictments of the system (p. 203ff.).
Another radio play, *Chief above and chief below* by Masinga and Hugh
Tracey was subsequently performed by the Bantu Theatre Company of
Cape Town – formed by George Makanya together with Teda de Moor
in 1952. It mounted a second production, *George's journey*, in 1961.
Finally, in May 1954 Dhlomo's play *Dingana* was put on by the Medical
Student's Drama Group of the University of Natal (the 'non- European'
section),[4] an event which Couzens describes in some detail:

Despite 'serious overcrowding' on the first nights when it was performed in
the University hall at Wentworth, the play was very well received by audience
and critics. The *Mercury* found the performance had a natural 'freshness' and
the *Daily News* said it 'must be a milestone in the indigenous theatre of this
country'. So strong was the demand, in fact, that a repeat performance was
scheduled for the Durban City Hall and an extra chorus of warriors (bringing
the cast up to nearly 40) was recruited. Thus on 16 and 17 August, 1954,
Dhlomo's *Dingana* was performed in the City Hall... Once again, the
performances were lauded.

However, despite this success lack of supporting capital or interest from establishment theatre ensured that the production and play rapidly disappeared again from public view.

In contrast to such and other somewhat conflicting endeavours in the 1940s and 1950s, white theatre and performance amongst the ruling classes continued doggedly to perpetuate colonial and imperial fixations. Kavanagh notes that in 1958 it was possible to write that 'ten years ago (i. e. in 1948) theatre was confined almost entirely to an occasional musical company from Britain or a Christmas pantomime' and although 'white theatre had expanded by 1958 – "in Johannesburg four professional managements fight for the rights of plays" – its repertoire was still predominantly foreign'.[5] While there is evidence of more theatrical activity than this before the 1950s, such theatre always offered merely a pale echo of current British and North American practice. The Johannesburg Repertory Players for instance which had begun activities in 1927, performed seven or eight plays a year on average, from the 1930s to the 1960s, none of them indigenous. Other companies such as one run in the 1940s by Gwen Ffrangcon Davis and Marda Vanne, the Munro-Inglis Company – both presented under the aegis of African Consolidated Theatres – and that formed by Brian Brooke from 1945 on, did the same.[6] As well, the Federation of Amateur Theatrical Societies of South Africa was founded in 1938 and the Johannesburg Afrikaans Toneelspelers in 1942.[7]

But the most significant event of these years was the formation of the National Theatre in 1947. An earlier rather different attempt had been made in 1941 to form what was called the African National Theatre, which while it existed, performed several 'popular political plays' including 'Routh's *Patriot's pie*, about a young African enlistee, and *The word and the act*, a satire of Prime Minister Hertzog's Native Administration Acts'[8] at the Gandhi hall:

Tau by I. Pinchuk showed how 'when a tribe is united, it can fight for its rights and win.' The play also portrayed 'the cruel way in which Africans are treated on the farms and also the way in which the Government oppresses the Africans.' It...showed up the way 'some Africans sell themselves to the masters and become enemies of the people.' *The Foolish Mistress* was a sketch by Guy Routh which dealt with mistress-maid relationships and *The Rude Criminal* was written by Gaur Radebe who was a leader soon after in the big bus boycott in Alexandria. The group also put on *The Hymn of the Rising Sun*, a very powerful play by the American Paul Green, a white who wrote a number of successful plays mainly about black Americans. This group seems to have been an attempt by the communists to help build a popular base through popular theatre.[9]

This account, of the African National Theatre, based on reports of performances of plays which, in the case of indigenous attempts, significantly do not appear to have survived in published form, provides a nice contrast with the activities and interests of the National Theatre, formed within the ruling classes, again significantly, with government funds in 1947. From its inception this organisation had no place for black creative participation, although reliance upon black labour for the carrying out of all menial tasks was not dispensed with. Members of the Board of Governors as well as actors together with all other theatre practitioners were white: despite the appellation 'national' the two companies formed were Afrikaans and English playing to white audiences only. Within a few years, the initial loan given to the company was waived and, further, a grant of £10,000 was made, increased in April 1949 to £15,000 pounds per year and in 1957 to £25,000 pounds annually.[10] The organisation also attempted to foster interest in the drama amongst the 'youth' – which one of its chroniclers takes to mean white pupils under the aegis of education departments for whites in the Transvaal and later the Cape and Natal. It risked two productions of Shakespeare, a *Macbeth* translated into Afrikaans in 1950 and *Twelfth night* in 1953. Whereas from 1948-62 those Afrikaans plays selected for production were often indigenous, only about five of over forty plays performed in English were by South Africans, and none of these by any member of the oppressed classes. An active member commented on the evident Afrikaans bias in the selection of indigenous plays for performance:

South African playwrights were constantly encouraged to submit their plays. Sadly this policy of promoting indigenous plays seldom payed off, this being particularly true where it affected the English-speaking population. While plays by W. A. de Klerk and comedies by Gerhard Beukes became hits on the platteland, those by Guy Butler and Anthony Delius met with a luke-warm response. The exception was a rewritten version of *Seven Against the Sun* [set in East Africa during the second world war], by James Ambrose Brown.[11]

But when it is recalled that theatres were segregated, and that the National Theatre in its behaviour, like the Nationalist Party government, seemed to mean by 'South African' only 'white South African', the National Theatre Organisation's record clearly appears to have been biased. It was prompted by disinterest in and in practice, discouragement or suppression of any alternative discourses – coming either from possible dissident white or black theatre practitioners – rather than by audience disinterest in the work of those English dramatists who were

C

acceptable to the National Theatre Organisation Board.

II Naturalising possession of the land in The dam and The dove returns

One dramatist favoured by the National Theatre was Guy Butler, whose play The dam won the first prize in the English section of the government sponsored Van Riebeeck Tercentenary Play-writing Competition in 1951. The director in the National Theatre Organisation production of The dam in 1952 was Marda Vanne, the well-known Afrikaans actress and producer whose real name was Margaretha van Hulsteyn. Some decades earlier she had been married to and then divorced J. G. Strijdom, subsequently appointed Nationalist Party Prime Minister of South Africa in 1954. Butler's next play, The dove returns was produced by the National Theatre in 1955. It is true that The dam was first per-formed at the Little Theatre in Cape Town, which had remained a multi-racial theatre since its opening, so audiences to performances of the play at this theatre may have been to some extent at least multi-racial, although there is no record of this. But the extent to which the vision of the ruling classes associated with the National Theatre remained indifferent to the existence let alone the culture of the oppressed classes may be seen in the message of the then Minister of Education Arts and Science, included in the programme, discussing Butler's play and the two Afrikaans plays which, together with The dam, won awards:

It is right that plays of other countries and other times are also produced by the National Theatre Organisation because that enables us to draw compari-sons and will serve as encouragement to our authors. But on the occasion of a national festival we are naturally more interested in our own cultural achievements and it must be a source of pride to us that our authors when called upon, responded so well.[12]

As compared with a dramatist such as Dhlomo, Butler was privi-leged in a variety of ways. A member of the ruling classes, he was born to a prosperous Cape family, descended from Quakers well disposed to the Afrikaans, and with connections through his mother to England.[13] After serving on the Western Front during the Second World War, he took a degree at Oxford and returned to a lifetime of service in tertiary education in South Africa, becoming, after a brief spell at Witwatersrand University, Professor of English Language and

Literature at Rhodes University, Grahamstown. By the end of the 1950s he was 'a member of the English-language establishment' (p. 15) editing the Oxford *Book of South African verse* which contained not a single black poet.[14]

Like Dhlomo, Butler – particularly as he was situated within the colonialist-oriented discourses of university English departments – was, in the very attempt to write plays about South Africa, contesting prevailing attitudes. Moreover, against the predilections of many of his colleagues, well into the 1970s he argued for the importance of the study of South African literature. This impulse was coloured, however, by the discourses on which it drew.

Dhlomo's attempt to engage in his plays with his world involves the construction of ruling class subjects whose lawless greed for power and land counteridentifies their alleged allegiance to Christianity and pretensions to ordered government. As the last chapter shows, Dhlomo often chose the frontier image in his plays in order to probe relations between dominant and subordinate classes. This may be understood as – to use Bakhtin's term – his chronotopic focus. 'In the literary artistic chronotope,' suggests Bakhtin,

spatial and temporal indicators are fused into one carefully thought-out, concrete whole. Time, as it were, thickens, takes on flesh, becomes artistically visible; likewise, space becomes charged and responsive to the movements of time, plot and history... The chronotope as a formally constitutive category determines to a significant degree the image of man(sic) in literature as well. The image of man (sic) is always intrinsically chronotopic.[15]

Dhlomo's choice of the frontier predicates a fluid situation in which there is still chance for the subordinate subject to be constructed with a positive cultural identity in positions of resistance and hostility to the colonial invader. Colonial and non-colonial space is there to be occupied, seized, fought for, stolen, appropriated and, if lost, crucially by implication, to be regained. Particularly in *Cetshwayo* Dhlomo's chronotopic focus may also be said to become the means whereby his text may address as well the time and space within which he himself is positioned, one, as we have seen, in which segregation was ominously intensifying in the social order.

Butler's concern, by contrast, is with a time and space in which ownership of the land by ruling class whites is an accomplished fact, treated in language that continually seeks to naturalise that possession. Thus *The dam*, performed for the first time as I noted at the Little Theatre in Cape Town in 1952, and *The dove returns*, first performed in 1955 in

Natal,[16] construct the white subject, primarily as member of patriarchal landowning farming families. In *The dam* the patriarchal figure Douglas Long comments to his family when his Dam has finally been built:

We stand here, on this particular place
Important to the history of our hearts;
And at a particular hour when the dusk
Draws all the mountains close to our shoulders:
We feel we belong; this bit of the world is ours,
Individually, and as a family. (p. 66)

Coetzee notes that in Afrikaans literature about the farm, by 'shedding his sweat or blood on the land' the farmer establishes or reconfirms his family's 'natural right' over it[17] – a view expressed too by the Englishman Jim Shaw in *The dove returns* when he asserts 'my family belongs to this soil,/Has paid for it with its courage, its work, its blood' (p. 79), and this claim to 'natural right' is given direct expression elsewhere when Sarah van Heerden tells her husband Karel, 'You own this farm,/You planted that orchard, sunk the bore hole' asseverating too that:

Man lives in families,
And families live in limited spaces, houses, towns,
So many morgen of land. (pp. 10,32)

Farm ownership and the labour of farming families is also mingled with a vision of progress that draws on Christian discourse. *The dove returns*, which depicts relationships between English and Afrikaans farming families during and after the Anglo-Boer War, culminates in a scene of reconciliation taking place, in the final act, on Good Friday 1905. Dramatic emphasis is placed firmly upon the capacity, within the characters, to grow as Christians, in this case especially, their need to practice Christian forgiveness. Their reconciliation is, moreover, enacted not only through the marriage between the Afrikaans daughter of the van Heerdens and the English Jim Shaw but through the promise that their oldest son will inherit the van Heerden farm of which Karel van Heerden, the patriarch who has lost his own son in the war, says 'This farm has been a van Heerden farm since the (eighteen) forties./ It takes time to know a farm: like a woman (sic)' (p. 80). Marriage ensures the continuation of the farm's existence within the familial line, 'sanctified' and blessed by a loyal and faithful serf figure, the 'coloured' servant Simon at the end of the play. Such presentations parallel what Coetzee has detected in Afrikaans farm literature, the construction of each farm as 'a separate kingdom ruled over by a benign patriarch, with, beneath him a pyramid of contented and industrious children, grandchildren and serfs'.[18]

In 1951, Horton Davies, who was at that stage, like Butler, at Rhodes University in Grahamstown published a book entitled *Great South African Christians*, describing eighteen white personalities together with one black. His introduction confirms the enduring strand, in South Africa, of an energetic, proselytising and paternalist Christianity. Thus, he indicates that amongst those chosen for attention, some:

were the first to apply old ideas in a new country. They were the pioneers who endured the dangers and discomforts of wild animals and savages for the sake of the gospel of Christ...Yet others were notable champions of the underprivileged Coloured and African people, enduring persecution and criticism for Christ's sake...Great Christians, in the writer's view, must be faithful, fearless, compassionate and humble.[19]

So evident in Waters's work decades earlier, this strand is present in Butler's plays as well. *The dam*'s primary concern is to foreground the interiority of Douglas Long, whose work is presented not only heroically but in religious terms, as a personal service to his God. When the first attempt to construct the dam ends in catastrophe, Long stands alone in the koppies, suicidal, and cries to his God for a sign. Saved, as he sees it, from despair by the arrival of his 'coloured' servant Kaspar who tells him his family wait for him, he acquires a newer, if still equivocal, understanding of those who serve him:

Do I matter so much to them? And you,
You have come after me like a faithful dog.
I have thought only of myself; you have thought of me
God forgive me. His light is upon me.
I begin to see myself and I am ashamed.
It was my selfwill, always my will, my will.
O God, help me to bear the sight of myself. (p. 50)

This curious mixture of religiosity and, at best, insensitivity, is followed by Butler's movement into the final coda of his play. Long's climactic understanding, helped by a loyal serf, quickly moves away from awareness of the subordinate classes altogether and into his own personal growth towards a better Christian consciousness, and the acquisition of a measure of humility, conveyed, for instance, in his comment, 'those who sign themselves with the sign of the Cross/Are not surprised at pain' (p. 62). The echoes of Eliot at this point in the

text, as elsewhere, are inescapable. It discovers providential significance in choric verses that proclaim 'In the beginning was the
Word...The Word that found the heart of a man/A year ago today'
(pp. 59-60). What Coetzee finds in Afrikaans farm literature is thus
true of constructions of the white subject here: the production of a
particular kind of self-realisation, a 'realisation of the self not as
individual but...as the transitory embodiment of a lineage' that
'becomes tied to landownership and to a particular kind of spiritual
experience available only to landowners'.[20]

What is striking about such moments of 'learning' from materialist
or anti-colonialist perspectives as well as from a Christian one, is the
way in which, despite any endeavour elsewhere in the text to engage
with the blacks who also inhabit the land, this impulse towards
Christian compassion and love is contained. Applicable to the Long
family and primarily to Douglas Long, it is also held in check by that
discourse deriving in part from white settler colonialist and racist/
segregationist formulations. Despite the intense religious commitment
of these farming families, the history that lies behind their 'white
proclamation of homestead walls' (p. 8) is, accordingly, never
interrogated. Secure within the colonialist and missionary discourse in
which it operates, it presents the former resisters of the settlers always
negatively. Their ghosts have retreated to the kloofs, which remain
haunted by 'Batsi the stubborn chief' who 'trapped at last,/Coughed
out blood and curses between the cliffs' (p. 8).

It is worth recalling here that the black sense of injustice over the
Land Act of 1913 had not been lessened by the slight increase in land
allotted for black ownership, in Hertzog's segregationist legislation.
When, just over a decade later, after the war the Nationalist Party came
to power in 1948 and replaced segregation with apartheid, the
problem intensified. Now that the land had for decades been secured
for mining and agricultural capital, the state turned its attention to
what it saw as the urgent task of formalised separation particularly in
urban areas, not only where the interaction of human bodies was
concerned but in terms of the spaces which those bodies would be
permitted to occupy. Legislation was passed aiming at 'the complete
separation of the various races, African, Coloured and Asian from each
other and from the whites, in separate residential areas in all urban
areas throughout the country'.[21] Such legislation was also directed at
removing black inhabitants living within or next to white areas,
including Sophiatown in Johannesburg, and placing them in often

specially created locations or townships. Other laws restricted the use of facilities – places such as beaches, as well as the areas where blacks might live, trade and work. Furthermore, all blacks throughout the country, in terms of the cynically named Natives (Abolition of Passes and Co-ordination of Documents) Act of 1952, were required by law to carry documents or passes validating their presence in white urban areas. This was to be extended in time to women. No black was permitted to be in an urban area for longer than seventy-two hours unless she or he had permission stamped in her or his passbook to be available day or night for police inspection. Neglecting to carry a pass was defined as a criminal offence. One of the points which Nelson Mandela developed at his trial focused on apartheid ownership and control of space and movement:

We want to be part of the general population and not confined to living in our ghettos. African men want to have their wives and children to live with them where they work, and not to be forced into an unnatural existence in men's hostels. Our women want to be left with their men folk, and not to be left permanently widowed in the Reserves. We want to be allowed out after 11 o'clock at night and not to be confined to our rooms like little children. We want to be allowed to travel in our own country, and seek work where we want to, and not where the Labour Bureau tells us to. We want a just share in the whole of South Africa; we want security and a stake in society.[22]

III Butler's representation of labour

There are, it is true, several moments when *The dam* addresses the existence of numerous non-English peoples, seen as part of a worrying other, who also inhabit this space and who, in the words of its character Dr Robert prompt 'demands upon our sympathy'. Robert, disturbingly a spokesman elsewhere in the play, for 'common sense' speaks here not only of 'the Afrikaners who find us alien and proud;/ The immigrants who find us hard and bright;/The Jewish refugees who dream at night/Of Julius Streicher or of Zionism' but also of

The Coloureds with the bloods of half the world
Fermenting in their veins; the Indians
Intelligent and small, chewing betel nut;
And all the motley tribe of ragged blacks
Playing a blind-man's buff between the mine-dump
And the mud-hut the war chant and the blues – (p. 35)

The stereotyping evident in this passage is paralleled early in the play when Douglas Long, gazing at the land, sees his black labourers:

O God of stars and stones and us between them
Touch these semi-savage things that sweat for me,
Half-warriors without a chief, still held
To the tribal womb by a tattered chord...
These migrant muscles in rags...
Touch them, dear God, touch me, and let us know
Your common touch. O let us hear one heart
Beat over the breadth of Africa, one heart...
O God let them not hate me, let not my dam
Be left as a futile relic here, to join
The bare Zimbabwe ruins as more dead evidence
Of another race that Africa defeated. –
A noisy white experiment which failed. (p. 26)

The emphasis on a 'half-savage' condition together with admission of the contentious issues of land and migrant labour only in the alliterative side-glance of the balanced phrase 'migrant muscles' reflects what Alvarez-Pereyre has noted as Butler's constant predilection elsewhere, at least during this period, for the term ' "tribesman"...to designate the African' commenting that Butler 'persists in talking of "primitivism" to describe the [black's] mode of life and civilisation'.[23] Such sentiments, notes Alvarez-Pereyre, fitted in well with the governing class's attempt to portray the blacks as a dependent and permanently subordinate race. E. G. Jansen, who became a minister of Native affairs observed in the mid-1940s that while 'the Boer regarded the Native as someone for whom he was responsible and from whom he would receive the labour expected of him' the blacks 'regarded the Boer not only as his Master, but also as a friend and helper to whom he could turn for help and advice in times of difficulty'.[24] This was a view essentially shared by the white United Party, which lost power after 1948 and was, throughout the 1950s, the official Opposition in the Houses of Parliament. The endeavour in both of Butler's plays to argue for reconciliation between English and Afrikaans may be said to complement or parallel United Party attempts to regain lost influence, if not power.

Yet historians have shown that labour realities were more complex than those suggested by the construction of blacks in Douglas Long's language. Indeed, within the urban landscape, blacks had provided nearly two-thirds of the increase in the labour force during the course of the Second World War.[25] Industry depended on them for goods strategically important or vital to the economy including foodstuffs, footwear, clothing, cement, coal, iron, gold, chemicals, explosives and munitions. The number of blacks employed in manufacturing rose continually so that 'at the end of 1948 they accounted for 80.8 per cent of unskilled employees, 34.2 per cent of the semi-skilled and 5.8 of the skilled in occupations regulated by wage determinations' (p. 554). Wages remained consistently lower than estimated basic needs throughout the period and in the decade preceding the appearance of Butler's play, strikes were on the increase (pp. 554-5). One of the most significant of these was the miners' strike in August 1946 which in turn provoked a bill in 1947 seeking to make trade unionism illegal, and to outlaw all strikes. 76,000 miners came out on strike, while the response of the Chamber of Mines, according to Simons and Simons, can be seen to draw on similar ideological discursive formations positing savagism and reflecting paternalism which Butler's language in Long's prayer evokes:

Encouraged by the willingness of white workers to scab, the Chamber refused to negotiate with the African miners' union. Migratory, tribal, peasant miners, the gold producers' committee argued… were 'not yet sufficiently advanced for trade unionism'. They did not want a trade union, 'had fallen an easy prey to control by alien interests', and showed 'a serious element of irresponsibility' in demanding 10s. a day.

On this, Simons and Simons comment:

In reality, the mine owners crushed every attempt by the men to think for themselves, follow leaders of their own choosing, and act collectively for the achievement of aims freely adopted. The Chamber, said the committee, pursued the national policy of European trusteeship and the preservation of tribal society. 'Conflict between the allegiance demanded by a trade union and those owed to the tribe would tend to disrupt tribal life, a result diametrically opposed to the basic principle of national policy'. This was an astounding and impudent distortion of the actual policy, adopted by a gigantic organisation that over the years had sucked millions of men, at the height of their manhood, into the degrading life of compounds. (pp. 573-4)

Within the rural landscape, peasant resistance to government attempts to implement rehabilitation measures and encourage cattle-culling had also increased in the reserves in the decade before Butler's play. As one spokesman observed:

Today our people are disease-ridden because of malnutrition; they haven't the oxen to plough; the majority of babies do not survive the first year because the mothers are too starved to be able to feed them...(Africans) have far too few cattle for their requirements. It is not that the cattle are too many, but that the land is too small. There is an appalling shortage of land.[26]

The fight against government policy intensified – annual reports of the Native (later Bantu) Affairs Department between 1948 and 1952 speak each year of ' "considerable organised opposition", "semi-secret organisation", "alarming reverses...serious retardation" of policy due to "malicious agitators" – which was to continue until a blanket of silence was draped over the topic by the new Minister, Verwoerd' (p. 274).

IV Enter the townships

The dam's recognition of Long's labourers was, however, itself significant. This contested the practice in much farm literature of marginalising black agricultural labour – in reality crucial to the farm system in producing the wealth of farming families. And when not totally ignored, in such literature, the existence of the oppressed class was usually admitted, as I have noted briefly, in the form of the submissive, loyal but peripheral serf figure. But elsewhere The dam expresses concern over the development of 'difference too deep for us to shift' while 'within our walls of privilege we Whites/live in a state of siege' (p. 36), and as the play draws to its close, it addresses urban space in a way that recognises that there may be looming problems in the land within which these farming families have found their sense of mutual understanding and religion. Susan Long describes the townships she encountered on a visit to Johannesburg:

the violence; and smells,
Degradation, the lurid colours, the dark
Of a primitive human storm. – How sweet
The air is here, how spacious, how secure
In the cities at this hour, and every day
Trains and trams pour out their thousands
Into space one tenth the size of this farm;
A horde of hovels hedged between a white
And well-lit suburb on two sides
And mine-dumps, depots, coal-yards on the other.
    People
Press down unlit, treeless streets, to meet
In houses struggling vainly to be homes,
Where twenty sleep in a room the size of our kitchen,

And love is violent, and laughter hard, and hatred
Rises like steam. (p. 65)

It is likely that this passage is based upon Butler's own experience of
Sophiatown, during his brief period as a lecturer at the University of
the Witwatersrand, through his knowledge of Father Trevor
Huddleston, to whom he dedicates the published version of The dam.
But despite the thrust towards sympathy, in the daughter's phrase 'the
dark of a primitive human storm' or, a little later, in the way she
describes the labourers celebrating the building of the dam with their
'grotesque heads thrown back, their mouths/Wide and moaning at the
indifferent stars' (p. 67) it is difficult not to detect strands of the more
paternalist aspects of assimilationist discourse. Moreover, the effort to
poeticise, to find the apt image, – hatred that 'rises like steam' – itself
contributes to a certain beatification of the suffering it presents. It is
true she refers to the workers in a brief phrase, as the dispossessed
inhabitants of a 'seasonless land' but, watching the labourers celebrating the completion of the dam, she also reflects:

The Coloureds see it
As a white man's undertaking, big and bold
As usual, but with a curse upon it,
Linked with the grave of Batsi the Chief.
And the blacks see it as a source of work,
Of sweating and swinging, and singing to falling picks.
And the promise of meat and mealie-meal;
And the lands below it are waiting its water.
Wild duck will find it, returning each season
And the south-west breeze like silver paper
Between smooth shadows of these hills. (p. 64)

These lines suggest as they unfold, the coloniser's and the proprietor's
gaze which encompasses not only the landscape but the inhabitants on
it, assumes that the (untranslated) voices of the oppressed denote
harmonious and joyful subjection, provides a version of the labourer's
needs that positions them at a very elementary level of aspiration,
swinging their falling picks rhythmically, dreaming of earnings in
kind. The easy movement to the final image suggests that, seen as the
ducks and the waters of the dam are seen, they are part of an integrated,
poetic, if slightly lugubrious, pastoral, property of the gazer.

What appears in the play to herald a broadening consciousness in
the text is, in other ways too, held in check and contained. Against
apparent expression of guilt and concern in this South African English

farming family, may be set the level of awareness about urban blacks that the language here, and the play as a whole suggests, when set against, again, what we may learn from the discourse of historians. Living conditions, on which Susan concentrates exclusively, were indubitably almost uniformly bad, in most of the black townships throughout South Africa. But there were also, to mention only one of many other important facts, in the period when the play was written episodes of resistance to the system that was producing those conditions in many parts of the country. Moreover, the black urban areas of particularly the eastern Cape, where Butler lived and worked, as well as the East Reef area were in the late 1940s and early 1950s notable sites of struggle.

Port Elizabeth, the home of South Africa's motor industry – through which people must usually pass from the relatively nearby Grahamstown to visit, for instance, Johannesburg – began to develop a black work force in the late 1930s and 1940s and, by 1951, over 60,000 blacks lived there.[27] Conditions were bad – for instance, Korsten, by the 1930s a huge 'rack rented, shanty village' had grown rapidly, until, in 1948:

> many of its inhabitants had to rent miserable rooms constructed from packing cases in which motor-car parts had arrived. Such dwellings were being built at the rate of 60 a month, with one 9' by 7' room housing as many as thirteen people. The problem worsened as farmers began to evict squatters and workers dependants from their land…In 1946 a local survey showed that Port Elizabeth – of six major urban centres – had the poorest African population; and by 1949 it was reckoned that Port Elizabeth shared with East London the worst tuberculosis rate in the world. (pp. 49-50)

Trade union consciousness and popular political participation was strong in Korsten, New Brighton, and elsewhere – evidenced in a number of strikes and in the bus boycott of 1949 which lasted for nearly four months in response to an increase in the bus fare (p. 52). In 1952 when a number of groups including the African National Congress announced the Defiance Campaign – which entailed various acts of civil disobedience – as a result of the Government's refusal to respond to its demands that crucially oppressive laws be abolished, the reaction in Port Elizabeth was particularly strong. Moreover, by the beginning of August, in the eastern Cape the Campaign had spread from Port Elizabeth to Grahamstown and elsewhere.

It is in such contexts, that Susan Long's need to travel up to Johannesburg to bring back news about black urban conditions to the Long family – of which any farmer or inhabitant of the towns in the eastern Cape might have received at first hand from her or his own area – should be seen. Moreover, the kind of Christianity to which Douglas Long in his prayer about his migrant workers, and the enduring survival of his 'white experiment' is given, was not the only version of Christianity possible in the eastern Cape of the time as Tom Lodge's account of the struggle in the Grahamstown-Port Elizabeth area makes clear:

A mood of religious fervour infused the resistance, especially in the eastern Cape. When the campaign opened it was accompanied by 'days of prayer', and volunteers pledged themselves at prayer meetings to a code of love, discipline and cleanliness. Manyanos [members of church-based township women's welfare groups] wore their uniforms and accompanied Congress speeches with solemn hymn singing, and even at the tense climax of the campaign in Port Elizabeth – where there were strong syndicalist undercurrents – people were enjoined on the first day of the strike to 'conduct a prayer and a fast in which each member of the family will have to be at home'; and thereafter they attended nightly church services'. (pp. 43-4)

And it is in this context too that the poeticised and spiritualised response Susan has to the townships – one which freezes the image of the urban African ignoring episodes of increasing resistance to suggest, by contrast, an icon of passivity – may also be understood. The language Butler gives her, it may be argued, seeks no discourse of resistance, but chooses rather to sanctify, an ideal that while it ministers to suffering remains unconcerned with attempts significantly to diminish or eradicate it. Susan ends her description of this space by noting that

also – at this moment –
The Angelus bell is ringing. All on the Mission
Pause; hands, fresh from tending the sick and the hungry
Rest on the heart of the Incarnation; and here
And there, halting in a purple mist of smoke,
A dark heart beats in unison with the bell...
Of God's own heart still beats and pleads. (pp. 65-6)

and this awareness finds its resolution in her personal decision to tend to that suffering by joining a mission.

In *The dove returns*, written after the Nationalist Government had won a second more convincing election victory in 1953, and after its thrust against English economic dominance was intensifying, Butler's concern with the oppressed classes, only, at best, secondary to his major themes in *The dam*, diminishes, becoming in the process even more equivocal. Urban space disappears while the black presence on the rural landscape is explored only through the sporadic presence of a minor Griqua servant, conforming to the faithful serf figure commonplace in much farm literature, speaking language that fixes him in position finally as the defeated inhabitant of a reserve trying to avoid with difficulty prevailing racist discourse.

Butler held from the 1950s and still holds an influential and highly respected position in South African education. In 1959, discussing the lack of any ballads in the South African literary tradition, he could observe lightly with little apparent concern that 'one possible explanation for this silence (as for so much else) is the presence of cheap indigenous labour: it meant that the lonely ruminative jobs of herding sheep and cattle were done by others',[28] he could note in some of the poetry he read 'it is fairly easy for a European poet to write sympathetically about a Zulu mother or a coloured child dancing beside a bus queue, but he becomes less sure of himself when faced with groups, with primitive rituals or barbaric customs' (p. xxxii) and in other poems addressing blacks he identified without further comment a 'civilised bewilderment in the presence of barbarism' (p. xxxii).

Such views in his critical writing as well as in his plays makes it perhaps not surprising that, unlike Herbert Dhlomo's difficulties with the performance and publication of his work, Butler had no problem with the two plays which he wrote in the 1950s. It seems likely that Douglas Long's prayer together with its general emphasis – as later in The dove returns – upon the need for co-operation between English and Afrikaans farm owners expressed also in language indicating acceptance of much prevailing paternalist and segregationist discourse, were in Butler's favour, in the matter of prize giving, as well as in the choice of his play for performance by the first state subsidised theatre.

V The appropriation of black performance

In other spaces, the struggle to promote theatre was harder. As well as theatrical endeavour amongst the oppressed classes, theatre historians trace the steady erosion in the 1940s and 1950s of independent attempts within the oppressed classes to maintain the performance arts or to explore the drama. These were inhibited not only by apartheid legislation but by the increasing involvement of white theatrical

practitioners, producers, entrepreneurs – in part, indeed, one consequence of that legislation. Whites tended to occupy powerful and often
controlling positions in the various theatrical and performance
ventures in which they collaborated. And 'professional artists who
wanted to reach out beyond their local audience had few alternatives'
because 'only a white employer could easily get performance permits
and the vital..."pass" entitling performers "to go to any town under
the European promoter, who is held responsible for their actions"'.[29]

Thus while Kavanagh observes that in the 1950s 'popular theatrical
activity based in the traditional culture hardly existed at all in the
Witwatersrand, except in comic sketches interpolated between musical
items at concerts',[30] he notes instances where traditional elements were
sometimes exploited commercially in a number of white directed
productions for white audiences (p. 49) – which had begun to happen
decades earlier to the Mthethwe Lucky Stars. Wilfrid Sentso, founder
and manager of the Synco Fans, was one of those who tried to keep
all aspects of black performance out of white hands.[31] His performance
school was established in the mid-1930s and for the next twenty-three
years he tried to maintain his independence, reaching perhaps his peak
in 1947 when the Grand Theatre in Vrededorp was hired for a week
of variety shows. But segregation and apartheid subsequently prevented further growth. Again, as early as 1942, white musicians who
feared competition from their black counterparts began to work for
the exclusion of black musicians from white city clubs. Although in
one way or another black players continued to find work until the late
1950s their position was always extremely vulnerable (p. 162). After
the war a white officer, Lieutenant Ilke Brooks, put on a variety jazz
show for white audiences called Zonk with great success. South African
conditions, to repeat, continually favoured such promoters because,
'they could command greater organisational and financial resources
and stand between performers and the mass of segregationist legal
restrictions that inhibited interracial contact and independent African
enterprises' (p. 151).

As segregation intensified, other attempts in the performing arts
were made to resist it. Es'kia Mphahlele and Khoti Mngoma had founded
the Syndicate of African Artists in the mid-1940s 'to bring serious
music and the arts to the doorstep of our people who were not allowed
to go to white theatre or concert halls'.[32] But the government refused
to grant it any financial support so long as the Syndicate insisted on
performing to multi-racial audiences. Nevertheless, appealing to the

people for support, Mngoma emphasised that the syndicate was 'beginning to create a cultural front in our struggle towards self-determination'.[33] In the end police harassment forced them to disband the Syndicate in 1956, after which there was 'no black-run theatrical organisation left in Johannesburg' although 'amateur dramatic societies and teachers like Bob Leshoi of Lady Selbourne High School in Pretoria continued to organise dramatic scenes for community concerts and some full scale productions (p. 204).

Writers such as Lewis Nkosi, Nat Nakasa and Bloke Modisane have described how they continued to be barred from white theatres and entertainment throughout the 1950s.[34] The Johannesburg Bantu Music Festival, initiated by the Johannesburg Non-European Affairs Department in 1947, an initial success, eventually collapsed because 'restrictive and petty apartheid regulations poisoned the atmosphere'.[35] And by the 1950s the dwindling opportunities for jazz artists, the interference of gangsters – largely unchecked by the South African Police force – in shebeen life which discouraged working-class and middle-class patronage of the drinking houses, and the advent of white promoters such as Alf Herbert with his Township Jazz shows designed primarily for white audiences, were all further factors working against independent black performers, many of them now 'caught between recording studios and the promoters' (p. 171) in an increasingly apartheid society.

VI Intersecting interests in Union artists

However, not all white involvement in the performing arts was negative. Coplan argues, for example, that white involvement at least helped keep music professionalism alive. Again, in the early 1950s, Ian Bernhardt member of an amateur white dramatic society, formed an all-black drama group called the Bareti players which drew on the tradition of theatre based on European models. They performed The comedy of errors in 1955 and several one-act plays on South African themes in the townships.[36] Bernhardt was also one of the founders, together with the trade unionist Guy Routh, Fred Thabedi an organiser of youth clubs, Dan Poho, Bob Leshoi and others of the Union of South African Artists.

The original aim of this group was to protect black artists from exploitation and it 'successfully arranged royalty payments to Solomon

Linda, Spokes Mashiyane, and Mackay Devashe' and 'engineered the boycott by British Equity of all segregated shows in South Africa' (p. 172). The Union also organised, in the early 1960s, the African Music and Drama Association which met at Dorkay House. When Routh left for England Bernhardt promoted the Township Jazz Concerts which were to culminate in the production of *King Kong*. The Union was, however, sporadically open to charges of exploitation and Kavanagh has argued that the support of white capital, including that of Anglo American, had a powerful impact upon productions and the general practice of the Union – 'here was "multi-racial" cultural and educational activity under white direction, in European cultural and artistic forms within a capitalist format.'[37] He suggests also that the Union diverted much energy away from popular music culture and that 'its main function rapidly came to be that of a body which discovered black talent and purveyed it to white audiences in South African and abroad, and did not hesitate [on occasion] even to call on the forces of the white state to settle its disputes with its labour force and contractors' (p. 92).

Despite this, it is important to add that the Union was directly or indirectly associated with or involved in several dramatic endeavours that were perceived at the time to be at least partly contestatory. Such plays were always the result of multi-racial collaboration. *No good friday*, for example, by Athol Fugard working with a number of black intellectuals from Sophiatown – who were most of them members of Union Artists – opened first in 1958 at the Bantu Men's Social Centre and then, for one evening, for white audiences at the Brooke Theatre. The significance of this play lies partly in the fact that it was devised, unlike those by Dhlomo and Butler, primarily within the theatrical situation by a group of people, amongst whom Fugard himself was working as much as possible in the theatre. *King Kong*, a musical promoted by Union Artists which drew on the growth of jazz in the townships, and the emergence of township variety shows organised in the 1950s by Alfred Herbert, opened at the Witwatersrand University Great Hall in 1959 to multi-racial audiences, and went on to play in London. This again was a work devised specifically for theatre performance. *Sponono*, the result of collaboration between Alan Paton and Krishnah Shah, and also promoted by Union Artists used black actors and opened in 1961.[38]

These ventures occurred within a social order in which there were still no theatres within the townships themselves and in which in the cities, apart from the Little Theatre in Cape Town which always accepted multi-racial audiences and the Witwatersrand University Great Hall, theatres continued to practise segregation. The productions that Union Artists helped to mount, or were in some way involved in, were therefore in the very fact of their occurrence, themselves part of the struggle to preserve multi-racial space in a social order where established theatre as well as government practice insisted upon segregation. Although the majority of the audiences who came to see these plays were drawn from the white middle classes, the fact that they were the result of multi-racial collaboration as well as the fact that performances took place in multi-racial space, was therefore, as I indicated – given the government's ever increasing apartheid thrust in restructuring the social order and implementing its laws – perceived by those undertaking it as, in important senses, subversive. Moreover, it worked against the policy of the subsidised National Theatre Organisation. Audiences attending a play that resulted from multi-racial collaboration might more fervently believe, together with theatrical practitioners, that they were, at least for the duration of the performance, occupying a space that contested the apartheid social order in which they were situated.

While Kavanagh does not perhaps pay sufficient attention to this aspect of these performances, the points he makes not only about Union Artists but about the particular ways in which these plays were produced are important. Thus in the case of *King Kong* he shows that black participants remained mainly performers while creative and administrative direction was white controlled. Performers were drawn from 'relatively uneducated professional singers and musicians'[39] while the white liberals who participated, together with the Union of African Artists to which they belonged, with its connections in English speaking capital, saw their role, he argues, as ' "agents" of the cultural hegemony of their group' (p. 94). Accordingly, Kavanagh suggests, they were anxious not to expose interests they in part represented – a crucial factor that determined not only the kind of achievement in these works but also the nature of their avoidances (pp. 59-64, 84-97).

The involvement in these productions of a highly talented group of black writers and journalists is also significant. Most of them worked for *Drum* the 'symbol of the new African cut adrift from the tribal reserve – urbanised, eager, fast-talking and brash'.[40] They worked too in an age which had seen, particularly in Sophiatown, 'a cultural flowering unequalled in the urban history of South Africa':

Principally in the pages of *Drum* magazine and the *Bantu World*, Henry Nxumalo, Can Themba, Stanley Motjuadi, Casey Motsisi, Arthur Maimane, Todd Matshikiza, Walter Nhlapo, Nat Nakasa, [Es'kia Mphahlele, Lewis Nkosi] and many others produced the best investigative journalism, short fiction, satirical humour, social and political commentary, and musical criticism South Africa had ever seen.[41]

But here, too, Kavanagh argues that although the writers on *Drum* 'opposed racism and certain aspects of apartheid and situated its stories and news within the culture produced by the urbanisation of blacks...it did not oppose the practices of mining capital, and its attitudes to the African nationalist organisations were ambivalent to say the least'.[42] Thus the black journalists in the cast of *No good friday*, whom he also sees as ' "agents" in the operation of what was clearly a form of English-speaking white hegemony',[43] together with the teachers and the educated intermediate classes who participated tended, he also argues, to draw largely – and sometimes equivocally – on assimilation-ist discourse in their struggle against apartheid.

Such intersecting interests in Union Artists, it may also be argued, had clearly identifiable results for the plays. Predominantly assimilationist discourse traverses *King Kong* and *Sponono* as well as *No good friday*. Thus the hero of *No good friday* is Willie, an intellectual with aspirations to escape African culture. *King Kong* is a boxer who hopes to succeeded in the great (white) world of boxing, while in *Sponono* the (white) superintendent of a reformatory struggles to persuade the young (black) hero to accept ruling class morality. Again, the plays choose to present dramatic conflict by means of a primary focus, as in Butler's plays, upon an interiority in the central characters, largely indifferent to the social order within which these characters are positioned. Thus in *No good friday*, Willie has a moral conflict which he resolves through the existential act of reporting a gang murder to the police, even though this ensures his own death at the hands of vengeful gangsters. Evidence in the play of community culture provides only the backdrop to his inner 'moral' conflict. *Sponono*'s main dramatic concern centres not only on the psychological struggle between the principal of the school and the young man Sponono whom he believes he is trying to reform but, again, on the 'moral' conflict within each of them. *King Kong*'s concern with its characters is more superficial, but the play is nevertheless a portrait of the promise and rise of an individual and then his fall into a life of crime and murder. And although there is in this play a slightly more developed concern for the social pressures that are breaking up Sophiatown and that are inhibiting black advancement, these, too, remain secondary.

VII Misreading the townships: King Kong, No good friday, Sponono

More significant than this, urban township space in all three plays is not perceived to any significant extent in terms of the actual space which people occupy and the conditions in which they live. Thus while they begin to register the existence of townships and a black population within an urban space, none of these plays focuses upon family life and its problems within the confines of apartheid, to which for example Mandela's statement at his trial at times pointed. Instead, the noticeable and recurrent association in the presentation of township life, is the foregrounding of gangsters and crime. In No good friday, the plot revolves around the stabbing of a rural worker who does not pay protection fees to a group of gangsters, shortly after his arrival in Sophiatown. The subsequent decision by the central character Willie, to report the murder to the police, is prompted by his sense that it is through the negligence of the township inhabitants themselves that gangsterism thrives. King Kong deals with the rise and fall of a champion boxer, played out in the context of the more sensational and negative surface elements of Sophiatown life 'such as drinking, stabbing, crime, gangsterism, sexual infidelity, and promiscuity'.[44] And Sponono is situated in a reformatory in which the main character who returns sporadically to the townships struggles against the life of gangsterism and crime that awaits him there. Moreover, each of these plays has a crucial stabbing scene on stage.

The preference for such superficial and sensationalist aspects of township life, rather than for more constructive aspects of communal township culture has been discussed by Kavanagh in the context of the formation of popular urban culture which, he notes, may be seen in terms of 'imposed and constitutive elements' (p. 72). Kavanagh observes that in South Africa the imposed elements are often brutalised and pathological, and result from the massive efforts at social restructuring undertaken by the ruling classes. On the other hand, Kavanagh argues that more positive resilient and inventive impulses exist within the townships which, if emphasised, would contribute to the formation of a different view of popular culture:

The existence of this dialectic presents the playwright with a choice which is as ideological as it is aesthetic. One can either emphasise one factor in the dialectic or the other, or one can depict the dialectic itself. In other words, the playwright can emphasise the positive elements of the culture or the negative ones, or provide a picture which shows their interaction. (p. 72)

If the major emphasis in the presentation of township life in these plays, despite their multi-racial ambience is negative, their avoidance (as in the case of Butler's plays) of political activism and community struggle that is part of the history of the townships in the 1950s is equally striking. For instance, after the Defiance Campaign in 1952, the executives of the African National Congress (ANC), the South African Indian Congress, the South African Congress of Democrats and the South African Coloured People's Organisation set plans in motion which culminated in a Congress held at Kliptown, a township near Johannesburg, in April 1955 at which the Freedom Charter came into being. This in turn led to extended harassment by the state. Bannings of key leaders were followed by the arrest of 156 prominent figures on charges of treason.[45] Furthermore, in 1958 complexities within the African National Congress led to a breakaway by Africanists, who, under Robert Sobukwe, in 1959 formed the Pan-Africanist Congress, which, Lodge describes, according to Sobukwe's presidential address stood for 'government by the Africans for the Africans' and, at least until liberation, sought to keep whites at a distance (p. 85).

The history of the 1950s is full, too, of evidence of community resistance. This includes the women's fight against the imposition of passes, the Alexandra and Evaton bus boycotts, the struggle against the imposition of Bantu Education, the politicisation of African trade unionism.[46] More specifically Sophiatown, in which both *No good friday* and *King Kong* are located, was a thriving urban suburb despite its troubles. Father Trevor Huddleston described it as 'reminiscent of an Italian village somewhere in Umbria':

in the evening light, across the blue grey haze of smoke from braziers and chimneys against a saffron sky, you see close-packed, red-roofed little houses. You see, on the farthest skyline, the tall and shapely blue-gum trees... you see, moving up and down the hilly streets, people in groups: people with colourful clothes: people who, when you come up to them, are children playing, dancing and standing round the braziers... In the evening, towards the early South African sunset, there is very little of the slum about Sophiatown.[47]

Lodge, who cites this passage, argues that the removal of Sophiatown and the surrounding neighbours in the Western Areas was important to the government primarily because they were perceived to be 'hotbeds of African resistance' (p. 99) and while it is true that there were powerful gangs in Sophiatown even this fact has been given an emphasis somewhat different from its treatment in these plays, none of which attempts, as Kavanagh points out, to relate the criminal phenomena to which it points to the social forces facilitating it.[48] Lodge observes that 'though it would be an exaggeration to assert that the working-class community saw gangs as fighters for social justice' it was 'popularly believed that gangs "seldom harm ordinary folk"' while 'most of their non-internecine violence was directed at universally disliked people: the more prosperous traders, the South African Police and the municipal "Blackjacks"'.[49] Elsewhere it has been argued that

The tsotsi subculture, through its value system, style and ritual, aggressively denied hegemonic consensus. Tsotsi values, such as brazen rejection of the law and glorification of violence, criminality and hedonism, were defined in direct antagonism to the consensus value system. Tsotsi style and ritual often drew on imagery familiar to the consensus culture but inflected and subverted the symbolic structure of those images.[50]

Yet, in these plays, whereas none of this receives acknowledgement the dramatisation of gangsterism remains the consistent feature, investing the constitution of the oppressed township subject with associations of criminality and danger. And, as in the case, in other ways, of Butler's texts, any impulse to subvert prevailing discourse – if undertaken with more energy by these plays – remains, in this, contained. Memmi has noted that:

In colonial relationships, domination is imposed by people upon people but the pattern remains the same. The characterisation of the role of the colonised occupies a choice place in colonialist ideology; a characterisation which is neither true to life, or in itself incoherent, but necessary and inseparable within that ideology…(the colonised) is disfigured…into an oppressed creature, whose development is broken and who compromises by his defeat.[51]

He also notes that after the Second World War, European colonial powers prohibited the showing of certain movies of resistance which emphasised 'the possibility of aggressive and free action' (p. 94) and which showed that 'poorly armed or even unarmed oppressed people did dare attack their oppressors' (p. 94). From such perspectives, it is the absence of any recognition of resistance and contestation in the construction of the oppressed subject in both rural and urban space in all these plays that is most noteworthy.

Notes

1 Couzens, *The new African*, p. 186.
2 Kavanagh, *Theatre and cultural struggle*, pp. 48-9.
3 See Coplan, *In township tonight!*, p. 149, 205.
4 Couzens, *The new African*, pp. 317-18.
5 Kavanagh, *Theatre and cultural struggle*, p. 49.
6 Brooke, Brian, *My own personal star*, Johannesburg: Limelight Press, 1978, p. 142.
7 Steadman, 'Drama and social consciousness', p. 75.
8 Coplan, *In township tonight!*, p. 204.
9 Couzens, *The new African*, pp. 187-8.
10 Stead, Rina, 'The National Theatre Organisation 1947-1962', in Hauptfleisch, Temple, ed., *The Breytie Book*, Randburg: The Limelight Press,1985, p. 66.
11 Stead, 'The National Theatre organisation', p. 67.
12 The programme is lodged with the Human Sciences Research Council Library.
13 Alvarez-Pereyre, Jacques, *The poetry of commitment in South Africa*, tr. Wake, Clive, London: Heinemann, 1984, p. 15.
14 Butler, Guy, *A book of South African verse*, London: Oxford University Press, 1959.
15 Bakhtin, M. M., *The dialogic imagination*, ed. Holquist, Michael, Austin: University of Texas Press, 1987, pp. 84-5.
16 Butler, Guy, *The dam*, Cape Town: A. A. Balkema, 1953; Butler, Guy, *The dove returns*, London: The Fortune Press, 1956.
17 Coetzee, J. M., *White writing*, Sandton: Radix, 1988, p. 85.
18 Coetzee, *White writing*, pp. 6-7.
19 Davies, Horton, *Great South African Christians*, London: Oxford University Press, 1951, pp. iv-vi.
20 Coetzee, *White writing*, p. 87.
21 Roux, *Time longer than rope*, p. 372.
22 Cited in Meer, Fatima, *Higher than hope*, Johannesburg: Skotaville, 1988, p. 194.
23 Alvarez-Pereyre, *The poetry of commitment*, p. 16.
24 Cited in O'Meara, Dan, *Volkskapitalisme*, Johannesburg: Ravan, 1983, p. 173.
25 Simons, *Class and colour in South Africa*, p. 554.
26 Cited in Bundy, Colin, 'Land and liberation: popular rural protest and the national liberation movements in South Africa, 1920-1960', in Marks and Trapido, *Politics of Race*, p. 269.
27 Lodge, Tom, *Black politics in South Africa since 1945*, Johannesburg: Ravan, 1983, pp. 48-9.
28 Butler, *A book of South African verse*, p. xix.
29 Coplan, *In township tonight!*, p. 171.
30 Kavanagh, *Theatre and cultural struggle*, pp. 48-9.
31 See Coplan, *In township tonight!*, p. 150ff.
32 Cited in Kavanagh, *Theatre and cultural struggle*, p. 47.
33 Coplan, *In township tonight!*, p. 169.
34 Kavanagh, *Theatre and cultural struggle*, p. 51.
35 Coplan, *In township tonight!*, p. 169.
36 Coplan, *In township tonight!*, p. 205.
37 Kavanagh, *Theatre and cultural struggle*, p. 90.

38 Fugard, Athol, No good friday, in Dimetos and two early plays, London: Oxford, 1977; Bloom, Harry, King Kong, London: Collins, 1961; Paton, Alan and Shah, Krishnah, Sponono, Claremont: David Philip, 1983.

39 Kavanagh, Theatre and cultural struggle, p. 95.

40 Nkosi, Lewis, 'The fabulous decade: the fifties', in Home and exile and other selections, New York: Longman, 1983, p. 8.

41 Coplan, In township tonight!, p. 179.

42 Kavanagh, Theatre and cultural struggle, p. 60.

43 Kavanagh, Theatre and cultural struggle, p. 60ff.

44 Kavanagh, Theatre and cultural struggle, p. 97.

45 See Lodge, Black politics, pp. 67-90.

46 See Lodge, Black politics, pp. 114-200.

47 Cited in Lodge, Black politics, p. 94.

48 See Kavanagh, Theatre and cultural struggle, pp. 75-8.

49 Lodge, Black politics, p. 102.

50 Glaser, Clive, L., 'Anti-social bandits: culture, hegemony and the Tsotsi subculture on the Witwatersrand during the 1940s and 1950s', paper presented at Department of History MA Seminar, 30 August 1988, p. 31.

51 Memmi, Albert, The colonizer and the colonized, London: Condor, 1974, pp. 88-9.

3

Body and state

While the impact of the colonial and imperial metropolis continued to be felt – and sought – in establishment theatre towards the end of the 1950s, the struggle to find identity on the periphery intensified as the grip of apartheid on the country grew ever tighter. On winning the General Election in April 1958 with an increased majority from within the minority white electorate, the Nationalist Prime Minister J. G. Strijdom was reported as declaring that 'the electorate had once again returned the party on its colour policy and this policy would be pursued resolutely as the only way in which the white race could be maintained in South Africa with justice to the non-whites and the only way by which racial clashes in South Africa could be avoided'.[1] The Nationalist Party's obsession with and exploitation of racist discourse, amongst other developments, after 1948 had initiated an 'unprecedented drive to reconstitute racial categories in South Africa'.[2] For purposes of control, the subject was to be decisively constructed in terms of bodily colour and sexual behaviour. As part of this process, a string of laws were passed to mark and categorise subjects according to bodily appearance and also, by working through bodily desire, to assert governmental authority and control. One of the first measures was the Prohibition of Mixed Marriages Act (1949).[3] The following year The Immorality Amendment Act (1950) prohibited sexual intercourse between whites and those who were not classified as white. The Population Registration Act (1950) helped to arbitrate on race classification and the consolidating Act of 1957 sought to define any kind of sexual act between those classified as whites and those not classified as white, not necessarily intercourse, as unacceptable.

Philip Fisher, considering 'what the present does in the face of itself, for itself, and not for any possible future' remarks that:

within the present, culture stabilises and incorporates nearly ungraspable or widely various states of moral or representational or perceptual experience. It changes again and again what the census of the human world looks like – what it includes or excludes – and it often does so in tandem with changes in social fact or legal categories that make, from the standpoint of a later perspective, the facts seem obvious.[4]

Towards the end of the 1950s and in the early 1960s a number of dramatists from within the ruling classes attempted to engage with the state's obsessive classification of race, in the endeavour to stabilise and incorporate 'the nearly ungraspable or widely various states of moral or representational or perceptual (apartheid) experience' that involved the body, and that were tearing more viciously than ever before into the social fabric. Lewis Sowden's *The Kimberley train* opened on 12 September 1958, in 1959 Basil Warner's *Try for white* appeared, while in 1960, when he was in Europe, Fugard acted in David Herbert's play *A Kakamas Greek* [5] and Fugard's *The blood knot* opened in Johannesburg in 1961. Each of these plays, in one way or another attempted to address the apartheid marking of the body.

The appearance of these plays, together with the outburst of activity in multi-racial theatre endeavours such as those discussed in the previous chapter, mark, after Dhlomo's largely unpublished but massive project in drama, and after Butler's two attempts in the early and mid-1950s, not only perhaps the most creative outburst in South African drama to date, but also a shift into the theatre space itself. While the origins of earlier plays – as well some current attempts – were to be found mainly or exclusively in the writing of them, this shift reflected the beginnings of an awareness of theatre space and the experience and contribution of the practitioners occupying it as important points of origin for the engendering of any play. The sudden efflorescence of dramatic activity in the late 1950s and early 1960s, as the apartheid trauma erupted with ever increasing ferocity through the social order, suggests also the extent to which dissident whites and predominantly elitist or petit bourgeois members of the oppressed classes began to discover and utilise the dialogic nature of theatre in the struggle for a self-identity that might contest and resist ruling class hegemony. But it must be emphasised that this efflorescence entailed always an ongoing struggle against an increasingly censorious state process coupled with the almost complete indifference of established theatre and capital.

1 The state's dramas of colour and treason

Ruling class obsession with skin pigmentation in the late 1950s and early 1960s was seeping everywhere into the education system, social life, the media, the courts and theatre. In 1958 newspapers, for instance, were full of often insensitive and racist accounts of state policing of the body. Thus one article headlined 'Is she white or not?' reported that a woman whose great grandfather's brother was a 'coloured' man and whose mother was married to a 'European' had been charged with 'unlawfully using the European woman's lavatory on Salt River Station'.[6] A day earlier, the following distasteful report on a young man who had been reclassified as 'coloured' but who had since managed to convince the authorities, and married a young woman classified as white, was published:

A European victim of the Population Registration Act told me today that 'an incredible letter' from Pretoria nearly wrecked his marriage and estranged him from his relatives. A young man with fair hair, blonde eyebrows and the features of a Viking told me voluntarily that he was planning to leave the country... He showed the letter [reclassifying him] to his fiancee's father who said: 'God, you're the whitest Coloured man I've ever seen,' then chased him out of the house... he said 'Although I knew I was a European it preyed on my mind so much that I began to think there was something in it...There will always be rumours – and what's going to happen to him?' He pointed to his four months old son.[7]

And another article, published when Athol Fugard was living in Johannesburg a few months before he produced No good friday, reported:

A 22 year old African Houseboy (sic), who wrote a letter to an 18 year old European girl expressing his love for her, had been rightly convicted of crimen injuria, it was held in the Supreme Court in Cape Town today...Giving judgement Mr Justice van Winsen said: 'No general principles as to what conduct is calculated to impair the dignity of persons living in our society to such an extent as to merit punishment can profitably be devised...In determining whether the writing of a letter constitutes crimen injuria one cannot lose sight of the fact that it was written by the accused to a person who was a total stranger to him and, that between them, there was not only a social barrier, but a colour barrier as well... That she ascribed her feeling of being involved to the fact that the accused was an African only serves to emphasise a fact to which our courts have frequently had regard – namely that the difference in colour between the complainant and the accused is an "aggravating" feature...In all the circumstances I am not disposed to differ from the magistrate's finding.' Mr Justice Beyers and Mr Justice Watermeyer agreed.[8]

The State, ever since its notorious arrests of major leaders of the Defiance campaign, had been preparing for its own drama over race and colour in the much awaited and infamous Treason Trial which opened on 1 August 1958. This was a formal and public attempt to prosecute and convict some of the most significant opponents of apartheid. Even the Main Street Diary, a daily column in the *Rand Daily Mail* which usually discussed trivia about personalities in social as well as civic life, ran extensive coverage of the judges and defence lawyers involved, over two days, including full accounts of their careers and photographs. 'Speculation,' it commented, 'puts the cost of the Government's seven counsel at ninety thousand pounds, but the total will obviously depend on how long the trial lasts. Opinion is that this might be anything from six months to two years.'[9] The trial had a sensational opening when the defence's request that two of the judges recuse themselves was accepted by one judge. But if it, with its continual strong police presence, was intended to dramatise the state's determination to punish opposition, the large crowds the trial drew from the oppressed classes who regularly gave the currently favoured thumbs up Afrika! sign and sang and danced outside the court in Pretoria – also regularly described and photographed in the press – provided evidence of continuing courage and the will to resist. Lewis Sowden, a journalist on the *Rand Daily Mail*, reviewing Antony Sampson's newly published book on the Treason Trial one day after its opening, observed:

No one can read his account of the growth of African National Movements and be complacent. Their leaders have been at loggerheads. The older generation has clung to a belief in education and persuasion; the younger generation has been demanding militant action. The older generation still has faith in the West; the younger is distrustful. But all this does not mean that African Nationalism need not be taken seriously. In the past it has seemed to lack leadership and direction, but it is fast acquiring direction and, as Mr Sampson suggests more than once, this trial may prove to be one of its binding forces.[10]

In theatre too, the consequences of segregation were intensifying. Although the establishment had never really opposed the traditional segregation in theatres, it now found itself faced with a British Equity ban on anyone coming to South Africa without performing to blacks as well as whites. Thus, in order to import a North American company giving *The pyjama game*, one performance at least to black audiences was necessary. In this way managements might satisfy Equity's demand without undoing segregation. Such a performance could not of course take place at His Majesty's Theatre now reserved solely for whites, and so the company had to move to the Witwatersrand University Great

Hall. And the newspapers did not conceal the reason either, informing readers that 'African Consolidated Theatres which brought the show to South Africa were forced to stage a performance for non-Europeans (sic) by Equity, the British actors union, which has ruled that British artists cannot sign contracts to perform in the Union unless non-Europeans (sic) are allowed to see them.'[11] Similarly, *Odd man in* was taken to the Bantu Men's Social Centre, complete with sets, at the end of its run – for only one performance. The *Rand Daily Mail* reported another proposal to pacify Equity on 9 January:

Plans for the provision of regular theatrical performances for non-European (sic) audiences are being worked out by the Theatre Managers Association...The basic proposal is that the dozen or so theatrical managements regularly producing shows should jointly undertake to present, at least six shows a year to non-European (sic) audiences. It is felt that this would permanently obviate the difficulties frequently created when Equity, the British actors organisation, demands that its members in South Africa should not play exclusively to white audiences. (p. 6)

The article goes on to note that these plans would be presented to the manager of the Non-European Affairs Department, Johannesburg, who, 'in a position to supply the accommodation which regular performances would require', had recently 'refused to allow *Look back in anger* to be played to non-Europeans (sic), considering that the play was unsuitable for the purpose (an opinion which found many people in agreement)'. This article ends by focusing on the 'untold difficulties' posed by the 'presentation of plays to non-European audiences' according to Mr Robert Langford, Secretary of the Theatre Managers Association, who complained that 'We simply haven't got the theatres' and then opined that 'giving regular shows to non-Europeans (sic) we should have a good answer to Equity when (as with *Look back in anger*) a particular show was considered unsuitable for non-Europeans (sic)'.

However, there were a number of theatre practitioners who realised the problem lay with segregation itself. Prominent amongst these was Leon Gluckman, actor and producer, recently returned from England and later to be involved in the collaboration that produced *King Kong*. He spoke pointedly about segregation:

Audiences are composed of the elite, many of whom have been educated or sophisticated to a certain point of view. We must reach the people who have never been to the theatre, or who, having attended it, do not like it. We must overcome the attitude towards the colour bar, which thwarts theatre, and approach the future with the Africans and Coloureds in mind.[12]

II 'Plays which deal with South Africa in its present situation': The Kimberley train

The establishment was also coming under attack because of its indifference to local culture. Berdine Groenewald was quoted in the press as asking where any good South African plays might be found, and criticising the National Theatre – in turn defended by the actress and producer Margaret Inglis – for not encouraging indigenous drama.[13] The beginning of 1958 for instance had seen Plaintiff in a pretty hat being performed at the Brooke Theatre, Summer of the seventeenth doll at the Reps Theatre and Listen to the wind directed by Taubie Kushlik – followed by Odd man in presented by Anthony Farmer – at the Library Theatre. A variety show presented by Hugo Keletti with largely white performers, entitled Variety under the stars was on at the Joubert Park Open Air Theatre, while at His Majesty's Theatre, under the aegis of African Consolidated Theatres, an American Company, as I noted, had been imported for a brief run of The pyjama game. Establishment indifference towards encouraging the growth of indigenous theatre was also raised in the press by Lewis Sowden, who argued that more support for new South African plays was needed, maintaining that

the trying out of new plays does not involve building a new theatre. Plays can be tried out in existing theatres or even in a rehearsal room. As for the amateur societies they have the same snobbish attitude to indigenous plays as other people. They are unwilling to experiment.[14]

But, despite this appeal for space for new plays, throughout 1958 the lights went down from time to time at the Library and Joubert Park Theatres, His Majesty's frequently resorted to cinema, and the YMCA Theatre as well as that at the Johannesburg Technical College were only sporadically used. The two professional theatre companies at the Brooke and the Reps theatres that managed to run continuously throughout the year performed only non-South African works including The chalk garden, Career, Janus, Thieves carnival, The boy friend, A dead secret, Grab me a gondola, Dear delinquent. An offer by Brian Brooke to give his theatre for Sunday Night try-out performances of new plays, echoed several months later at a Reps Committee meeting, and a promise from Antony Farmer to form a panel of producers and others who would undertake the reading of new scripts does not seem to have produced any rush into production.[15]

Indeed, Lewis Sowden who had, as I noted, entered this debate, was the only one really to benefit from this sudden offer from members of establishment theatre. His own play The Kimberley train was 'discovered' by the committee and in due course, produced by Cecil Williams at the Library Theatre – at first anonymously in view of his position as drama critic as well as Assistant Editor on the Rand Daily Mail.[16]

This work, like all others in the late 1950s, was not interested in or able to address the Defiance Campaign or the Treason Trial – nor was it directly concerned with the State's dramatically declared hardline stance – soon to be underlined by the election after the death in August of the conservative Strijdom of the extremist racist Verwoerd to the premiership. But, as in the case of Butler's plays, The Kimberley train reflected at least the growth of the perception amongst members of the ruling classes that theatre should and could emerge from the South African context. It is also the first of those several plays appearing at this time which reflected, in different ways, what the changing social facts and legal categories based upon race meant for imaginative or cultural concepts of the subject in South Africa. Thus it deals with a 'coloured' woman who tries to pass for white and who is, by the end of the play, exposed. The play, performing to the white middle classes was a sell-out every night, 'the biggest success in Johannesburg for many years', prompting Cecil Williams to proclaim 'the success of this play shows that Johannesburg wants plays which deal with South Africa in its present situation'.[17] A reviewer saluted it as 'intensely moving' in the way it 'deals with race relations, race prejudice, the yearnings of the have-nots, the indifference of the haves, the shock to both systems when the two come into collision'.[18]

The 'coloured' people to whom Elaine Miller and her family in The Kimberley train belong, were descended from the Dutch/Afrikaner and other European settlers together with 'many strands in South Africa's past: Late Stone Age hunter-gatherers and herders, collectively known as Khoisan; slaves from the heterogeneous trading networks of the Dutch East India Company in the Indian Ocean; descendants of Indonesian Muslims sent to the Cape as political prisoners or enslaved artisans'.[19] But, whereas in the nineteenth century the term 'coloured' had been used to refer to all 'non-European' peoples, in the early years of the twentieth century it came to apply to what was now an 'artisan and petty-bourgeois class of non-European people' who 'found in the ethnic identification of their position in isolation from the rest of the non-European people a protection against their future disenfranchisement

and impoverishment'.[20] Before 1948 they won a measure of preferential treatment, in comparison with blacks, from successive govern-
ments. When they came to power the Nationalists continued the policy
of preferential treatment to 'coloureds' both in the attempt to retain their
'loyalty' and in the pursuance of their policy of ethnic fragmentation
(p. 171ff.) But at the same time Nationalist Party measures to separate
'coloureds' from whites intensified. Passing for white, which had been
relatively easy earlier in the century – it has been estimated that 'by
1936 38 per cent of the people classified as white in the Cape province
were of "mixed descent"' (p. 169) – became more difficult in the face
of Nationalist determination to implement their notions of 'race purity'.
Laws were passed to introduce segregation on trains for 'coloureds',
separate their living areas from whites and deprive them of the vote.

But although The Kimberley train recognises and expresses a measure
of concern in the text about race classification, and is ostensibly by a
journalist who was contesting establishment theatre practice, it
submits to prevailing notions within the South African social order as
to what the human body is and may signify. The central relationship
in the play, between Elaine Miller and the son of a wealthy middle-
class clothing manufacturer, John Powers, around which revolves what
dramatic plot and tension there is in the text, is unable to resist, once
Elaine's 'origins' are exposed, the insistence in prevailing discursive
formations that the body should be defined primarily in terms of
colour. In its presentation of a romance between the offspring of two
families divided by social and political constraints, the play avoids any
extended scrutiny of their personal relationship or the interaction of
their bodies. During the course of a rare physical embrace, John
observes:

There's something about you that seizes all of me and holds me... Something
in you that's gentle and fierce at the same time... primitive. (p. 20)

while in the final scene, when Elaine's family have been discovered,
and the two lovers are ostensibly struggling against their world, this
'something' in Elaine proves too powerful to ignore. She herself speaks
in a way that shows her own subjection to racist ideological discursive
formations:

Don't you understand: It's not enough to pretend to be white. You have to
know of the colour within you and not care a damn! That's what makes people
white. I wasn't able to do it. That's why I refused to marry you...when I could.
(p. 73)

No Romeo, John's few protesting remarks rapidly dwindle into submission. It is significant that the two are alone together on stage only during half of one scene in the first act and never again. And their crucial final attempt to evade dominant relations and discourse occurs in public and is contained by the repressive presence on stage of John's parents, the largely submissive Miller family and, for a while, even a policeman. All witness what the text presents as a hopeless attempt. John's cry: 'We're trapped, Elaine, we're trapped!' (p. 75) complements the implicit affirmation of blood 'difference' as decisive.

III Miscegenation and degeneration

Scholars have identified the coded concern with blood that so powerfully underlies the concern with 'miscegenation'. It is a concern that in one way or another is particularly prevalent in South African literature, including the work not only of Sarah Gertrude Millin, but in the late 1950s and early 1960s – from a markedly different and more liberal perspective – that of dissident novelists from the ruling classes such as Nadine Gordimer in *A world of strangers*. It derives not only from the influence of the Nationalist exploitation of certain doctrines in Calvinism, which I explore later in this chapter, but also from social Darwinism and the 'explosion of biologically based racial science in the second half of the nineteenth century' which set itself 'the task of classifying the world's races according to a natural hierarchy'.[21] Eugenics, 'the so-called science of "racial stocks"...was founded on the idea that social ends could be efficiently achieved by the deliberate manipulation of genetic pools' (p. 72). By the twentieth century, as I noted briefly in chapter 2, social Darwinism and related doctrines contributed in South Africa to crucial areas of political debate: 'speculation about the relative intelligence of blacks and whites; the almost universally expressed horror of "miscegenation"; and fear of racial "degeneration" following upon the uncontrolled development of a black and white proletariat in the cities' (p. 75).

The ways in which racist discourse operates with notions of intelligence, miscegenation and degeneration involves too, as J. M. Coetzee shows, particular conceptions of blood, thought of as the 'locus of life and identity'.[22] If blood is that which defines 'the inherited social status of the individual by flowing supratemporally through him and all his blood-ascendants and descendants' (p. 146),

D

Coetzee observes that race theories 'take up' the conception of the blood – as the 'fluid of generation and as the home of the germs of generation – as material for fantasy' (p. 146) and gives the example of Gobineau:

The word degenerate, when applied to a people, means... that the people has no longer the same intrinsic value as it had before, because it has no longer the same blood in its veins, continual adulterations having gradually affected the quality of that blood... Great peoples, at the moment of their death, have only a very small and insignificant share of the blood of their founders...The blood of the civilising race is gradually drained away by being parcelled out among the peoples that are conquered or annexed. (p. 147)

Thus in the work of Sarah Gertrude Millin, Coetzee argues amongst other things that 'flaw can thus be thought of as "black blood" insofar as this blood is invisible – that is, hides in "white blood" – but also insofar as it threatens to erupt in the future, throwing off its white disguise' (pp. 140-1).

Such ideological discursive formations are repeatedly manifest in The Kimberley train. Mr Philips, the leader of the gang formed to protect the interests of those who pass for white, asks Elaine's brother, Wally, threateningly, 'You're Coloured, aren't you, both of you? Part white, part a slice out of the chocolate cake. Answer me' (p. 14). Similarly, Mr Powers's reference to police methods of hunting out blacks who pass for 'coloured', 'If it falls out, he's Coloured...he passes. You know, coffee with a dash, white grandpa' (p. 28) and Elaine's mother Bertha's assertion that 'In our family there's the best blood' (p. 42) point to the preoccupation with mingling of blood, miscegenation, 'colour'. This is postulated as inescapable as well as insuperable – when they discover Elaine is 'coloured', Powers observes, 'It's odd about colour. You live in the middle of it all your life, and when it touches you you jump' (p. 64). At one point in the play Mr Powers asks his 'coloured' maid what she thinks of blacks who pass for 'coloured'. In a way that would have pleased the Nationalist Party and its ideologues in the South African Bureau of Racial Affairs, she opines: 'We're a higher class, Sir. We're second class, and they're third' (p. 27).

IV Towards an authentic South African drama

Athol Fugard was in Johannesburg working on No good friday in 1958 when The Kimberley train, opened. Whether he saw it or not, his experience in *A Kakemas Greek*, also on a related theme, must have been suggestive for the writing of his own play about two brothers who share a shack in Korsten, just outside Port Elizabeth. They have the same black mother, but Zach has a black father whilst his brother Morrie's father is white. With no easy ride to performance by the National Theatre Organisation, *The blood knot*, opened in Johannesburg on 22 October 1961 at Dorkay House, in a rudimentary theatre created out of space on the top floor of a building, fronted on the one side by Eloff Street, a main traffic thoroughfare and, on the other, by a recreational area for workers from a nearby mining compound. Although Fugard had been permitted a few performances of *No good friday* at the Brooke Theatre, what he was attempting in *The blood knot* was extraordinary not only because of its concern with a crucial ruling class fixation in South Africa, but also because of his decision despite segregation to act on stage himself with a black actor. He had no hope of support or facilities from the establishment. Accordingly, rehearsals took place in Fugard's Hillbrow apartment which he shared with his co-actor in the production, Zakes Mokae. The theatre in which the play opened, under the aegis of Union Artists, contrary to general theatre practice, seated at the opening performance an invited integrated audience (of about sixty – although, very quickly, often double that number attended). A review in *The Star*, was favourable and the play moved to the YMCA theatre where it played for white audiences only, after which it went on tour for six months. This was a staggering and unusual success for a play that was, in an aggressively apartheid oriented social order, presenting its audiences with, for the first time, a multi-racial cast. Nadine Gordimer wrote of the 'white audience streaming in week after week to sit as if fascinated by a snake'.[23] The play was subsequently performed abroad, filmed and shown on BBC Television, and has been revived many times in South Africa.

Fugard himself was born in the semi-desert sheep farming area of the Karoo to an Afrikaans mother and an English-speaking South African of Liverpool-Irish descent, who was crippled in an accident and never able to provide the main support for the family. They moved from what was a primitive shanty in depressing circumstances to Port Elizabeth where Fugard's mother ran a cafe and was the family's major earner. Fugard commented that 'in terms of white South African social categories' his background could be described as 'lower middle class... more or less the bottom social rung because you don't really have a white labouring category in South Africa' and added that 'judged by the considerable degree of affluence enjoyed by white South Africa, both in my childhood and still to this day, it was a relatively poor situation' (p. 15). He attended a technical school and left Cape Town University at the beginning of his third year to hitch-hike up Africa. After several adventures including imprisonment in the Sudan for being an illegal immigrant he worked as a sailor on board a ship with a multi-racial crew which, he has since said, cured him of racism. On his return to South Africa he was employed as a clerk in Fordsburg for a Native Commissioner's Court, about which he observed, 'I knew that the system was evil, but until then I had no idea of just how system-atically evil it was. That was my revelation. As I think back, nothing that has ever happened to me has eclipsed the horror of those few months' (p. 26). After the performances of his first play No good friday, Fugard had worked for a while as a stage manager for the National Theatre Organisation and then left for England with his wife to acquire greater theatre experience, but the Sharpeville massacre prompted him to return to South Africa, where he wrote The blood knot.[24] Unlike the essentially literary attempts at drama which had until now been undertaken by Dhlomo and Butler, Fugard's struggle to discover on stage self identity and a sense of place within the periphery grew out of his own active involvement in and commitment to the theatre from the start of his career.

As I indicate briefly at the end of chapter 5, 'A green leaf on a burnt tree', his work, because of his chosen focus upon essentialist versions of interiority and existentialism, has been easily and frequently appropriated by traditionalist critics both in South Africa and abroad. Writing from America, one of the most recent of these observes:

Fugard's ultimate concern is the universal human plight rather than the particular South African one. Man's (sic) isolation, his lonely search for warmth, intelligibility, and meaning in an alien world, his avowal of human dignity, affirmation of his identity, and temporary recourse to dreams and illusions before embracing a present bereft of consoling myths – these are themes so fundamental they cannot be delimited to a single society that will someday crumble from its inherent contradictions.[25]

But Fugard's plays can be responded to or read in more than one way. If from some points of view the focus on interiority in The blood knot, encourages such readings, the play nevertheless reflects as well, more than any other drama of this period, the way in which in South Africa the subject is constructed in terms of the body. Its initial reception in South Africa as well as the interest it aroused abroad and its subsequent revivals attest to its significance. Rather than, as in The Kimberley train , simply transmitting or echoing some of the dominant and racist ideological discursive formations which flow through the social order, its far more interrogative presentation of crucial ways in which the body is used within South Africa invites close examination.

V Calvinism, the body and existentialism in The blood knot

On the one hand the text depicts attitudes to and the handling of the human body within the familial structure: here the body, in its search for love, comfort and pleasure is presented as a subject with needs, requiring care. The body is identified too as a source of mystery and fear – producing fear of defilement or incontinence, fear of uncontrolled desire and its need for gratification. However The blood knot on the other hand, also presents attitudes to and treatment of the human body within the context of the state: here the body provides the focal point for surveillance. It is a means for the state of categorisation and control.[26]

Fugard's own interest in interiority is evident in the presentation of familial relations in the play. Morrie and Zach, it becomes clear very quickly, have different attitudes towards their bodies. Morrie, in his interaction with Zach and in his attitude to desire, reveals an unease, anxiety and guilt about human physicality, evident in his vicarious involvement in not only providing relief for, but also cleansing Zach's body with its 'stinking feet' and sweat after labour, the 'rude odours of manhood'.[27] This uneasiness about the body – the need to control what is perceived as the excessive and unattractive aspects of its physicality – suggests in turn a fear of incontinence, a fear of being overwhelmed by that very physicality. Morrie's unease is evident too in his response to human desire, both in his brother and in himself. He defines Zach's love of music, company and sexual pleasure as 'the passing of time, and worthless friends' (p. 62). When the play begins he has already prevailed upon Zach to abandon his former life in favour of their companionship and his dream of a different future. And when Zach reminisces about his sexual past, Morrie disciplines him:

Morris. All right, Zach!
[Pause.]
Zachariah.That was Connie.
[He broods.]

Morris. Feeling better?
Zachariah. A little.
Morris. Talking helps, doesn't it? I said so. You find the answers to things. (p. 64)[28]

The plan to acquire a pen-pal is a further means of controlling desire and Morrie's encouragement of Zach's move into chastity. Moreover, what he sees as the continual purification of his brother's as well as his own body, is aided by regular readings from the Bible. Some of Fugard's cuts in his new version of the play published in 1987 when examined foreground the obsession with defilement and debilitation that recurs in the original as, for example, in scene 2 when, during one sequence, Morrie emphasises to Zach that 'a man can't spend his life with only one thought' (p. 29) and suggests that Minnie aged because 'it happens…to men…before their time…after women and too much life' (p. 30). Against this picture Morrie posits the safety of their present parsimony and abstinence as well as the possibility of the pen-pal Ethel who will 'fill those empty hours without wasting you away' (p. 30).

This attitude to the body suggests most obviously, in South Africa, Calvinist discourse. Fugard edits out a long speech from The blood knot where this seems particularly evident:

Do you think a man can't hurt himself?…What's to stop him dreaming forbidden dreams at night and waking up too late? Hey? Or playing dangerous games with himself and forgetting where to stop? I know them, I tell you, these dreams and games a man has with himself. That. There in your hand. To Miss Ethel Lange, Oudtshoorn. You think that's a letter? I'm telling you it's a dream, and the most dangerous one. Maybe, just maybe, when the lights are out, when you lie alone in the darkest hour of the night, then, just maybe, a man can dream that one for a little while. But remember, that even then, wherever you lie, breathing fast and dreaming, God's Watching With His Secret Eye to see how far you go! You think he hasn't seen us tonight? (p. 46)

Protestantism, it is often observed, took away the mediation of the church between the individual and her/his God.[29] Morrie's language resonates guilt and fear about human desire – anxiety about the fevered imaginings to which a young man might be given in bed alone at night. His insecurity suggests the belief that the individual must face her/his God directly. What are construed as impure thoughts about the body will be immediately apparent, he asserts, to the deity's alert surveillance. It is this that makes Morrie at times so tortured about his brother's body and its welfare as well as, by implication, his own.

Fugard's mother was Afrikaans – moreover, Fugard observed about himself in 1984, 'For all my much vaunted emancipation, I now realise I'm actually a Calvinist at heart. I remain a Calvinist'.[30] But if we wish to suggest the Calvinist nature of Morrie's attitude to the body, it is important to recognise as well that in South Africa Calvinism is not merely confined to the Dutch Reformed Churches. Elements of it appear also in the Anglican, Methodist and Presbyterian Churches.[31] Indeed, Morrie's anxiety to cleanse and maintain the purity of the body and to avoid defilement may be said in important ways to be part of Western religious discourse in general. To illustrate this we may glance briefly at Kristeva's examination of the emergence of the pure/impure distinctions in the Bible.[32] She argues that impurity develops as a metaphor for idolatry, sexuality and immorality and traces the development of such basic distinctions with particular reference to passages in Leviticus:

> The pure will be that which conforms to an established taxonomy: the impure that which unsettles it, establishes intermixture and disorder... Thus initially what appeared to us as a basic opposition between man and God (vegetable/ animal, flesh/blood), following upon the initial contract 'Thou shalt not kill', becomes a complete system of logical oppositions. (pp. 98-9)

Kristeva shows how dietary laws developed the notion of the self's clean and proper body which was to 'bear no trace of its debt to nature 'but remain 'clean and proper in order to be fully symbolic...Anything that leaks out of the feminine or masculine body defiles' (p. 102). The transitions she registers relating to blood impurity take in the following:

> prohibition of meat diet (following upon the prohibition against killing), the postdiluvian classification of meat as in conformity or nonconformity with the divine word, the principle of identity without admixture, the exclusion of anything that breaks boundaries (flow, drain, discharge). (p. 103)

Fugard may have used the first passage in the Bible from which Morrie quotes in scene 1 because the detailed concern in it with making distinctions complements Morrie's own obsessive preoccupation with distinguishing between what he considers acceptable and unacceptable in the human body. Whether this is so or not it is interesting that the passage he chooses comes itself from Leviticus:

> And if thou bring an oblation of a meat offering baken in the oven, it shall be unleavened cakes of fine flour mingled with oil, or unleavened wafers

anointed with oil; and if thy oblation be a meat offering baken in a pan, it
shall be of fine flour, unleavened, mingled with oil. Thou shalt part it in pieces
and pour oil thereon. It is a meat offering. (p. 66; Leviticus 2:4)

Morris is not the first to attempt to handle the body with recourse to
such discourse.

By contrast with Morrie, Zach, from the beginning of the play, is
far more at home with his body.[33] It may be that in the presentation
of Zach's strong sensuality and his longing to live, in the present,
through his body, the text may nevertheless also resonate those
currents in Calvinism as well as in Western religious discourse
generally, that postulate the dangerously seductive nature of the
physical being and that warn against transgression. But the effect of
Zach's sensuality, set against Morrie's fevered fear of the body is
positive. As well as this, it is worth recalling that the text appears during
a period of liberal reformism in sexuality.[34] Strong in Britain, this was
permeating through to a South Africa still very much subject to colonial
cultural influence. Commentators detect a more permissive attitude to
sexuality developing after the Second World War in which sexual
enjoyment became more permissible: there was 'an increase in the
availability of contraception and contraceptive advice and... fashion
eroticised the body more explicitly'.[35] Fugard's text is not concerned
with these developments; nevertheless in the presentation of Zach's
attitude to his body there is an ease that contrasts with Morrie's
attitudes and, tangentially at least, points to the more permissive
possibilities.

All the scenes of the play are located within the home and within
the family unit and in terms of this aspect of Fugard's concern the play
may be seen as partly concerned to explore the struggle of two young
men in the safety of these confines to find, through games, fantasy,
discussion, argument, within their bodies, identity. Zach agrees to try
his brother's alternative which suggests a measure of affection for his
brother, as well as a need to secure a way of life that may improve upon
what he knew before the arrival of his brother. Moreover, as the play
unfolds, it is Morrie, too, who reveals a measure of ambivalence about
his own attitudes. When Zach shows curiosity about his brother's
sexual life Morrie replies with a mixture of desire, defensiveness and
self-righteous justification (see p. 73) but later in the play he has no
answer when Zach again probes his secret attitudes (p. 81). The sense
that Morrie is slowly being seduced away from his Calvinist impulses
and his ambivalence are most evident in the scenes which follow, in

which he is yet again seduced into the fantasy of potency as a result of Zach's insistence that he try on the newly purchased suit. And if, at the beginning of the play, Morrie seems to live vicariously through the care he takes in the comforting and purifying of Zach's body, once Zach realises Ethel Lange is unattainable for him, he becomes involved vicariously – even if partly aggressively – in helping his brother enact the fantasy of sexual potency and achievement. In the course of the play, each brother cares for the needs of the other in terms of what each understands to be appropriate for the body and for desire. This struggle is one that fluctuates and alters as each attempts to handle a need, the fulfilment of which, for the duration of the play, remains unresolved, unattained, absent.

This activity of caring may also be set more deliberately within the context of existentialism, within the context of Fugard's own observation that:

the essence of The Blood Knot is the problem of one person trying to cope with the reality of another existence, of someone else whose pain he feels, whose suffering he witnesses. It is the existentialist's dilemma of one person trying to relate to another.[36]

This interest in existentialism in The blood knot has often been remarked by critics although not always fully explored. Existentialism, we may recall, 'repudiates all the absolute categories, religious and secular, through which we have claimed significance for ourselves'.[37] In consequence it entails 'anguish at our meaninglessness, affirmation of human responsibility' and, on occasion, 'recuperation of religion' (p. 101). Fugard, who also mentions Sartre in his comments on the play, clearly draws on this discourse not only in his portrayal of the struggle of the two brothers throughout the play to attain appropriate bodily identity, but also in his presentation of the world they inhabit.[38] The waste that has polluted the lake just outside their window, the shack they live in, the extreme poverty they are required to endure all suggest a bleak and indifferent world. This is of course intensified by the continual reference to the racism that operates explosively within that world. Located in such conditions, they search for understanding and their attempts to identify appropriate bodily needs and their fulfilment, the plans they make and abandon, the commitments they accept and then change may be seen as part of an existentialist struggle, in what is postulated as a meaningless/absurd world, to assume responsibility for themselves and for one another. The use of the alarm clock and the use of time may similarly encourage existentialist readings. Time is to be inhabited in the play with the help of self-created timetables and plans to impose order, but there is nothing beyond that: time can easily become entrapment. It also postulates loss; if the two brothers separately and together yearn for their lost mother, they also are left alone, in the present, without her.

VI Blood, colour and the state

If, however, we may detect Fugard's interest in existentialist discourse in these and other ways, the world Fugard evokes is also significantly different from that in existentialist writing or that, for instance, in *Waiting for Godot*. The 'muckheap' in Beckett's play serves powerfully as metaphor for a metaphysical condition. But the dead lake at Korsten suggests, more particularly, industrial waste.

Early in the play Morrie expresses unease about the extremities of poverty in which he and his brother are situated, which , like his unease about the body, he endeavours similarly to control with language. Here he brings into play not the talking about sexuality, the letter writing or the prayers he uses with Zach, but, instead, language that postulates an alternative future on a farm which the brothers will own, in the open country:

> You think I like it here more than you? You should have been here this afternoon, Zach. The wind was blowing again. Coming this way it was, right across the lake. You should have smelt it, man. I'm telling you that water has gone bad. Really rotten! And what about the factories there on the other side? Hey? Lavatories all around us? They've left no room for a man to breathe in this world. But when we go, Zach, together, and we got a place to go, our farm in the future...that will be different. (p. 60)

The dead lake, the shack at Korsten, the sense of economic exploitation Zach especially registers as both worker and 'consumer', the poverty of the two brothers and the bleakness of their prospects all denote the material conditions which prevail within existing relations of domination and subordination in the social order from which the play comes. Such conditions subject these bodies to a life of deprivation, continual need and labour without adequate comfort or rest.

It is true that these conditions are presented in some respects in a general way – of which Marxist critics particularly are critical.[39] But it is not merely poverty that pressurises the subject in the play. The text shows that thrusting against the attitudes to the human body evident within the family structure, upon which the brothers draw, in the attempt to locate their bodily identity, is the discourse fostered by the state which the text sees as imposing upon these subjects, continually, an entirely different identity. It may be argued from this point of view that through the emphasis – in terms of prevailing discourse, ideology and the operative legal system – on such identities for the human body, the state can assert its own authority and position and contribute further to the legitimation of existing relations of domination and subordination.

We may perceive this, in the argument of materialist and Marxist discourse, by glancing briefly at the way in which in South Africa, in this context, ideology has functioned to obscure as well as to identify actual conditions. Dan O'Meara's formulation of this concept is useful here.[40] He reminds us that 'ideologies form the lived and imaginary (i.e. ideational) relation with their real conditions of existence – the ideational forms of representation through which the economic, social and political relations and contradictions are lived and fought out by men and women' (p. 15). At the same time 'ideologies are partially adequate but misrepresentative forms of cognition of the real world' (p. 12). And finally:

if ideologies arise out of everyday experience and mirror and guide such experience in both a partially adequate yet misrepresented way, they do not adequately represent the conditions of existence of such everyday experience. Here is the source of the illusory character of ideology. (p. 13)

In chapter 1, I noted the argument that one of the ways in which the dominant classes remain in control is through institutions which privilege their preferred discursive ideological formations. What is important in the present discussion is the extent to which, as I suggested earlier in this chapter, prevailing discursive formations in South Africa have worked particularly powerfully through the human body and doctrines about skin pigmentation attached to it. Yet materialist examinations of developing conditions of existence in South Africa identify as crucial 'inter alia, the consolidation of capitalist production in a period of monopoly, the monopolisation of the means of production in the hands of white capitalists, the dispossession of African producers' (p. 13).

It is worth looking a little more closely here at one particular way in which, as O'Meara argues, changing conditions in the 1940s affect the emergence of Afrikaner Nationalist discourse. O'Meara traces the rapid disintegration of the old economic relations during this period:

The apartheid concept crystallised and condensed the responses of various class forces to...transformations. It reflected the farmers' concern over their declining labour supply and inability to compete for labour against the higher wages paid in industry and commerce. It encompassed the concern of emerging Afrikaner business for a cheap labour policy to ensure their own accumulation. And it pandered to the fears of specific strata of white workers at being displaced in the new industrial division of labour by cheaper African labour. (p. 173)

O'Meara refers to a series of 'long authoritative articles on "The Racial Question in Our Country" in Inspan in 1947' which argued that 'the racial question had developed above all into a question of labour...South Africa's economic development "has been built on, and is dependent upon, the cheap labour-power of the native"' (p. 174). Thus the broad outlines of the new apartheid policy became clear:

It would concern itself firstly with measures to restrict the flow of labour from the rural areas to the town, but above all from the white farms to the towns. Secondly it would exercise the tightest possible control and discipline over the African work force, permitting no form of organisation which challenged the ...existing division of society. Thirdly, measures to maintain low wages and regulate the conditions of work so as to permit an intensification of exploitation would be introduced. Fourthly, the jobs and superior positions of white workers within the industrial division of labour would be protected from competition from cheaper African labour. And finally, since any conception of 'racial equality' encompassed all the evils inherent in the changes experienced during the 1940s' segregation would be reinforced and extended in all fields. (p. 175)

Total segregation, however, was not envisaged and 'the new government was urged to limit itself to the practical task of improving the system of influx control, developing the native reserves, and segregating public places and certain residential areas' (p. 175).

All this supports the argument that the problem of labour in South Africa is of primary significance. Yet many of the laws passed in the 1950s, as the opening to this chapter showed, were to develop social segregation, while often, the way in which South Africa was described suggested the problem to be one of colour rather than labour. If we glance briefly at the thinking of some other Afrikaner Christian Nationalists of the 1940s, we may understand part of the reason why this came to be so.

In 1942 Dr P. Meyer, speaking to students at a National Conference, observed that 'To Afrikanerdom belong only those who by virtue of blood, soil, culture, tradition, belief, calling form an organic unitary society'.[41] In 1945 Dr G. Cronje published a book called '*n Tuiste vir die Nageslag* – (A home for posterity) – in which he asserted:

The more consistently the policy of apartheid could be applied, the greater would be the security for the purity of our blood and the surer our unadulterated European racial survival... (cited in de Klerk, p. 218, my emphases)

One interesting aspect of this mode of thought may be seen in the way in which an internal obsession with bodily purity/impurity, central, as we have seen, to much Western religious discourse, is put to use. The concept of impurity is not any longer emphasised as part of a private, inner dilemma. It comes to be applied to some bodies and not to others, and is treated, indeed, far more importantly for the politicians than the danger of defilement facing the private, struggling soul. Defilement becomes, more intensely the mixing with 'different' blood and 'different' skin pigmentation. Moreover Christian Nationalist politicians were helped by Calvinist doctrines of hierarchy which they, again, put to good use.[42]

Notions of purity and notions of hierarchy provided for Christian Nationalist politicians and then for the state after 1948 a means for entrenching authority and strengthening control. The concern with bodily purity and impurity – so disturbing to Morrie – affords a special opportunity: the predilection to fear impurity within the body and within the self can be turned to good use to predicate impurity in the other. The human subject is encouraged to believe fervently that impurity is more importantly to be located in the bodies around her/him rather than within her/his own body. Or, if a member of the subordinate classes, the subject is defined by prevailing discourse, held in position, as impure. In terms of this it is interesting that, as he expresses desperation about their physical location (p. 60), Morrie draws upon language suggesting faecal waste. It is to cope with this sense of defilement, encouraged in these subjects, defined by the state as labour units, located in living conditions on the poverty line or below it, that Morrie resorts in his final comments to fantasy about 'when we go... and we got a place to go, our farm in the future...that will be different' (p. 60).

Such perspectives argue also that, as the power of those utilising such discursive formations about the body increases so do the laws encouraging this view and so does the transmission of this racist ideology, through cultural institutions, education, the media, and the theatre. As my references to O'Meara suggest, from this perspective also, this particular aspect of ideology helps to hide rather than reveal the underlying conditions that centre on the need for cheap labour and the means brought into play to ensure its continuation.

VII Body and state in The blood knot

I will now examine two ways in which Blood knot/The blood knot suggests or depicts the state's contestation over the body and shows, too the state's attempts (regardless of the subject's search for her/his own integral bodily identity) continually to work through language about the body in order to assert its control.

The one obvious way in which this may be demonstrated is in the frequent, although fluctuating indications of interpellation in the play, indications that show the subject hailed by prevailing discursive formations and held in position by those formations.[43] This is not only to be found in the cry of Zach to his mother in scene 6 that he is also beautiful, which implies a measure of acceptance of the 'impure' associations attached to darker skin, nor in the mother's implied preference for her lighter skinned son. It is most evident in aspects of Morrie's language.

He appears to regard his brother's skin as evidence of misfortune: 'When I hear that certainty about whys and wherefores, about how to live and what not to love, I wish, believe me, man, I wish that old washerwoman had bruised me too at birth' (p. 94). He fears the power of the state and its ability to discover Zach's still hypothetical involvement with a white woman: 'I'm telling you now, Zach, burn that letter, because when they come around here and ask me, I'll say I got nothing to do with it' (p. 80). And he believes, intermittently, the dominant ideology about the potency of a white skin. His own sense of sexual potency increases when he imagines himself as a white middle-class suitor: 'Don't be a bloody fool! You got to buy a whole suit to get a breast pocket...How do you think a man steps out to meet a waiting lady. On his bare feet, wearing rags, and stinking because he hasn't had a bath?' (p. 98). The extent to which this merges with dominant discourse about the body emerges directly when he observes in scene 5:

The clothes will help, but only help. They don't maketh the white man. It's that white something inside you, that special meaning and manner of whiteness...this whiteness of theirs is not just in the skin, otherwise...well I mean...I'd be one of them wouldn't I? (p. 103)

If Morrie's language evidences interpellation he also actively imagines the surveillance that will not only expose the two pen-pals but will also incarcerate them:

And what about your dreams Zach? They've kept me awake these past few nights. I've heard them mumbling and moaning away in the darkness. They'll hear them quick enough. When they get their hands on a dark-born boy playing with a white idea, you think they don't find out what he's been dreaming at night? They've got ways and means, Zach. Mean ways. Like confinement, in a cell, on bread and water, for days without end. They got time. All they need for evidence is a man's dreams. Not so much his hate...It's his dreams that they drag off to judgement. (p. 92)

Here Morrie ascribes to the body that dares to desire, the same fate that in his Calvinist view of himself he has assigned through his Calvinist God. But this time it is the state that is the omnipotent observer. It is all the more significant that Morrie's response, to police his brother and himself, under the assumption that they are already being watched and will inevitably be discovered, takes place long before an attempted seduction that will in fact never materialise beyond the letter itself.

It is worth recalling here Foucault's well-known description of one effect of the panopticon, an architectural design of incarceration where the prisoner is placed under the continual scrutiny of a hidden observer in a central tower who is at the same time invisible to all the prisoners, in separate cells whom he may nevertheless observe at will. By these means the actual presence or absence of the warder makes no difference to the prisoner's sense of being held continually under surveillance. In this way, 'a state of consciousness and permanent visibility that assures the automatic functioning of power' is induced in the prisoner.[44] We may argue that, instead of the architectural apparatus within South Africa, the Immorality and related Acts together with legislation about race classification were designed to produce a similar consequence: a surveillance that is perceived to be 'permanent in its effects even if it is discontinuous in its action... [so that] the perfection of power [renders] its actual exercise unnecessary' (p. 201). The result of such arrangements is that the inmates of the panopticon or the subjects of the state are 'caught up in a power situation of which they are themselves the bearers' (p. 201).

Thus Morrie schools Zach as to the state's view of his desire for a white woman and as to the state's definition of his bodily colour. When Morrie expresses his fears of being overheard, of being confined by the state, not only has no actual incident of sexual contact occurred or no meeting between the brothers and Ethel Lange taken place, but no agent of the state is even remotely aware of the existence of these brothers or what they struggle to understand in their hut in Korsten. In an important sense then, the text presents Morrie as thinking and acting in complete subjection to prevailing ideology and its manifestation in the laws and institutions of state.

The evidence of interpellation and subjection which I have been tracing is, however, as I remarked earlier, intermittent in the text. This is because Morrie himself, when he can, attempts to struggle against the state's definition of bodily identity. For one thing he returns to his brother having given up the attempt to try for white (which, in the practice of deception, also yields to the dominant ideology's assertion of the importance of colour). His guilt about his desire to escape into the dominant class is itself evidence of resistance to the imperatives in prevailing discourse. His concern is to revivify the family structure and to find identity within that. And his attempt to live vicariously through his brother, to invade his body, is not, as some critics have asserted, an attempt primarily to dominate so much as an attempt to understand his brother's body in a way the state has forbidden – that is, not as impure, but as the body of a brother related to him by blood. This is evident at crucial moments in the play – early on when he puts on his brother's coat:

It's been a help to me, this warm old coat. You get right inside a man when you can wrap up in the smell of him. It prepared me for your flesh, Zach. Because your flesh, you see, has an effect on me. The sight of it, the feel of it...It feels, you see...I saw you again after all those years ...and it hurt, man. (p. 67)

and later when, confessing to his past actions and his guilt over them he also seeks expiation:

So what was stopping me? You. There was always you. What sort of thing was that to do to your own flesh and blood brother? Anywhere, any place or road, there was always you, Zach. So I came back. I'm no Judas. (p. 107)

The play also presents most powerfully a series of incidents in which the thrust towards brotherhood, towards the affirmation of a physical bond of oneness is continually contested by the imposition of, within the social order and as a means of consolidating existing economic relations, racist ideology. Thus although all the scenes take place within the home and the family structure, many of the games the brothers play, or the fantasies they enact take them out of the home and into the social order of which they are part. And it is when this happens that we see prevailing racist discourse about the human body work in ways that divide them, lead them to hostility and to fracture, subject them to its insistence, not on the bonds of blood and brotherhood but on the body's skin pigmentation, the notions of purity and impurity the state has so skilfully incorporated into its bid for domination. After the initial recognition of exploitation through the word game played with 'prejudice' and 'inhumanity' that confirm Zach's actual position as a labour unit, seen without compassion, within the social order, each subsequent game becomes more and more frightening. The extent to which the roles defined by the state, through its use of language about the body, decisively redefines their relationship and threatens their family becomes more and more evident.

Zach schools Morrie in the art, within the social order of seeing him as a labour mechanism and treating him accordingly. And Morrie, when he assumes the fantasy of being white in the larger social order, finds it irresistible to project on to his brother all that he senses is impure within himself – project this, in the terrible racist insults he flings at Zach. Some critics have valuably explored Fugard's interest in psychodrama in these scenes, but what the brothers learn and perceive most powerfully in these games is what the social order does to their bodies.

This tension between body and state which remains throughout the play and is not resolved at its end points profoundly and penetratingly to the social order from which this play comes. We may recall furthermore, in this connection, that, as Derrida in some eloquent senses has argued, in another context, it extends much further: 'Apartheid constitutes…the first "delivery of arms," the first product of European exportation'…The 'survival of Western Europe' depends upon… 'the stability of the Pretoria regime'.[45] 'There is no racism', says Derrida:

without a language. The point is not that acts of racial violence are only words but rather, that they have to have a word. Even though it offers the excuse of blood, colour, birth, – or rather, *because* it uses this naturalist and sometimes creationist discourse – racism always betrays the perversion of a man, the 'talking animal'. It institutes, declares, writes inscribes, prescribes. A system of marks, it outlines space in order to assign forced residence or to close off borders. It does not discern, it discriminates. (p. 292)

The blood that ties the two brothers together in the play is born out of love, the enactment of desire in the human body. The two struggle in the course of the play, at times to realise this, at times to deny it, to see, at the end that they cannot separate. But the state is unrelenting in its pressure to redefine with its own discourse, their bodies, to demarcate, in ways that both entrench its authority and legitimate the actual conditions of domination and subordination within the social order. The knot at the terrible and moving final moment of the play, then, we should add, remains tied, but only for the moment, and only just.

Notes

1 *Rand Daily Mail*, 18 April 1958, p. 1.
2 Goldin, Ian, 'The reconstitution of Coloured identity in the Western Cape', in Marks, Shula and Trapido, Stanley, ed., *The politics of race, class and nationalism in twentieth century South Africa*, Harlow: Longman, 1987, p. 166.
3 See, for what follows, de Klerk, W. A., *The puritans in Africa*, Harmondsworth: Penguin, 1983, p. 243, pp. 270-2.
4 Fisher, Philip, *Hard facts*, Oxford: Oxford University Press, 1987, pp. 3-4.
5 See Hauptfleisch, Temple and Steadman, Ian ed., *South African theatre: four plays and an introduction*, Pretoria: Haum, 1984, , p. 241. The manuscript of *Try for white* has disappeared. See also Vandenbroucke, Russel, *Truths the hand can touch*, Johannesburg: Donker, 1986, pp. 40-2.
6 *Rand Daily Mail*, 26 February 1958, p. 3.
7 *Rand Daily Mail*, 25 February 1958, p. 11.
8 *Rand Daily Mail*, 8 March 1958, p. 3.
9 *Rand Daily Mail*, 4 August 1958, p. 4.
10 *Rand Daily Mail*, 2 August 1958, p. 4.
11 *Rand Daily Mail*, 10 January 1958, p. 5.
12 *Rand Daily Mail*, 29 January 1958, p. 9.
13 *Rand Daily Mail*, 19 February 1958, p. 6; 24 February 1958, p. 8.
14 *Rand Daily Mail*, 25 February 1958, p. 8.
15 *Rand Daily Mail*, 20 February 1958, p. 6; Hofman, *They built a theatre*, pp. 157-8; *Rand Daily Mail*, 24 February 1958, p. 6, 25 February p. 8.
16 Sowden, Lewis, *The Kimberley train*, Cape Town: Howard Timmins, 1976.
17 *Sunday Express*, 5 October 1958, p. 7.
18 *Sunday Express*, 14 September 1959, p. 21.
19 Marks, Shula and Trapido, Stanley, 'The politics of race, class and nationalism', in Marks and Trapido, ed., *Politics of race*, p. 27. See also Goldin, Ian, 'The reconstitution of coloured identity in the Western Cape', in Marks and Trapido, ed, *Politics of race*, p. 158.
20 Goldin, 'The reconstitution of coloured identity in the Western Cape', p. 163.
21 Dubow, Saul, 'Race, civilisation and culture: the elaboration of segregationist discourse in the inter-war years', in Marks and Trapido, *Politics of race*, pp. 71-2.

22 Coetzee, *White writing*, p. 145.
23 Cited in Vandenbroucke, *Truths*, pp. 67-8, from which these details are taken. See also pp. 13-28 from which the biographical details following mainly come.
24 Fugard, Athol, *The blood knot*, in Fugard, Athol, *Boesman and Lena and other plays*, Cape Town: Oxford University Press, 1984. Fugard has also produced a new shortened version *Blood knot*, in Fugard, Athol, *Selected plays*, Cape Town: Oxford University Press, 1987. Where possible, for consistency I have quoted from *Blood knot*; critics in discussion usually refer to the earlier published version of the play.
25 Vandenbroucke, *Truths*, p. 262. See too pp. 64-5; Green, Robert, 'The cripple and the prostitute: Fugard's *Hello and goodbye* in Gray, Stephen, ed., *Athol Fugard*, Johannesburg: McGraw-Hill, 1982, p. 163; Hauptfleisch, Temple, 'Fugard's dramatic expression of the freedom concept in *Boesman and Lena*', in Gray, *Athol Fugard*, p. 188.
26 I am indebted in this chapter to Michel Foucault, *Discipline and punish*, Harmondsworth: Penguin, 1982.
27 Fugard, *Blood knot*, pp. 55-7. See also Morrie's comments on the packet of salts (p. 54) and the verses Zach quotes (p. 57). See also pp. 6-7 in *The blood knot*.
28 See too Zach's fantasy in *The blood knot*, p. 45.
29 See for example,. Jordan, Winthrop, *The white man's burden: historical origins of racism in the United States*, New York: Oxford University Press, 1974.
30 Quoted in Macliam, Garalt, 'Fugard, Bryceland and the seventh wave that is "Mecca"', *The Star Tonight*, Johannesburg, 21 November, 1984, p. 11.
31 See, for example, Dakin, A., *Calvinism*, London: Duckworth, 1940; Sinfield, Alan, *Literature in Protestant England 1560-1660*, Beckenham, Kent: Croom Helm, 1983; Garson, N. G. 'Calvin's Institutes and the English Reformation', in 'John Calvin's institutes his opus magnum', Proceedings of the Second South African Congress for Calvin Research, Potchefstroom University for Christian Higher Education, 1986.
32 Kristeva, Julia, *Powers of horror an essay on abjection*, New York: Columbia University Press, 1982.
33 See *The blood knot*, pp. 61, 64, 28-9.
34 See Dollimore, Jonathan, 'The challenge of sexuality' in Sinfield, Alan, ed., *Society and literature 1945-1970*, London: Methuen, 1983, pp. 51-85.
35 Dollimore, 'The challenge of sexuality', p. 60. Fugard was in London in 1960 when the trial over *Lady Chatterley's lover* took place.
36 Fugard, Athol and Simon, Barney, 'The family plays of the sixties', in Gray, *Fugard*, p. 40.
37 Sinfield, Alan, 'Varieties of religion' in Sinfield, ed., *Society and literature*, p. 100.
38 See Fugard, Simon, 'The family plays', p. 40; Walder, Dennis, *Athol Fugard*, London: Macmillan, 1984, p. 53; Maclennan, Don,'The palimpsest: some observations on Fugard's plays', in Gray, ed., *Athol Fugard*, p. 219.
39 See for instance Mshengu [Kavanagh], 'Political theatre in South Africa and the work of Athol Fugard', *Theatre research international*, VII, 3, 1982, p. 171.
40 O'Meara, *Volkskapitalisme*.
41 Cited in de Klerk, *Puritans*, p. 214, my emphasis.
42 O'Meara, *Volkskapitalisme*, pp. 174-5.
43 See Althusser, Louis, 'ideology and ideological state apparatuses' in Althusser, Louis, *Essays on ideology*, London: Verso, 1976.
44 Foucault, *Discipline and punish*, p. 201.
45 Derrida, Jacques, 'Racism's last word', *Critical enquiry*, 12, Autumn 1985, p. 295.

4

Staged silences

If *The Kimberley train* and *The blood knot* tried from within South Africa to identify in what ways the body was being marked and categorised, a third play *The rhythms of violence* by Lewis Nkosi, writing in exile in the 1960s, also attempted to address the problem. Nkosi's play emerged at a time of great repression and it was banned at once from performance or publication within the country. Several other plays that were to emerge in the 1960s, by contrast, from writers situated within the ruling classes, seemed actively to collude, as other plays have done, with state censorship, remaining entirely indifferent to current struggle within the social order. However, a number of township dramatists produced plays which won audiences much larger than those attending establishment theatre or other ventures, barring perhaps *King Kong* and *The blood knot* . These plays were also unique because of the minimal involvement, if at all, of dissident members of the ruling classes. But they too were, in conditions of repression and censorship, unable to deal with the social problems they raised in any contestatory way. Moreover, despite their success, they remain to an important extent marginalised, never having appeared in published form. As Hilda Bernstein has commented, ruthless government action had drawn a 'net of silence' all over the country,[1] and drama in the 1960s did not escape.

I Violence and the body in *The rhythms of violence*

The terrible deaths at Sharpeville on 21 March 1960 of sixty-nine blacks including women and children, shot by police during a peaceful protest, did not of course initiate the violence that has always informed ruling class behaviour in the implementation of segregation and apartheid. But it precipitated the intensification all over the country of urban protest and resistance. Moreover, in the rural areas uprisings had occurred towards the end of the 1950s in Zeerust, Sekhukhuneland, and, by 1960 Pondoland.[2] The government responded vigorously to this and to the founding of the Pan-Africanist Congress (PAC) in April

1959, mentioned in chapter 2. After the massacre at Sharpeville a State of Emergency was declared and, amidst further demonstrations and resistance in Langa, Nyanga and Cape Town itself, both the ANC and the PAC were banned. As a result of the bannings the National Committee for Liberation (later the African Resistance Movement – ARM), Umkhonto we Sizwe and Poqo, a movement aligned in mood and temper with the PAC, began, as I noted in chapter 2, campaigns of sabotage, with Poqo also 'at its most threatening carrying out random attacks against groups of whites' (p. 74, 92). But the head of Umkhonto we Sizwe, Nelson Mandela, was captured in 1962 and over the next four years ARM and Poqo were eventually broken while 'the underground Communist Party was infiltrated and badly crippled'. Thus, although 'in the first six months alone of 1964 there were 203 cases of sabotage, in 1965 as a whole there was none' (p. 94).

Lewis Nkosi was a highly talented young journalist on Drum who had also worked with Fugard on No good friday. He chose exile in 1961 in order to take up a scholarship awarded him at Harvard University and since his departure he has never returned to South Africa, becoming a well-known writer, critic and academic who is currently situated at the University of Zambia. Nkosi has been described as 'an intellectual standing between the black masses and the white world, with a "pass" into the world of the liberal intelligentsia, but regarded with contempt by African nationalists.'[3] His play, The rhythms of violence, written in the early 1960s shortly after he left South Africa was published by Oxford University Press in 1964, – staggeringly indicative of hegemonic processes, it seems to have been only the second play in English by a black South African to have appeared by then in print.[4]

Nkosi's play was written close enough to his departure to retain a direct experiential link with life lived within the apartheid regime, produced without the formidable restraints that were closing in on cultural expression within South Africa. As well as its use of widespread detentions and arrests, the government had acted swiftly in the 1960s to intensify its control over the arts and literature.[5] With the advent of multi-racial endeavour in drama in the 1950s had come also the Nationalist government's determination to enforce at every level the traditional practice of segregation in theatres. In 1958 a proclamation 'prohibited the attendance of blacks at cinemas in white areas without the minister's permission'.[6] The Group Areas Act of 1960 'forbade the association of different races in clubs, cinemas, and restaurants.[7]

Racially mixed casts could still perform before segregated audiences but this loophole was closed with the Group Areas Act of 1965 in which 'racially mixed casts or audiences were prohibited from public entertainments unless a permit was secured' (p. 47). Theatre practitioners were further inhibited by the rapid succession of wide- ranging laws intensifying the process of censorship in the country.[8] At the same time the government experienced as the decade unfolded, and once its reaction had taken hold, a period of economic security and growth.

The central plot of The rhythms of violence turns on the love between Tula Zulu, a member of the oppressed classes, and a white Afrikaner, Sarie Marais. When Tula learns that Sarie's father intends to resign at a Nationalist Party rally at the City Hall, where a bomb, planted by his brother Gama and a multi-racial group of student activists, is due to explode, he rushes there in an attempt in some way to save him. But Tula as well as Sarie's father dies in the explosion. The text recalls the events at Sharpeville to emphasise that it is the government that has begun the use of 'violence against unarmed people' (p. 84) and the play opens with the assertion that 'we can no longer tolerate white domination, subjugation, and repression' (p. 73).

Perhaps for the first time in South African stage history, Nkosi in his play repeatedly manifests a readiness on stage to identify directly rather than merely to allude to the actualities of the police presence in South Africa (as is, perhaps, done in the more muted scenes involving the police in The Kimberley train). The opening scenes of The rhythms of violence explore and depict in detail the racist ideological discursive formations that inform police attitudes and registers as well their predilection for the use of unrestrained force.Thus two policemen seated in the foyer of the City Hall in the first scene, hearing the noise of the political gathering and speeches outside, reassure themselves repeatedly that 'We are armed and the kaffirs haven't got guns' (p. 72) and speak with patent insensitivity about their shooting of 'natives': 'Ugh, man! Got sick over him! It's not enough you rip open a kaffir's skull! You must get sick over him too!' (p. 72). The language of the play often pointedly reflects prevailing racist discourse about blood, miscegenation, the body. When Tula approaches the two with a petition, he is repeatedly insulted and told 'all Natives are bloody stupid' (p. 76), while elsewhere too (p. 77) the policemen's racist obsessions unfold at length.

Set against its foregrounding of police violence and state repression, The rhythms of violence evidences a commitment to the belief in multi–

racialism, which, current at the end of the fifties, was thought to be the only way to counter the segregationist thrust of the state. This allegiance in the play has been criticised by, for instance, Wole Soyinka, who argues that Nkosi's 'makeshift instance' of the 'ideal goal for South Africa (which no one denies)' of a 'multi-racial society', is an example of 'hankering for a Christian salvationist ethic'.[9] But, as Nkosi himself claimed, there is evidence in the play of recognition that the discourse of multi-racialism was fast becoming inappropriate within conditions of escalating violence. The play not only recognises inherent racism within the police force but dramatises an attempt at sabotage. Nkosi's recognition of the shift to a more militant political stance in the early 1960s was paralleled, it is worth noting, in novels by other writers in exile such as Peter Abrahams's *A night of their own* and Alex La Guma's *In the fog of the season's end*.[10]

Nevertheless, if the text, as Nkosi argued, warns of the eclipse of the validity of the discourse of multi-racialism, its predilection for multi-racialism remains clear and, in terms of his presentation of love and the body in the play, Nkosi explores that belief in multi-racialism even further. In its concern with the body, common to several plays of the period, *The rhythms of violence* privileges individual relationships and repeatedly offers counteridentification of prevailing discourse about the body as means of contestation. Not only the relationship between Tula and Sarie, but that between Gama and Mary and Jimmy and Kitty, offer alternatives to prevailing discourse about the way the body may behave – as one of the signs on the wall of an undergraduate party has it 'interracial sex is a historical fact' (p. 79) while racist fears of miscegenation are mocked in the course of it. But unlike its more explicit and courageous treatment of the shift to violence in the social order, in the presentation of the body *The rhythms of violence* remains, despite its subversive impulses, largely subject to the avoidances which fixation upon colour within the South African social order appeared to promote.

The presentation of the relationship between Tula and Sarie is, as in the case of the young couple in *The Kimberley train*, in this respect striking. Meeting at a student party they are drawn to one another and talk, about their families, about love as an abstract concept, about politics, about Sarie's father. They do this, moreover, in public – the audience never sees them alone together on stage. And they do not, for the most part, interact as lovers; their expressions of affection remain strangely formalised – given the fact that it is on the basis of this feeling that Tula will soon risk all to save Sarie's father. At one point their attraction to one another is placed by their friends in the context of race classification (p. 89), and the closest the two lovers come to any intimacy is when they dance together. But the stage directions indicate that 'everybody is watching them' (p. 91) and Gama teasingly interrupts them. The moment of physical intimacy – of transgression against prevailing discourse – becomes very quickly a public one requiring comment.

The other two relationships between Gama and Mary and Jimmy and Kitty, overtly patriarchal, used to complement this central one, are already accomplished facts by the start of the play and throughout its duration. Although in these cases the dramatic action does include some physical intimacy between the partners, they too manifest a certain self-consciousness. Their conversation is fixated on the taboos and stereotypes they challenge. Nkosi attempts to capture the high spirits, erotic abandon and wildness of undergraduates in the dialogue, but the power of prevailing discourse is never forgotten in their frequent use of stereotypical phrases such as the 'sweet flower of European womanhood' (p. 80), 'dark and lascivious Moors' (p. 82), and references to dark virility as compared with 'sex starved white men' (p. 83).

If the ironic tone of the young speakers, strives against the stereotypes it uses, this language also reproduces those stereotypes: despite the ostensibly ironic tone with which they are partly spoken, there is no substantial exploration of any one relationship in the play to set against it. Without, then, detracting from the play's demonstrably contestatory concerns when it first appeared, it is important to note an element of unease in the treatment of the body which suggests, even for someone freed (recently) from the restraints of censorship and seeking alternative discourses, the difficulty of evading prevailing ideological discursive formations. We may recall here Raymond Williams's identification of 'alternative and oppositional initiatives... which are made within or against a specific hegemony' and his argument that this hegemony may set 'certain limits to them' or may succeed in 'neutralising, changing or actually incorporating them'.[11] He also distinguishes 'other kinds of initiative and contribution which are irreducible to the terms of the original or the adaptive hegemony, and are in that sense independent' (p. 114). While Nkosi, no longer subject to direct censorship by the South African state, endeavours to contest prevailing discourse about the body, in *Rhythms of violence*, he does not, in these terms, manage finally to attain a point of independence, a fact that, as I suggested, testifies as much as anything to the difficulty of doing so. The ironic jibes designed to trivialise prejudice evoke at the same time, the stereotypes of virile and passionate (lecherous and primitive) black man and over-refined (civilised but impotent) white man[12] stereotypes with a long lineage in assimilationist discourse. It is worth recalling Nkosi's observation, which bears similar traces of stereotypical thinking, even though there can be no doubt that he is powerfully motivated against the discourse of racism in his work:

In no time we learned what we had not suspected, that many white South Africans, despite their wealth and privilege, envied us the township for what they supposed to be its vivid colour, its extravagant, if precarious life. We, on the other hand, had envied them the white suburb for what we considered its discipline and control, its sense of orderliness and thrift. This was the supremest irony of South African life... *Passion and craft, instinct for life and passion for technology, Europe and Africa; how these things would have found a perfect wedding in South Africa!* (my emphasis)[13]

II People and human passions in Manson and Butler

Establishment theatre in the silent 1960s continued to function as it always had in earlier decades with complete indifference to the development of a South African theatre culture. In the late 1950s and early 1960s a number of theatres subsidised by municipal and civic authorities as well as several others were built around the country. These included the opening of the Bloemfontein Civic Theatre in 1959, the Ernest Oppenheimer Theatre in Welkom, the Guild Theatre, which opened in East London in 1962, others in Oudtshoorn and Pretoria and the opening of the Johannesburg Civic Theatre in 1962. None of these theatres or those that were to be built in the next two decades has ever provided a space for emergent South African plays. They have frequently been used for performances arranged by the Performing Arts Councils which came into being in 1963. One for each province in the country, these Councils replaced the subsidised National Theatre and were designed, according to a brochure issued by the government Department of Information 1969 entitled *Performing arts in South Africa: cultural aspirations of a young country*, 'not only...to provide drama productions in two languages [Afrikaans and English]' but also 'to pamper the tastes and cater for the interests of the balletomane, the music-lover and the devotees of opera.'[14] As chapter 9 will illustrate in a little more detail, these Councils were concerned to pursue the Eurocentric and North American compulsions and fantasies of a small minority within the white minority group of the country. At the same time so far as the government was concerned they could be cited, presumably for the benefit of the metropolis of which they considered themselves part – during the silent, repressive 1960s and within a continuing, enormously exploitative social order – as evidence of South African 'Civilisation':

The standards by which a people's degree of civilisation should be measured are bewildering in their complexity and diversity. In any assessment... numerous social activities must be taken into account – activities such as a nation's preoccupation with its standard of living and medical services, its economic development and scientific research projects. There is, however, a single barometer from which a nation's measure of maturity can be gleaned at a single glance: the vitality of its cultural life and its achievements in the fields of art, literature, theatre and music. (Introduction, *Performing arts in South Africa*)

The Performing Arts Council of the Transvaal performed the following plays in English in 1963 and 1964, to provide, presumably, to its post-colonial imperial centre, evidence of its 'cultural' credentials: *The affair, The cherry orchard, Romeo and Jeanette, Playboy of the western world, Rookery nook, Hamlet, Ring around the moon, The miser* and *Rashomon*. In this selection as well as in its choices for the remainder of the decade and after, the Council made no attempt, as I remarked, to foster the development of any indigenous English South African drama despite the fact that it was heavily subsidised. It was in this no different from professional theatre companies such as the Reps and the Brian Brooke theatre company who chose for their repertoires mainly commercially successful British and American plays and musicals including *Boeing-Boeing, Come blow your horn, The mousetrap, Oklahoma, Stop the world I want to get off, Irma la douce* and *Grab me a gondola*.

It is true that in contrast to this unadventurous and thoughtless conformity to prevailing ideological discursive formations evident in the practice of establishment theatre, some indigenous dramatic attempts did emanate in the silent 1960s from members of the university English establishment. Occurring at a time of great repression in the country, and with the luxury of university support systems to help them surface, these plays, however, offer no reference to or engagement with the move towards violent resistance and the equally fierce reaction of the state in the contemporary South African reality such as is found in Nkosi's play. The space they dramatise is inhabited primarily by individual powerful and patriarchal (white) protagonists who control and shape their environments and other inhabitants largely through self-assertion and the acquisition of 'faith'. Their focus is heavily located within interiority. Such works were always directed at and played – when they were performed – before white audiences.

Thus H. W. D. Manson, an intellectual attached to the middle classes, working in the English Department at the University of Natal, Pietermaritzburg, wrote a number of plays that embody his view that the drama should 'deal primarily with people and human passions', which he privileged above and separated from any 'political impli-cations'.[15] He maintained that drama should also concern itself with 'challenges' that 'always demand more of those who have to evaluate their ultimate worth in actual and difficult situations'.[16] These 'actual situations', rejecting as they did any merely 'fashionable' concern with 'some modern African man' (p. xx) were understood in fundamentally psychological and 'moral' terms and, in most of his plays, he refused to engage with the South African space, setting them either in allegorical locations or in places such as Japan, medieval and Anglo-Saxon England, Scotland. Only one, *Pat Mulholland's day*, is set in South Africa, although as Manson himself reassured potential audiences and readers, there is nothing in the play that prevents it from being presented as if occurring elsewhere.[17] It was produced in 1964, according to admirers 'with some eclat' by the Iscor Dramatic Society near Pretoria' – a group not noted for any other achievements either before or since this event.[18] It concerns the interior dilemma of a patriarchal sculptor Pat Mulholland, who is suddenly told by his doctor that he is likely to die at any moment. The play explores the way he copes with this news, first in the company of an old friend, and then with his long-suffering family (a mother and daughter). Set in Pietermaritzburg and its environs – like any other town or city in South Africa, inhabited by a majority of blacks – no blacks at all appear in the play.

Manson's Leavisian focus on character, motivation, interior moral worth and capacity for feeling was complemented by attitudes be-speaking the old assimilationist and colonialist discourses. Thus he observed 'for those of us who live in Africa, and particularly for those, like myself, who were born in very recently settled countries (as

Tanzania was when I was born there) the impact of civilisation and Christianity on primitive peoples is a fascinating and dramatic thing'[19] and his colonial loyalties ran deep – he broadcast what he called the 'Freedom Radio' dedicated to a separatist movement that wished to keep Natal as a British colony when South Africa, having been more or less thrown out of the Commonwealth, became a Republic in 1961.[20]

Manson's plays were hardly ever performed beyond his own university, but he had little difficulty in publishing them, through Natal University Press as well as the Afrikaans publishers Nationale Boekhandel and Human and Rousseau. Equally significant is the bizarre admiration of and extravagant claims for him offered by some of his colleagues, also holding important teaching positions within the university. Unlike the 'arid nihilism of successful plays like Waiting for Godot, or the blinkered domestic dullness and squalid pettiness...the sterile insecurity of the Kitchen Sink school',[21] Manson, two of his most ardent devotees were to claim tellingly in 1972, writes in language that 'quivers with delicate life – delicate and yet strong and deep... concerned with ultimates' (p. 22), even as he remains situated in a

country, huge and still comparatively empty, but not long ago much emptier and wilder. Large tracts of it are very dry, and it is nearly always full of sunshine everywhere; it is peopled, where it is peopled, by human beings, black and white and coloured, whose lives and natures differ greatly from those of the British. Life was very rough for everybody here not long ago, and people were hardy; and everything is not yet tamed and subdued even for the whites. (pp. 15-16)

Even for colonisers 'reconciled to the sun, the heat and the dry earth', writes Memmi, their 'homeland' looks 'misty, humid and green', features in turn invested with quasi-ethical qualities that, by implication, are absent in the African terrain.[22] It is only the mother country that is not wild, that 'combines...positive values, good climate, harmonious landscape, social discipline and exquisite liberty, beauty, morality and logic' (p. 60).

On Settlers Day 1967, the day chosen to commemorate the arrival in South Africa, of amongst others, the English 1820 Settlers, Guy Butler, now professor of English for several years at Rhodes, premiered his new play Cape charade or Kaatjie Kekkelbek at the Rhodes University Theatre in Grahamstown,[23] and saw it subsequently performed in Cape Town. As in the 1950s Butler's concerns stay largely with the establishment of a 'South African English' identity. He remains crucially dependent upon the colonialist and assimilationist discourses on which he drew in the previous decade. These had clearly still, well into the second half of the twentieth century, strong currency within English departments in various South African institutions of education. Repeating his patriarchal impulses in *The dam*, Butler concentrates this time upon the dramatisation of a figure from history, the pioneer roadbuilder Andrew Geddes Bain.

Presentation of his hero resonates traditional supremacist and eugenicist views. The patriarch Bains is set within a dutiful if suffering family (wife and daughter) and a range of 'coloured', and in the style of colonialist discourse, stereotypically inferior 'serf' figures who surround him. It is true that Butler tries here as in his earlier plays to show in crucial ways how his protagonists are to an extent both 'humanised' and redeemed by sometimes very brief contact with members of the oppressed classes who accordingly serve, when they are not comic characters, as functions of white regeneration. His attempt again, in his work of the 1960s, to incorporate these figures into the space presented in his plays contrasts with the indifference to them of a dramatist like Manson. But his subjection to prevailing discourse despite his continued endeavour to encompass 'coloured' and black people in his view of the world, remains striking. The trait of idleness detected in the 'coloured', and – to quote Butler's hero – the view of 'coloureds' as a 'drunken, lecherous, insolent, irresponsible lot' (p. 24), if ostensibly implicitly criticised in the text, nevertheless informs Butler's presentation of his own characters such as the 'coloured' servant Kaatje Klauterburg and her husband Klaus. Such discourse is evident, also, in the presentation of some 'coloureds' as 'loafers' in *The Kimberley train*. Moreover the version of the 'coloured' in Butler's play as infused with 'a love of music' and 'an invincible instinct for happiness' (p. 24) despite predilections to rascality is present in his portrayal of another 'coloured' character, the musical but potentially criminal Dirk. At one point, in a way that demonstrates too the paternalist and supremacist discourses upon which Butler still draws, both the 'coloured' husband, himself depicted as a rascal, and Bain, whom he serves on one of their expeditions, describe the roadbuilder's relationship with his 'serfs':

Klaas : The cold wind was in our teeth. At last we Hotnots could go no further. We sat down in the water, in the drowning dark, with our horses' bridles in our hands. It got so cold that at last we found it less terrible to lie down, on our sides in the water. (Klaas lies down, followed by Bain) We all lay together, in Mr Bains's shadow. His back broke the wind.

Bain : My brain began to die. Then somewhere inside me a sort of earthquake started. An animal cry for warmth…I tried to get up. My limbs were so stiff I fell, twice. (he manages to stand) I shouted to the others to get up. They refused. It never occurred to me to leave them there, in the mud. I kicked them. They wouldn't budge. Then I took the sjambok to them. (p. 40)

Such traits, which Butler gives to his 'coloured' characters, repeat, it is worth adding, what V. A. February has identified as typical of the presentation of the 'coloured' as stereotype in South African literature.[24] Noting that 'stereotypes function as a means of social control and repression' (p. vi) February observes that 'one of the direct consequences of colonialism and racism is that the colonised or the discriminated invariably become the dupe of a series of rationalisations whereby the power-holders (i.e. the whites) justify their dominant position in society' (p. vi). Thus early representations in literature of the Khoi and the San, the original inhabitants of South Africa, produce them as 'lazy, they love to drink, they swear and fight at the slightest provocation and are generally immoral' (p. 1). And February argues that 'the stereotype of the present day "coloured" draws…on a fairly continuous tradition starting with the depictions of the Khoi in literature…In general…writers portray the "Hottentot" characters as carefree, comical, witty, loud-mouthed, fond of liquor, and prone to fighting easily' (pp. 23, 26). That such presentations of the coloured, as well as such a portrait of Bain could be undertaken by another theatrical practitioner emanating from an influential position within the university establishment, together with, as the cast list of actors from the ruling classes reveals, future South African scholars, academics and performers, is also indicative of the nature of prevailing discourse in the universities of the 1960s, as well as amongst many in the audiences and press who received the play. Thus one white reviewer wrote in *The Cape Argus* of the play's presentation of the 'irresistible instinct for happiness of the Coloured people',[25] a remark which, like the play itself occurred whilst the government's attack upon District Six, a freehold suburb in Cape Town that had for over a century been inhabited by its largely 'coloured' population was under way in conditions of state brutality, and intense anger, resentment and bitterness on the part of the people themselves removed to the Cape flats.

III Township theatre in the 1960s

Leaving aside the work of Athol Fugard, to which I turn again in chapter 5, and the township tradition of performance which Union Artists at least in part promoted, most of the plays which had emerged in South Africa by the mid-1960s continued still to be dominated by literary models. Thus if Dhlomo was subject to conservative English literary influences that, critics have argued, impeded the dramatic impact of his writing, Manson as well as Butler tried to write dramatic verse, impressed no doubt, as I have also remarked, by Eliot, rather than, say, Auden and Isherwood. It has been suggested that Nkosi's writing, too, suffers from an impulse to the literary rather than the dramatic, although it must be added that his attempts in The rhythms of violence to concentrate repeatedly on the presentation of the visual image of the integrated couple, and his use of jazz marked a movement away from the strict realism of established theatre. But all of these writers seem to have had their eyes fixed upon the printed page more clearly than upon theatrical performance.

Moreover, if realism and naturalism were the primary modes of this theatre, from the perspective of, for instance, Boal, this may be said in some instances subtly to have complemented that prevailing discourse that argued in favour of maintaining segregationist structures rather than breaking or changing them. It can thus be noted that the static realism of set design in The Kimberley train, encourages the sense of fixed and unbreakable structures. The movement from a heavily realistic set suggesting the middle-class wealth of the white family's flat in the affluent northern suburb of Johannesburg, Killarney, to what the stage directions describe as a set that must capture the vulgar petit bourgeois nature of the 'coloured' family's home in the centrally urban and semi-working class Jeppestown and then, in the final scene, back again to the first set complements the play's subjection to those ideological discursive formations that argue the fixity of divisions within the social order even as it dramatises the impossibility and futility of attempts at mobility and change.

Against these tendencies the performance traditions upon which the musical King Kong tentatively in part aspired to draw, and, especially, the work of dramatists originally associated with Union Artists in the townships in the 1960s initiated a more fluid theatre-based and less literary dramatic practice that was to be enormously influential for the theatre of later decades. But while playwrights such as Manson and Butler had no difficulty in finding publishers, township dramatists in the 1960s, like Dhlomo before them, although not, like Nkosi, banned, were never published. Butler's and Manson's published plays were at best exposed only to small English-speaking audiences within the minority ruling classes; the Performing Arts Councils received enormous subsidies but, like professional theatre, their audiences also came from a minority within the white middle classes. By contrast, in the townships, Gibson Kente and Sam Mhangwane made an enormous impact upon huge audiences – in extent and size exceeding anything either Manson, Butler or other theatre patronised by the ruling middle classes even remotely achieved. To date, however, research into this work remains sparse. But, although it continues to be marginalised, some of the innovatory aspects of this theatre practice have been recorded by historians, and may be noted briefly here.

The township theatre movement evolved out of various theatrical activities amongst blacks in the 1950s and 1960s. This included the various endeavours of Union Artists, Sowetan Wilfred Sentso's production of *Washerwoman*, performed in the City Hall, Johannesburg, together with his production of *Frustrated black boy* in 1961 with a cast of seventy-five actors and the work of Basil Somhlahlo and of Cornelius Mabaso, who wrote *Shaka*.[26] Companies formed by Union Artists also played in schools, in youth clubs and in community centres, stimulating interest in drama based on African folk tales. In 1960 Ronnie Govender and Muthal Naidoo formed a theatre group, founding the Shah Theatre Academy in Durban in 1964 together with Bennie Bersee, which staged a number of Western plays as well as Govender's own work.[27] Also in Durban, Alan Paton, inspired by *King Kong*, produced *Mkumbane* in an attempt to portray the daily life of blacks in Cato Manor township, while in Johannesburg in 1962, Ben 'Satch' Masinga 'produced his own jazz musical in Zulu, *Back in your own back yard*, for Soweto audiences only, and Union Artists declined to help him'.[28] Gibson Kente, who came originally from Grahamstown, also inspired by *King Kong*, put on *Manana, the jazz prophet* in 1963, which he too designed primarily for township audiences. His next production, *Sikalo*, in 1966, enjoyed moderate success with multi-racial audiences at the Witwatersrand University Great Hall, but was a hit after it opened at Soweto's Mofolo Hall in the townships. After this Kente broke completely with Union Artists. Together with Sam Mhangwane, also to become a highly successful township dramatist, Kente recognised that in the current highly repressive conditions 'black-produced black acted shows for black audiences were the only viable direction for black theatre to take' (p. 207). Growth of drama in the townships was encouraged also by 'increased urbanisation and greater spending power and therefore a potential audience capable of supporting, albeit on a small scale, professional entertainment.'[29] The thrust towards total segregation in theatre which 'broke the monopoly of the English-speaking whites by making performances in town impossible' and which cut 'the links between black and white urban areas' (p. 52) was a further factor.

The plays that resulted from this move into the township were located within a township reality, but tended to focus on love, adultery, alcoholism, and, as in the case of some of the1950s' plays, crime. Thus, after producing a township melodrama in 1963 called *Crime does not pay* Mhangwane wrote the *Unfaithful woman* , 'a sexy musical portrayal of social immorality and retribution...which toured continuously for the next twelve years'.[30] His next play, *Blame yourself*, the 'melodramatic realism' of which 'resonated with Africans' experience in the townships...remained popular...until the late 1970s' (p. 212). Kente produced *Lifa* in 1968 and *Zwi* in 1970 (pp. 207-9). He became 'the most widely known and best–paid black stage producer in Southern Africa',[31] devising a means of coping with the lack of theatre space in the township where practitioners had to depend upon any available space and preferably – even in the 1960s – space that would not require them to be subject to government control. The resulting need for mobility that would be crucial to swift adaptation to a variety of theatre venues was something that Kente understood, recognising 'that the costly sets, crew and equipment required by white theatre was not necessary in the townships and would serve only to reduce (that) mobility' and so, 'packing young, newly trained actors, simple costumes and a few crudely painted flats and backdrops into an old bus, the company performed under the house lights to standing-room-only audiences in township halls all over South Africa, and so became a major force in a rejuvenated black community showbusiness'.[32]

Many of the techniques upon which Kente drew during this period were, moreover, in the context of more establishment forms of theatre, importantly innovatory. His development in his plays of a 'synthesis of narrative, mime, movement, vocal dramatics, music and dance found in traditional oral literary performance into a township melodrama using urban experience and cultural resources' (p. 210) was particularly significant. Moreover, he used 'virtually every medium and style of performance found in the streets and social occasions of the townships so that working-class Africans unfamiliar with formal theatre could recognise themselves up on... stage' (p. 210). It is true that historians always comment on the fact that his plays remained fairly consistently concerned with social problems thus colluding with the silence about conditions of domination and subordination in the period. But while this may be seen as at least partly a consequence of the repressive nature of the 1960s, it should not be allowed to diminish the fact that Kente, particularly, was in a profoundly practical sense popularising theatre. He was, too, exploring drama that was firmly located within an, until then, either totally marginalised or misrepresented township life. Even if he was reproducing some of the prevailing ideological discursive formations about that life he was establishing a tradition that would lead in the 1970s, particularly, to more contestatory attempts at indigenous popular drama. It is for such reasons that his contribution to theatre, for those practitioners to follow him in the 1970s and beyond, was to be so important despite the avoidance in his work in the 1960s of conditions of struggle within the social order. The break with realism and naturalism in later plays, into more fluid and less static modes of production, continues to occur, as a recent collection of plays acknowledges, within his shadow.

Notes

1 Cited in Clingman, *The novels of Nadine Gordimer*, Johannesburg: Ravan, 1986, p. 94.
2 See Clingman, *The novels of Nadine Gordimer*, p. 91. See chapters 3-4, on which the following is based.
3 Kavanagh, *Theatre and cultural struggle*, p. 62.
4 Nkosi, Lewis, Rhythms of violence, in Wellwarth, George E., *Themes of drama*, New York: Thomas Y. Crowell, 1973.
5 See Clingman, *Nadine Gordimer*, pp. 75, 94; Coplan, David B., *In township tonight!*, Johannesburg: Ravan, 1985, p. 209.
6 Kavanagh, *Theatre and cultural struggle*, p. 51.
7 Vandenbroucke, Russell, 'Chiaroscuro: a portrait of the South African theatre', *Theatre quarterly*, VII, 28, 1977-8, p. 46.
8 See Akerman, Anthony, ' "Prejudicial to the safety of the state": censorship and the theatre in South Africa', *Theatre Quarterly*, VII, 28, 1977-8, pp. 54-7.
9 Soyinka, Wole, *Myth, literature and the African world*, Cambridge: Cambridge University Press, 1976, pp. 71, 70. See Kavanagh, *Theatre and cultural struggle*, pp. 62-3.
10 Shava, Piniel Viriri, *A people's voice: black South African writing in the twentieth century*, London: Zed, 1989, p. 52ff.

11 Williams, Raymond, *Marxism and literature*, Oxford: Oxford University Press, 1977, p. 114.

12 See Steadman, 'Drama and social consciousness', p. 134.

13 Nkosi, Lewis, *Home and exile*, London: Longman, 1983, pp. 23-4.

14 *Performing arts in South Africa: cultural aspirations of a young country*, Pretoria: Department of Information, 1969, pages unnumbered.

15 Manson, H. W. D., *Captain Smith*, Cape Town: Human and Rousseau, 1966, Preface, no pagination.

16 Manson, H. W. D., *Magnus*, Pietermaritzburg: University of Natal Press, 1970, p. xx.

17 Manson, H. W. D, *Pat Mulholland's Day*, Cape Town: Nasionale Boekhandel, 1964.

18 Van Heyningen, Christina and Gardner, C. O., *H. W. D. Manson*, New York: Twayne Publishers, 1972, pp. 152-3.

19 Manson, *Magnus*, Preface, p. xix.

20 I am grateful to my colleague Jonathan Paton for this information about H. W. D. Manson.

21 Van Heyningen and Gardner, *H. W. D. Manson*, p. 18.

22 Memmi, *The colonizer and the colonized*, p. 60.

23 Butler, Guy, *Cape charade or Kaatjie Kekkelbek*, Cape Town: A. A. Balkema, 1968. All references to the text are taken from this edition.

24 February, V. A., *Mind your colour*, London: Kegan Paul International, 1981.

25 *The Cape Argus*, 5 September 1967, cited in Butler, *Cape charade*, p. 89.

26 Steadman, 'Drama and social consciousness', pp. 91-2.

27 Larlham, *Black theatre, dance and ritual*, p. 79.

28 See Coplan, *In township tonight!*, p. 207ff., on which the following is largely based.

29 Kavanagh, *Theatre and cultural struggle*, p. 52.

30 Coplan, *In township tonight!*, p. 209.

31 Horn, *South African theatre*, p. 219.

32 Coplan, *In township tonight!*, p. 209.

5

A green leaf on a burnt tree

David Coplan observes that 'as the darkness of apartheid dimmed the lights of interracial theatre in Johannesburg' during the 1960s, in the face of government restrictions, 'most whites simply gave up'.[1] By 1968 Fugard was to comment that 'the legislation that governs the performing arts in various forms makes it impossible for an African and me to get together on the stage as we did five or six years ago…it's an appalling deterioration'.[2] The sense of desolation, despondency and aridity for dissidents located within the white ruling classes as well as members of the oppressed classes attempting to find ways to contest prevailing relations of domination and subordination at this time, is suggested in Barney Simon's remarks in the mid-1960s on the formation of the Phoenix Players in order to produce Fugard's *Hello and goodbye*:

After some of my friends had been kicked out of the country or sent to jail, I decided to make the best of it. Athol referred to us as a green leaf on a burnt tree.[3]

Fugard continued in the 1960s, however, to explore the potential of theatre as a means to self-identity and, as well, as a means to represent the South African place. He did so mainly from a marginalised position, often working with township groups and struggling to find both the capital and space for making theatre. He also produced three of his own plays, each of which in different ways attempted to engage with the social order.

I Fugard's theatre-based drama

In the late 1950s Fugard together with his wife began a small theatre group in Port Elizabeth called the Circle Players. Later, after his theatrical activities at Dorkay House in Johannesburg, his work in Europe in the late 1950s and early 1960s and his success with *The blood knot* Fugard continued to work with theatre groups both in Port Elizabeth and sometimes in Johannesburg. His ongoing experience in theatre inevitably underlined for him the importance of the theatre space itself, a recurring theme in his diaries of the period. On Eliot, a model at least for Butler and possibly Manson, he commented: 'He is so ignorant of theatre and its meaning, in a scholarly, assured way. To discuss, as he does, the fate of "verse" in dramatic writing, is in no way an appreciation of the function of "poetry" in drama. Beckett is a greater poet in the "theatre" than he (Eliot) has been or ever will be. Eliot goes on and on about blank-verse as if the poetic imagination in playwrighting must drag this ball and chain.'[4] And he noted elsewhere after meeting with Alan Paton, 'I could not really talk to him about theatre because he knows nothing about the medium. Incredibly naive – a naivety at the level of tools, craftsmanship, of realising what can be done on the stage, of what has been done. Ignorant even of what is possible with his own plays, like *Sponono*' (pp. 68-9). After a performance of a play at St George's Hall in November 1962, he wrote, 'again it has been proved: a play is an actor before an audience. We had nothing else' (p. 65).

In May 1963 he noted the visit of Norman Ntshinga, who made 'the old old request. Would I do a play for them? I say "request", actually it is a hunger. A desperate hunger for meaningful activity – to do something that would make the hell of their daily existence meaningful. He is coming again with a few friends and we will start a local branch of Union Artists' (p. 81). This was to be the beginning of the formation of the Serpent Players with whom Fugard worked frequently in the 1960s. Fugard recorded, after the success of performances of their first play, again, his sense of a new discovery: 'a completely bare stage except for one black applebox, and then the actors – on and off, running about etc. in a series of short pithy scenes. For the first time I feel I really sense the potential in truly improvised theatre' (p. 94).

Fugard's diaries also confirm his continuing preoccupation with the effects of apartheid. Concerned with plans for a new production and noting some of the problems his Port Elizabeth group faced, he compared them with difficulties he encountered in Johannesburg: 'Meeting with the group last night, our immediate problems are to find rehearsal space and a backer for the play. How different these men, and the local mood, are from Johannesburg. There I spent half of my time dreaming and bitching, with the Rehearsal Room group. Here we act. Also, these men are so much more responsible. I can see now how the patronage and "help" of well-meaning whites has sapped away the initiative in Dorkay House' (p. 96). Again, Fugard's comments on the first rehearsal ever of the Serpent players suggest the harassment to which he and those he worked with were subject in the 1960s:

The group – a clerk, two teachers, a bus driver and the women domestic servants or doing cleaning jobs. Most encouraging start. Potentially there are three or four talents up to Johannesburg standard. Enthusiasm incredible...In the middle of our reading the Special Branch burst in. Five of them, with I believe a squad car of uniformed police parked outside the university. The cast and I took it easily. SB took all our names and addresses – read the play, went through the papers I had... Du Plooy – head of the local SB – spent some time chatting to me about the London production of *Blood knot*... I did remember later that he could have taken me away and locked me up for 90 days without trouble. (p. 92)

In September 1962, returning to Johannesburg from Port Elizabeth to work on *Waiting for Godot* with a black cast, Fugard noted in his diary, 'I told the cast that Vladimir and Estragon must have read the accounts of the Nuremberg trials – or else they were at Sharpeville, or were the first in at Auschwitz. Choose your horror – they know all about it' (p. 62). And in April 1963 he recorded that

Not a day passes now without me reading in the paper, almost as a commonplace, of some fresh outbreak of violence, another outrage to justice and decency. I turn with fear from the thought of the final reckoning. We will have to pay and with lives and hope and dignity for all of these that we destroyed. (p. 79)

He knew several individuals who were subsequently imprisoned for their political activities, including Govan Mbeki – news of whose attempt to organise a hunger strike in jail he noted in January 1964. And he recorded in the same entry a visit from one of the Serpent Players who, extremely bitter and frustrated, talked of leaving the country. Doubtless such awarenesses prompted him on many occasions to wrestle with the problem in theatre of boycotts and censorship. In his Notebooks in June 1962 he asked 'Can I any more work in a theatre which excludes Non-Whites (sic)?' (p. 59) deciding 'I think my answer must be No' (p. 59).Then, struggling with his sense that 'plays must be done and the actors seen (even on a segregated basis) not for the sake of the bigoted and prejudiced – but for the sake of those who do believe in human dignity' he ends:

in my case...the crux of the matter is that here in South Africa at the moment (Jhb., C.T., P.E., Durban, Pretoria, Pietermaritzburg) there are venues where a play can be presented to mixed audiences. Some of them are barns – but then, Christ Almighty, does one need to point out that a theatre is made by

an audience, the actors and the play, and not by soft seats, well–equipped
stages, etc! (pp. 59-60)

In July 1962 he recorded the Equity resolution preventing British
entertainers coming to South Africa unless all performances were for
mixed audiences and again explored his dilemmas:

Here in South Africa it has been attacked, as expected, by the Afrikaans press,
the English press and our theatre managements. Their arguments are too
peeved, stupid and in many cases downright wrong to repeat. The old story
– white South Africa (English–liberal) doesn't mind talking about the injustice
of apartheid provided it involves no sacrifices. If our society is morally
bankrupt, the sooner the whites feel this as a reality, the better...For me there
is still a problem – an area in which I am feeling my way. Last night I suddenly
said to Sheila [his wife]: 'It's as simple as this. Compromise is the rule for
staying alive, for getting from one day to the next. But it will do no more
than that. Ultimately there comes a time when you have to make a stand –
and then compromise means death. You can only "win" by sticking to your
principles.' Special performances for 'Non-Whites' – then sooner or later also
special or certain plays only (p. 60).

In June 1963 'with the support of the Anti-Apartheid Movement,
276 playwrights from around the world refused performing rights "in
any theatre where discrimination is made among audiences on the
grounds of colour"'.[5] Fugard supported this boycott but in 1968 he
was to reconsider the issue again and to argue at that point against
continuing the boycott – 'anything that will get people to think and
feel for themselves, that will stop them delegating...functions to the
politicians, is important to our survival. Theatre can help do this.'[6]

II Existentialism and the South African space in Fugard's 1960s plays

In 1963, the state's indifference towards and its readiness to interfere
with theatre was expressed particularly blatantly, when the Minister of
Education took the unprecedented step, in October, of banning
performances of *Who's afraid Of Virginia Woolf?*, currently being produced
at the University Great Hall. Although the play was not banned for any
alleged political concern, the fact that a contemporary non-South
African play could be stopped because it dealt, in frequently sexually
explicit language, with marital problems and a childless marriage, was
a measure of the puritanical or Calvinist – in South African terms –

climate within which theatre practitioners of the 1960s worked. More important, it was an overt demonstration to the nation of government power and government readiness to act against what it deemed subversive or inadmissible, in theatre as well as everywhere else. Nevertheless, Fugard worked on and completed his first version of *People are living there* during this period, although it was only performed towards the end of the decade. He also completed *Hello and goodbye* and, in the latter part of the 1960s, *Boesman and Lena*.[7] These three plays reflect Fugard's impulse, already evident in his earlier work, to address his own time and space directly. Moreover, influenced particularly by Sartre, Camus and Beckett, he repeatedly draws upon European existentialist discourse, as he had earlier done in *The blood knot*.

People are living there develops a strongly European-influenced diagnosis of *ennui* amongst the poor white inhabitants of a small rooming house in Braamfontein. The central dramatic struggle in the play is located in the need to discover some viable assertion of 'self' in the face of what is presented as a desolate and arid world. In South African terms this foregrounding of 'self' may also be seen in terms of liberal discourse, which was increasingly under attack in the 1960s, with its concern to construct the subject in terms primarily of a series of individual 'rights'. Such concerns complemented not only existentialist emphases but the strong predilection within the South African system of education to draw on romantic constructions of the 'self' as well as its reliance upon individualistic notions of psychology. Milly's crisis of self-confrontation in *People are living there* juxtaposes her current malaise – 'its gone... a little left but mostly in the way of time' (p.157) – against her memory of a childhood full of a sense of presence and against the assertion at the end of one of her long speeches 'Mildred Jenkins, you are still alive' (p.158). In this the play works to suggest via the stage image of aridity and the text's focus upon private and personal angst a series of equivalents for putative psychological (liberal) hardships in the world of the audience against which the response of the central characters may be measured and, in the case of instances such as Milly's for certain critics at least, recuperation achieved.[8]

Both *Hello and goodbye* and *Boesman and Lena* may be said to draw similarly upon existentialist discourse. The stage image of a desolate poor white home in Port Elizabeth where a brother and sister confront the meaninglessness of their lives on the one hand, and the open flats of the Eastern Cape where homeless and desperate 'coloureds' and a black man – in a world often strongly reminiscent of that in *Waiting for Godot*

– attempt to cope with the absurdity of their existence on the other no doubt also provided some metaphoric equivalent for the feelings of desperation in the dissident 1960s audiences watching the plays. Such feelings clearly found sustenance in that existentialist discourse that identified forms of alienation and withdrawal from the social order.

But all three plays, and particularly the latter two, may be said, in their chronotopic focus, to point significantly not to modes of existentialist discourse, but rather to operative relations of domination and subordination within the time and space within which these plays were written and performed. As in The blood knot the space Fugard dramatises in People are living there is a poverty–ridden domestic South African one, although this time he chooses the poor white context of a Johannesburg rooming house in Braamfontein. (It is of course, in comparison with Morrie and Zach's hut at Korsten, relatively more comfortable, and the text makes brief acknowledgement of the relatively privileged stratum of these poor whites, in its reference at one point to job reservation). Fugard constructs similar or related spaces in Hello and goodbye and Boesman and Lena. In Hello and goodbye he dramatises again an indigent domestic space, inhabited by a poor white working family, while, in Boesman and Lena, significantly, two landless and exploited victims of apartheid repeatedly attempt to erect for themselves some domestic space within the vast rural/urban inhospitable terrain in which they are located. In constructing such spaces or representing the struggle to hold on to such spaces that are all the time under material and, to a degree, it is acknowledged in the last of these plays especially, political pressures, Fugard, as in his earlier work, authenticates the periphery and endeavours to abrogate the colonial and imperial centres. And his chronotopic focus, moreover, suggests, as I have remarked, from the perspective of liberal and existentialist discourse, an eroding liberal position, one increasingly stifled by a highly exploitative and repressive system busy restructuring space and segregating, arresting and persecuting all difference and opposition.

III The struggle over Calvinism in Hello and goodbye

Hello and goodbye and Boesman and Lena also suggest, in their increasing concern with material and political pressures, recognition of some of the ways in which the subject may not be merely a construction posited on essentialist notions of 'self', but may also include the at least implicit recognition that interiority itself is partly the product of material and social pressures as well as the prevailing discourse operative within the social order. *Hello and goodbye*, the first of these plays to be produced on stage, was performed in 1965 in the Library Theatre, Johannesburg, under what were for Fugard difficult and equivocal circumstances. Although in the early 1960s mixed casts and audiences were still possible in certain theatre venues, a 'mitigating' factor to which Fugard, as I noted, clung, in February 1965 a government proclamation prohibited mixed casts as well as mixed audiences in all public theatres – only small private theatres might from then on still function in a non-segregated way. After a week of non-segregated performances in a private venue, Fugard, although very critical of establishment theatre practice in South Africa and afraid of compromise, decided to permit performances of *Hello and goodbye* to segregated audiences at the Library Theatre. He was strongly criticised for this amongst others by Dennis Brutus [9] and has often since then wavered on the issue, but he has in the end tended to maintain, as I indicated earlier, that he 'would rather go on talking, even in compromised circumstances than be silent...Silence is, I think, a sort of treason in my country.'[10] In fact the performances at the Library Theatre were very poorly attended, prompting journalists to complain of Eurocentric middle-class uninterest in South African work. The South African actress Molly Sklaar, who took the part of Hester, recalls the difficulty she found in playing with a South African accent, which all actresses and actors in their training were at that stage warned to avoid.

In its focus upon a poor white family, *Hello and goodbye* dramatises the spectre which obsessed Afrikaner politicians for several decades after the great depression, as they sought to encourage Afrikaner economic ascendancy. The rise of Afrikaner capitalism, in the view of some historians, was in part at least a result of Afrikaner determination to alleviate 'the great destitution in which a large section of the volk, [or people] lived' especially during and after the depression of the 1930s.[11] The Afrikaner's self-proclaimed 'legitimate struggle to assert himself in the economic domain' (p. 109) intensified in the 1940s and 1950s and their increasing involvement in capital growth was embodied amongst others in Anton Rupert, one of the most successful of Afrikaner businessmen, financially one of the most powerful in South Africa, who, as head of the Rembrant Tobacco Group, was to declare towards the end of the fifties: 'I am a man with a Christian conscience, child of Christian civilisation. I am Afrikaner-born. I am a South

African. I belong to the Western world. I am a world citizen.'[12]

But the concern in Hello and goodbye with white poverty works towards rather different ends from those of the Afrikaner ideologues and politicians. From the perspective of existentialist discourse, the material deprivation of the Smit family provides the opportunity to explore a crisis of meaning within a situation in extremis. But this crisis of meaning in the play centres too on the discourse of Afrikaner Calvinism and Fugard draws upon existentialist discourse to construct a view of the subject that differs from and dialogically challenges that postulated by Calvinism, which, the play shows, flows powerfully through the structures within which the dramatic characters find themselves, and lies deeply imbricated within their consciousness.

Johnnie's well–loved narrative of his father's working life which he delivers in Act 2 provides one instance of the power of Calvinist discourse in his and his family's life. Recalling the depression, he enacts his father's mediation of physical suffering through biblical language, citing the day 'in the kloof the other side of Heuningvlei' when his father thought his end had come:

His back was hurting like never before, his blisters were running blood. So he cried in the wilderness. 'Why has thou forsaken me Lord?' Like Moses.'Why has thou forsaken thy lamb?' (p. 217)

The father, moreover, interprets his suffering as divinely designed because 'when they reached Graaff Reinet' he meets his future wife so that 'the Lord's purpose in all suffering was revealed'. And Johnnie's narrative concludes:

'I was there in the wilderness – like Moses. The sleepers bent my back, the Lord bent my spirit. But I was not broken. It took dynamite to do that!' Hey? (p. 217)

Johnnie's father speaks language that reproduces the Afrikaner Calvinist belief in 'an active sovereign God, who calls the elect, who promises and punishes'.[13] The notion of punishment as part of a divine plan was one of the ways in which adversity – 'a sacred history made up of two cycles of suffering and death – the Great Trek and the Anglo-Boer war' – might be endured:

In the Christian tradition...suffering is not always seen as a sign of God's chastisement and rejection. God tests his innocent servants, and righteous suffering may be taken as assurance of God's favour... Calvin puts it well: 'How much can it do to soften all the bitterness of the cross, that the more we are afflicted with adversities, the more surely our fellowship with Christ is confirmed.' (p. 12)

Thus in 1938 Henning Klopper testified that: 'Disasters, adversity, privation, reversals and suffering are some of the best means in God's hand to form a people... These are the tests by fire which refine a people and determine its worth' (p. 13).

The narrative's emphasis upon a wilderness of suffering, together with its biblical resonances, thus also points to the movement of the Trekkers into what they saw as another, later wilderness. And in this context the belief in a God 'who brings forth life from death in the course of history' is yoked to confidence in the deity's interest not in the individual alone but in the individual as part of an Afrikaner people, 'a community of the saved...it is a whole nation with its distinct language and culture, its own history and special destiny' (p. ix). In terms of such reasoning the Afrikaner sense of personal suffering was easily invested with communal significance.

But against these Afrikaner Calvinist resonances, the accident in Johnnie's father's experience challenges, in terms of existentialist discourse, any providential notion of the universe. If it took dynamite to bend the Smit father's spirit, the consequences of this have been more material. The explosion deprives the father not only of his leg but of his ability to support his family. The dynamite that breaks the father's working life thus heralds the subsequent hardship and suffering of the Smit family. And in Act 1, in another narrative performance equally lovingly undertaken, Johnnie recalls the story of this accident in greater detail (p. 201). Here too biblical references attempt to contain or mediate the fact of the accident and those consequences that must at least interrogate or threaten the very religious discourse called into play to grapple with it, but the narrative nevertheless reports an act of transgression. Johnnie's father has chosen a moment of forbidden pleasure, taken time off 'when the others weren't looking' (p. 201), to eat prickly pear. And in the account of the moment of the explosion itself (p.201), the biblical references are at a minimum.

The accident posits an irrational and destructive world: dynamite, as Johnnie says, is 'a hell of a word' (p. 201) also because if the father has been careless in moving up the mountains, not only were the safety precautions probably less than adequate, but there has been no substantial compensation for the accident. These facts, together with the knowledge of an act of transgression and together with the Smit's subsequent life of indigence and hardship makes the father's insistence upon Calvinist discourse all the more urgent as a way of coping with contingencies – not only the aberrance of the accident and the severity of the father's crippling, but the ensuing difficulties in their material condition – that continually challenge that discourse. As Hester observes:

all our life it was groaning and moaning and what the Bible says and what God's going to do and I hated it! (pp. 181-2)

How the deeper layers of the structure of utterance are 'determined by more sustained and more basic social connections with which the speaker is in contact',[14] and how the language which flows through the social order may crucially operate in the constitution of identity is suggested in other ways in Hello and goodbye. When the play opens Johnnie grapples with the death of his father – the care of whom has occupied most of his time – a fact that has materially affected his own ability to function. He desperately seeks a suitable language to contain or control his recurring sense of panic, insecurity, emptiness. His panic is evident in the awareness he expresses of existing in time and place without meaning. This intensifies with the arrival of the sister who has spent fifteen years in Johannesburg and who exemplifies rebellion and rejection of the Calvinist world in which the two have grown up. To resist her he draws too on a variety of linguistic formulations – when Hester becomes personal about his life he turns to the language of consumerism, literally reading advertisement and medical literature to avoid facing his sister's questions. Or, when Hester confronts him with his decision not to go to the railway school it is to the language of cliché that he clings, another means of masking or denying what later in the text emerges as, in existentialist terms, a failure of growth. And, especially as his father draws upon Calvinist discourse to mediate not only the accident but family life at the Smit's home, so Johnnie, it is clear, by retelling his stories, has been using this language, drawn from the familial and social situation in which he is placed, in the immediate context to cope with the death of his father, but also, over the years, to live through such stories and such language and so, again in existentialist terms, escape responsibility for himself.

His struggle to constitute an identity out of the language formulations available to him within the social formation culminates in an existentialist climax of angst 'I NEED SOMETHING! LOOK AT ME!' (p. 227), but it is followed by rejection of the language his sister speaks, and more determined submission to the narratives of his father and to the Afrikaner Calvinist discourse that those narratives perpetuate, a discourse drawn on not only by his father, but by the ruling classes of the South African state. As Hester's search for the fictionary compensation becomes more insistent, and the inevitability of her discovery that her father has already died, approaches, his fear drives him ever more doggedly into fragments of religious formulation:

> This is…was…will be for ever and ever…Let us pray: Oh Lord… something… our daily bread, brown bread, the broken loaf…and Amen. Grace at supper. By the grace of God, you me and him in the light of the lamp with our heads bowed at supper. (pp. 228-9)

The text emphasises that the language Johnnie – unable to respond to his sister's invitation to move into the 'other', to leave the past and join her in a new life in the city – chooses to define himself is, in the use he makes of it, crippling, by having him, no cripple, literally take up the crutches at the end of the play, as, through the well-loved narratives about his father and through that Afrikaner Calvinist discourse to which the father was devoted, he 'assumes' his father's identity. And, as in certain instances of interpellation in *The blood knot* and again in *Boesman and Lena*, Johnnie's subjection to the discourses which flow not only through his family unit but also derive ultimately from those discourses privileged by the ruling classes suggests aspects of Gramsci's description of the 'complex and well-articulated civil society, in which the individual can govern himself without his self-government thereby entering into conflict with the political society – but rather becoming its normal continuation, its organic complement'.[15]

The struggle within this discourse to resist alternative ways of perceiving the human subject is especially evident in the play in the attitudes expressed by the Smit father and son about Hester. She, in her language and in her account of her past manifests an independent spirit that seeks more than can be had in the narrow confines of the known world of her childhood. But father and son define her as representative of that which must be forbidden, that which transgresses, that which is impure. And so, as both Hester and Johnnie recall, it is, within the family, Hester who comes to demarcate the distinction so important to Calvinism between what is deemed pure and the punishable impure. Johnnie remembers, 'you weren't a real Afrikaner by nature, he said. Must be some English blood somewhere, on Mommie's side' (p.197). Moodie observes that the notion of pure and impure in Afrikaans Calvinist thinking is inextricably bound up with the sense of a separate, Afrikaner community:

English-speaking prejudice and discrimination proved God's election and at the same time ensured the separate existence of the Afrikaner consciousness. Maintenance of this separation came to be a sacred duty. In the light of God's intention to create another republic, everything which emphasised Afrikaner uniqueness – their language, their Calvinist faith, their customs and conventions, their very dress – took on sacred significance... The notion of 'Englishness' thus evoked for the Afrikaner the three great evils which threatened his separate existence – imperialism, capitalism, and egalitarian liberalism.[16]

The Smit father draws on this discourse to position his daughter, to cope with her non-conforming and non-submissive, adventurous response to life. Johnnie, in his recollections of childhood, describes this rebelliousness, 'her fingers in her ears and shouting or singing at the top of her voice to drown my crying' (p. 189), and her troublesome assertion of difference. But as he reminds Hester of this, he also imposes the burden of guilt as transgressor upon her:

You're a rotten egg. There's one in every dozen. (*Shouting to father's room.*) Hold on! I'm coming! (*To Hester.*) For your sake I hope this works. (p. 199)

The urgent stress upon the sinful daughter in the Smit family enacts also the Afrikaner Calvinist belief in the possibility of lapsing from a state of holiness, an anxiety that even for the elect, remains. This is because of the arbitrary notion of God's righteousness, which prompts Calvin to provide 'both subjective and objective assurances of election':

who are those who have been called..? Only God and the individual really know. Even for the individual himself, uncertainty may reappear. 'Anxiety about our future state steals in,' says Calvin, 'for Christ shows that "many are called but few are chosen." Indeed Paul himself also dissuades us from overassurance: "Let him," he says, "who stands well, take heed lest he fall." Again: You are grafted into the people of God? "Be not proud but fear." For God can cut you off again that he may engraft others.'[17]

From this point of view Hester's 'impurities' may provide a continual and necessary example that is also a warning for father and son of the dangers of lapsing. Yet Hester's impulse to transgress is after all paralleled, as I remarked, in the father's own impulse to escape the rules and the monotony of work to eat prickly pears. To submit to the discourse, entails inevitably hardship and sacrifice, must require effort and a commitment that may regularly renew itself through the repeated example of the daughter. The temptation to pleasure may be contained by the discovery of what is deemed aberrant behaviour that must be punished in the other.

Appropriation of one discourse then – in this case Afrikaner Calvinist discourse within the Smit family – not only exerts control and demands submission but entails in this way the continual identification of transgression, of transgressive discourses, as part of the process of submission – or, the structuring of ethnicity. In a similar way we may argue,the racist discourse which inscribes the view of black workers in Johnnie's narrative of the 'bad times...no jobs, no money' when the Smit father 'queued for a week to get the job – laying sleepers' whilst black workers were only able to 'sit and watch the white man doing kaffir work – hungry for the work...dying by the dozen' (p. 217) enables Johnnie to regard them as inhuman objects, part of an 'other', against which his father may more fully emerge as a member of the suffering elect.

Gramsci observes in his discussion of the State and civil society that:

Every man, in as much as he is active, i.e. living, contributes to modifying the social environment in which he develops (to modifying certain of its characteristics or to preserving others); in other words he tends to establish 'norms', rules of living and behaviour... A father is a legislator for his children, but the paternal authority will be more or less conscious, more or less obeyed and so forth.[18]

and he also argues that such norms often derive ultimately either directly or indirectly from the efforts of the ruling classes to privilege and promote certain discourses within private as well as state bodies and organisations in order to maintain their hegemony. It may be argued that the family unit in Hello and goodbye suggests one such private unit that is subject to just such a process in ways that, although less formally and deliberately than Gramsci goes on to describe, nevertheless point to the formation of the kind of subjectivity about which he speaks:

In general, it may be said that the distinction between ordinary men and others who are more specifically legislators is provided by the fact that this second group not only formulates directives which will become a norm of conduct for the others, but at the same time creates the instruments by means of which the directives themselves will be 'imposed', and by means of which it will verify their execution. Of this second group, the greatest legislative power belongs to the State personnel (elected and career officials), who have at their disposal the legal coercive powers of the State. But this does not mean that the leaders of 'private' organisms and organisations do not have coercive sanctions at their disposal too... The maximum of legislative capacity can be inferred when a perfect formulation of directives is matched by a perfect arrangement of the organisms of execution and verification, and by a perfect preparation of the 'spontaneous' consent of the masses who must 'live' those directives, modifying their own habits, their own will, their own convictions to conform with those directives and with the objectives which they propose to achieve. If everyone is a legislator in the broadest sense of the concept, he continues to be a legislator even if he accepts directives from others – if, as he carries them out, he makes certain that others are carrying them out too; if, having understood their spirit, he propagates them as though making them into rules specifically applicable to limited and definite zones of living. (p. 266)

But it is against her father and through him her brother, as 'legislators', that Hester struggles. She draws dialogically on existentialist discourse to counteridentify the claims to Christianity and goodness, made by the father in his use of Calvinism within the Smit home. She attacks her father's hypocrisy in the application of that discourse, juxtaposing against his reliance on his religion, his treatment of his family, 'God help you. God help us. No chance of that my boy. He never gave a damn about what happened in this house…' (p. 218).When Johnnie tells Hester of his missed opportunity to become the engine driver he longed to be, and of his father's response to something convenient primarily to his own comfort – that this is the 'will of God' – she identifies the element of manipulation in the father's response, 'He did that to Mommie…Said God and you all felt like sinners' (p. 226). And similarly, her view of her parents' marriage interrogates the validity of religious discourse in terms of the hardships of their actual family life. Furthermore, the notions of propriety which she attacks in her account of her train journey home as well as in her recollections of family life, are contested too by her more general recognition of the hypocrisy of the urban bourgeois world she has found in the city. She registers the way in which her material poverty, which has led her into prostitution, defines her in the city as impure but turns on the double standards of the ostensibly respectable. Despite the emphasis they may place on 'Sunday and sin', she tells her brother, because of her economic vulnerability they are ready to exploit her sexually, and she has 'hoered all the brothers and fathers and sons and sweeethearts in this world into one thing…Man' (p. 204). Her attack, throughout the play, upon the use of Afrikaner Calvinist religious discourse – its notions of purity and family, its demand for conformity – climaxes, even as her brother clings more frightenedly to that discourse, in an overt rejection of it:

JOHNNIE: God's will be done...
HESTER: You already look like him...
JOHNNIE: in hell as in heaven...
HESTER: And sound like him...
JOHNNIE: I am his son. He is my father. Flesh of his flesh.
HESTER: That's right. Lick his arse, crawl right up it until your feet hang out. Be HIM.
JOHNNIE: God forgive...
HESTER: That's what you want isn't it?
JOHNNIE: God forgive you for what you are saying.
HESTER: THERE IS NO GOD! THERE NEVER WAS! We've unpacked our life, Johannes Cornelius Smit, the years in Valley Road and there is no God. Nothing but rubbish. (p. 227)

IV Commissioned by society

Fugard continued to work with the Serpent Players in the mid- and late 1960s. Repeatedly in his notebooks he mentions encounters with political activists, some of whom were members of Serpent Players, noting several times meetings with ex-political prisoners, recently returned from Robben Island. In December 1966 he writes, 'Welcome, released about a week ago, came out with the group last night for what was supposed to be a small Christmas reunion party. It proved impossible for any of us to get "high"...his stories about Robben Island, the thought of Sharkie, Norman and Simon still there and the new spate of trials – 77 now recharged and found guilty just as they were on the point of release.'[19] He notes in September 1967: 'An evening with Norman, who was released ten days ago, after two years in gaol – most of that time on Robben Island. He talked almost non-stop, acting out his hilarious-terrible stories about life on the Island' (pp. 150-1).

Fugard also repeatedly records, throughout the second half of the decade, the continuing struggle of the Serpent Players to find a space to perform, and the harassment of various kinds to which individual members or the whole group were subject. Thus in November 1966 he mentions that:

The local Native Commissioner has given his permission for a play-reading by Serpent Players before the (white) Theatre Appreciation Group provided three conditions are observed:
1. It must not be public – members only.
2. Serpent Players may not use the toilets at the hall.

3. They must leave immediately after the reading – no social gathering or discussion...

– what should have been our last rehearsal for tomorrow night's reading was instead a moving, absurd, sensible and idiotic discussion – given all the pros and cons – of whether, with the possibility of the Special Branch being in our audience, we should proceed with The Coat as a group venture or as a reading by myself alone. (p. 142)

In March 1967 Fugard decided to refuse the government subsidised Performing Arts Council of the Transvaal permission to perform People are living there, although it had not yet been produced and observed:

Offer was extremely generous – large advance royalty etc. At first I was quite confused – so many principles seemed involved, on both sides, for and against. Most important of all was my distaste at the thought of association with a Government-sponsored theatre, but if I said No, did this involve surrendering my right to talk here and now, even under segregated circumstances – a compromise I'd already accepted with Hello. Then tonight a sudden clarity. It comes down simply to decency and doing the job properly. I just couldn't work in that complacent, self-satisfied world. I couldn't make 'good' theatre under those conditions. No question of principles, but of taste. I'd rather work here, decently, with impoverished Serpent Players. (p. 149)

In June of the same year the government withdrew Fugard's passport. A few months later he noted that the Players had at last found a church hall in Korsten to rehearse Brother Jero 'after a badly dislocated four weeks' (p.157). And he continued to record incidents of harassment, mentioning in the following year an 'interview with two Special Branch policemen on the rocks yesterday... they found me down there after being told at the house I had gone fishing. Someone had phoned them with information about the Black Sash organisation and said he was Athol Fugard. Who was playing games? And with whom?' (p.165). The group was also inevitably subject to the danger of informers. Thus, reporting a social gathering including a member of the Serpent Players recently released from Robben Island, Fugard describes how a 'down-at-heel man suddenly produced an expensive camera and flash apparatus and wanted a picture of "the group", all of whom scattered in panic...and the evening broke up on a sour note of suspicion and fear' (p.144). In June 1970 he notes: 'whole of Serpent Players session devoted to discussing informers (impimpi). Impossible to believe, but the Group suddenly find X very suspect. Evidence from New Brighton suggests he is closely involved with Special Branch' (pp.184-5).

Such experiences must have intensified Fugard's awareness of the processes of domination within the social order and his notebooks provide evidence that not only in the production of plays but also in his reading this was being strengthened. In 1964 his production of Brecht prompted an extended discussion:

Struggling with apathy and confusion in the group to get *The Caucasian Chalk Circle* understood and started. By and large they are as bourgeois in aspirations and morality as most white people in this country. Masters and their slaves. The fight is for a slice of the same cake. No-one wants to bake a different one. This is the hardest – showing that the *Chalk Circle* is a different recipe.

And for myself again the suspicions and doubts about my work that contact with Brecht always provokes. Above all else I am overwhelmed at this moment by the 'usefulness' of the *Chalk Circle* – so much a tool, the edge honed to a bright decisiveness by this great dramatist. A man wants to dig a vegetable garden – I talk to him about the nourishment and health to be had from vegetables; Brecht gives him a spade and seeds. I have it now – my pessimism! Brecht has optimism. All is not said in that of course – there remains anti-individualism as opposed to my inability to see man – a man – as the sum total of his social relations; but pessimism and optimism define modes of thinking about man... Disturbing to realise how much a product I am of Western morality – and what could possibly be a better school in that morality than the back-streets of Port Elizabeth, and how different had my milieu not been so anarchic but productive of a social conscience. (p. 119)

In 1966, he notes of a reading of his play *The Coat*, on which he has been working, 'The piece is pure Brecht. *The Messingkauf Dialogues* did it. Improvisation and discussion, improvisation and discussion – and behind an apparent easy carelessness, a logic' (p. 143); over the years he makes repeated reference to Brecht's 'ease'. He was also reading Fanon and comments in 1966: 'Reading Fanon's *The Wretched of the Earth*. The most moral of all conscious acts: Rebellion. "I (we) have had enough!" An awareness (discovery) of self and circumstances' (p.138). Fugard's well attested predilection for interiority in liberal and existentialist terms was here clearly being stretched. Again in 1968 he notes: 'Survival can involve betrayal of everything – beliefs, values, ideals, – except life itself. Fanon on this subject. The schizoid condition of an oppressed people. The cure? Obviously nothing short of a revolution in the social order can give a man in that condition a chance of hoping (striving) with some possibility of realisation, that he can achieve this integration (balance) of self with the world in which he lives' (p.164). And his last entry for 1968 shows that such preoccupations persist:

For some weeks now have been reading Ernst Fischer's *The Necessity of Art* – his Marxism and advocacy of social realism seems finally to be expressed in his description of an artist as being 'commissioned by his society'. My whole dilemma, specifically in *Boesman and Lena* focused on this. Do I want a commission? Have I got one? Must I function without one? Is my context irremediably bourgeois? Can I align myself with a future, a possibility, which I believe in (hope for) but of which I have no image? My failure of imagination? More than ever before in my life a sense of how much the blindness, apathy, indifference of people holds us back, bogs us down in this morass of self – indulgence and limp, useless consciences. *Our hell (history) is man-made, to that extent it can be unmade by men* (my emphasis). (pp. 178-9)

Such concerns need to be set against the oft-quoted reflection of Fugard's in 1968 whilst working on *Boesman and Lena* that he was fascinated by Boesman's and Lena's predicament at a level 'neither political nor social but metaphysical…a metaphor of the human condition which revolution or legislation cannot substantially change' (p. 168). And it helps to account not only for his concern expressed also in 1968, that 'possibly one of the reasons why I have not used an African character and township setting in any of my last three plays is that I think and feel about it in too shallowly "political" terms' (p. 168), but also his worry in March of the following year about 'the "social content" of *Boesman and Lena*. Nagging doubts that I am opting out on this score, that I am not saying enough. At one level their predicament is an indictment of this society, which makes people "rubbish". Is this explicit enough?' (p. 181). It helps to account too for the extent to which despite Fugard's view of the characters as 'metaphors of the human condition', and despite such anxieties, *Boesman and Lena* more overtly than in his two previous plays depicts the power of apartheid laws in determining the pattern of individual existence.

Fugard's practical experience in theatre particularly throughout his period with the Serpent Players no doubt prepared him too, it is important to add, for what he registered as a seminal experience in his concept of theatre, his discovery of Grotowski:

he was in every sense the *agent provocateur* at that moment in my career. His book…made me realise that there were other ways of doing theatre, other ways of creating a totally valid theatre experience. That it needn't be the orthodox experience I had been retailing for so many years since *The Blood Knot*.[20]

Thus he records in working on *Boesman and Lena* in 1968 a 'greater honesty about, and use of the unreality of the stage'[21] and by 1970 notes 'Boesman and Lena for Durban – on stage all that the actors will need – props, the material for the pondok, clothing – dress for Lena, hat and old jacket for Boesman, balaclava and old overcoat for Outa. No curtains – black surround. When the audience is in, without dimming house lights, actors come on – barefoot, rehearsal clothes – and in front of audience put on their "character"clothes' (p. 185).

This movement away from the theatre Fugard had until then himself written, which included the greater flexibility and mobility that results from the decision not to use a realistic stage set, as in Fugard's previous productions of his own plays, but an open stage was, like Kente's work in the townships, particularly significant. South African theatre practitioners subsequently were increasingly to explore the potential in such techniques. They invited from the audience greater imaginative participation, heralding some weakening of the separation between audience, proscenium arch and stage so beloved in bourgeois theatre. They also suggested, in contrast to the fixed structures implied in the realism of most South African theatre hitherto, not only a space evoking deprivation, but a space affording maximum focus upon the potential of actress and actor as primary agents in the constitution of meaning. While these were still only tendencies in Boesman and Lena, they also provided a significant innovatory parallel to the developments in township theatre I noted in chapter 4.

V Afrikaner nationalism and Boesman and Lena

If Hello and goodbye suggests aspects of the impact of Afrikaner Calvinist religious discourse, within the South African social formation, Boesman and Lena conveys some measure of the impact which the political version of Afrikaner Calvinism, Afrikaner nationalism and its rule has had in prescribing particularly the kind of space within which the oppressed subject may exist. The apartheid restructuring of space in South Africa involves forced removals of which the South African Review has noted that since 1960 over 3.5 million removals have been effected; still another 1.3 million people have been under threat of removal since 1983.[22] As recently as 1977 a Nationalist Senator remained unrepentant about the process when he spoke in parliament:

We make no apologies for the Group Areas Act, and for its application. And if 600,000 Indians and Coloureds are affected by the implementation of that Act, we do not apologise for that either. I think the world must simply accept it. The Nationalist Party came to power in 1948 and said it would implement residential segregation in South Africa, out of the chaos which prevailed when we came to power, created order and established decent, separate residential areas for our people.[23]

In his book *The discarded people*, published in 1969, Cosmas Desmond, documenting removals, describes part of a very different reality:

I have seen the bewilderment of simple rural people when they are told that they must leave their homes where they have lived for generations and go to a strange place. I have heard their cries of helplessness and resignation and their pleas for help. I have seen the sufferings of whole families living in a tent or a tiny tin hut. Of children sick with typhoid, or their bodies emaciated with malnutrition and even dying of plain starvation.[24]

The state has consistently claimed that its actions have been in the name of race harmony, order and peace between people categorised as different and therefore irreconcilable, whose best resort and welfare lies in complete enforced segregation. In the detail of its enactment on stage *Boesman and Lena* repeatedly interrogates these claims. It is about two coloured squatters who have had their last hut demolished but who have established another makeshift abode for the night. They are joined by an old black man who dies while in their company. At the play's conclusion the two move on again. The Stage Directions for the opening of the play present an empty landscape on open terrain, and two characters who in their predicament and ensuing experience will suggest the thousands upon thousands of squatters who still inhabit present–day South Africa. One enters, 'heavily burdened', carrying amongst other things a blackened paraffin tin, an old mattress, a piece of corrugated iron (p. 239). After only a few lines of dialogue, Lena recalls why they are on the move, '*Vat jou goed en trek!* [Take your belongings and move] Whiteman says *Voetsek!* [Get away] *Eina!*'' (p. 240) and a little later she recalls one of the petty agents of the dominant order, who prompted them to abandon their previous refuge:

It was after Redhouse. Collecting prickly pears. Then they found our place there in the bush. *Loop, Hotnot* [Run Hotnot] So Hotnot *loops*....No, we ran! The *boer* had a gun. When he showed us the bullets. Boesman dropped his tin and went down that road like a rabbit. (p. 247)

Other details in the text suggest too what this process together with influx control were designed to facilitate: a steady supply of cheap labour, and the perpetuation, in consequence, of the master/mistress– servant relationship – in which the master/mistress can dictate all because the labourer s/he deals with has no rights of domicile, no home ownership, no right to live with her/his family, and is therefore totally vulnerable and insecure. Boesman, alluding bitterly to what he sees as the hopelessness of Lena's complaint that she is sick of it all, 'You want to live in a house? What you think you are? A white madam?' (p. 254), sarcastically instructs Lena in the way she must speak to prospective employers (p. 272). His recognition of the discursive formations to which this cheap labour is reduced in order to find work if it can, extends fairly quickly into relatively direct recognition of that deprivation of land and the process of removal which leads people, in the working class, to the kind of vulnerability we find in *Boesman and Lena* at the start of the play. And the allusions which Lena as well as Boesman make to the image of the 'whiteman's bulldozer' repeatedly signify that process to which the two are subject.

Part of the dramatic tension in the play stems from the ways in which the individual struggle to win some private domestic space and also to establish a viable sense of identity or interiority – primarily in existentialist terms – is continually broken down by the social forces within which it is situated. The best example of this may be found in Boesman's use of the word 'freedom', to which he attaches in his first account of the demolition of their last shelter, a predominantly psychological sense, 'There was room for me to stand straight.' This prompts Lena to taunt him: 'You still got it *ou ding* [old thing]? she asks sarcastically, 'you lost it?' (p. 275) and, as he proceeds with his description of their walk, his language about freedom changes:

I saw that piece of *sinkplaat* [corrugated iron] on the side of the road. I should have passed it. Gone on! Freedom's a long walk. But the sun was low. Our days are too short. (p. 276)

His initial description of the destruction of their previous shelter resonates a great measure of self-detestation, anger and frustration at hardship but now his sense of the meaning of the word 'freedom' produces a different realisation that includes a sense of the impossibility of escape from their pondok-existence (p. 284) within current relations of domination and subordination:

You think I haven't got secrets in my heart too? That's mine. *Sies!* Small little word, hey. *Sies.* But it fits. (*Parodying himself*) 'Ja Baas! Dankie, Baas!' *Sies*, Boesman!' And you? Don't ask me what you've done. Just look. You say you can see yourself. Take a good look tonight! Crying for a bottle, begging for bruises. *Sies*, Lena! Boesman and Lena, *sies!* We're not people any more. Freedom's not for us. We stood there under the sky...two crooked *Hotnots*. So they laughed. (pp. 283-4)

There is, it is true, as many readings of the play have amply explored, a struggle between Boesman and Lena to find in such conditions a sense of their own relationship. Boesman's silences in the first act, as his speeches in the second act bear out, are partly possible only because as the two finally realise, underlying his brutality is the agonising fact that she articulates the pain that he feels, that they both share. And this has prompted critics to privilege this realisation and, as in the case of other Fugard plays, to discover in it recuperation. But such readings need to be set against the text's powerful and repeated acknowledgement of the processes of the apartheid structuration of space, and the brutal removals that go with it, which determine, finally, their existence. Thus the assertion at the end of the play of their relationship, the clear description of the exact terrain through which they have been forced to move that Lena has sought throughout the play to identify is not recuperative. Boesman gives Lena a clear indication of place – where they have been and where they now are but his description suggests the movements of refugees, victims of war or grave economic or ecological disaster. And Lena, hearing this, says what Boesman, in turn, knew at the beginning of the play, 'Is that the way it was?...It doesn't explain anything' (pp. 292-3). Audiences may be impressed in this context by Lena's realisation that her relationship with Boesman too means something, as she decides to follow him, but her statement 'I'm alive Boesman' (p.293) is set too firmly in a relentless world, one still full of political extremism and exploitation, and one that does not go away at the end of the play. It concludes with an image on stage of two people on the road, without land, without a roof over their heads, without the prospect of employment and no right to stay anywhere:

Next time you want to kill me, do it. Really do it. When you hit, hit those lights out. Don't be too late. Do it yourself. Don't let the old bruises put the rope around your neck.
   Okay. But not so fast. It's dark. (p. 293)

VI Responding to, appropriating and suppressing *Boesman and Lena*

In the early 1970s, Fugard again changed his mind about government-subsidised theatre groups and allowed The Performing Arts Council of the Cape, CAPAB, to produce both *People are living there* and *Boesman and*

Lena. He stipulated that the plays had to be performed as well to township audiences. This was adhered to by CAPAB which drew large, white audiences and claimed that it had also won large attendance at the performances – far fewer – which it arranged for black audiences. *Hello and goodbye* and *Boesman and Lena* have since then repeatedly played successfully overseas as well as in South Africa.

The tensions in Fugard's construction of subjectivity primarily in terms of liberal and existentialist discourse and his increasing sensitivity to the impact upon the subject of relations of domination and subordination tends to be erased in many although not all reviews of performances or in much traditionalist criticism of his work (as I remarked briefly in chapter 3). Thus, although when *Boesman and Lena* opened Stanley Kaufman, with an anti-apartheid predilection, responded: 'the specifics of their wretched lives are caused by the history and policies of their country...the reason that his play achieves towering height...is because it *includes* the agony of apartheid, and shows that *apartheid* is not devil inflicted but man made', [25] and although in South Africa, after the play's opening, the *Eastern Province Herald* commented that Boesman and Lena 'are people who have been bruised to the soul by life in South Africa today and in vain retaliation they have bruised each other...their situation as homeless "hotnots" is itself comment on the time we live in', other reviewers tended to generalise and universalise the import of the play.[26] The *Evening Post* asserted that 'the play is simply a comment on misery; the aimless drifting of two low-class coloureds wallowing in the mud of life, both incapable of pulling themselves out of the mire' – a reaction that reproduces prevailing racist ideological discursive formations [27] while *The Star*, after the Johannesburg opening later in the year observed that 'the characters exist basically as metaphors and not as real and living people'.[28] Literary critics within South Africa as well as abroad also elect often to foreground narrow versions of interiority.

Thus one South African sees Boesman and Lena almost as itinerant gypsies 'who travel and live together in the area surrounding Port Elizabeth... scrounge around for something to eat and enough to drink, stay on until evicted, and then move on to the next place, where the whole process repeats itself...crossing and re-crossing the same piece of earth year in and year out' in order to discover that although they are 'in bondage' (unexplicated) they both discover an inner (recuperative) 'freedom'.[29] And one of Fugard's most recent North American critics, whom I have already cited in chapter 3, in part, perhaps, explaining

Fugard's success with some North Americans, lunges more and more determinedly after not one but several metaphors himself in the endeavour to detach the 1960s plays from their chronotopic location:

Throughout their performances Fugard and Bryceland used less and less make-up to make them look coloured. Boesman and Lena could be white, middle-class or productively employed...In a sense, Boesman and Lena are flotsam drifting down the Swartkops past the Smit's Valley Road bungalow and the Korsten shack of Morrie and Zach. In the sea they become one with the other souls drifting in the abyss. Up against an existential wall, Fugard's characters fight for a time, then resign themselves to the inevitable. Boesman and Lena have wandered about on the darkest night in one of the universe's blackest holes. They keep on trekking, but it is a night, and a hole, from which there is no escape.[30]

Such readings no doubt help to account for the selection of these plays by government-dominated organisations for performance. They are to be found in Britain as well. B. A. Young, of the *Financial Times*, with the few instances when Boesman and Lena draw on racist discursive formations – suggesting interpellation – in mind, confirmed when the play opened in London that colonialist and assimilationist discourse was still alive and well in Britain:

Athol Fugard...illuminates the eternal truth that even from squalor it is possible to snatch an occasional gleam of happiness...The play isn't as I see it, an attack on South African racial policy, though of course it is undoubtedly an attack on South African housing policy. What emerges from the racial point of view is that the coloureds despise the natives as much as the whites despise the coloureds...The moral that I find uncomfortably evident is a different one, that when we try to teach primitive peoples the European way of life they have as much right to our faults as to our virtues. If we aspire to set ourselves up as the arbiters of behaviour, our weaknesses must be concealed at least. Shakespeare,who knew everything, knew exactly how Boesman would behave, and even wrote a line for him: 'You taught me language, and my profit on't is, I know how to curse.'[31]

Nevertheless, despite such readings, the power of *Boesman and Lena* as in part a dramatisation of aspects of the apartheid structuration of space has not been lost on members of the ruling classes. As recently as 1985 when it was set as a school text in the Cape, although thousands of copies had been purchased, officials within the Department of Education there – presumably encountering the play after it had been set by a committee for the first time, banned it for schools and sent out orders for all copies that had already been purchased by the Department to be burned.

Notes

1 Coplan, In township tonight!, p. 209.
2 Cited in Coplan, In township tonight!, p.209.
3 Cited in Vandenbroucke, Truths the hand can touch, pp. 77-8.
4 Fugard, Athol, Notebooks 1960/1977, ed. Benson, Mary, London: Faber and Faber, 1983, p. 78.
5 Vandenbroucke, Truths the hand can touch, p. 78.
6 See Fugard, Notebooks, p. 159.
7 Fugard, Athol, People are living there, Hello and goodbye, Boesman and Lena, in Boesman and Lena and other plays, Cape Town: Oxford University Press, 1984.
8 See Raymer, John David, 'Eight recent plays by South African Dramatist Athol Fugard', thesis for the degree of PhD, Ohio University, 1975, Ann Arbor: University Microfilms International, 1981, p. 73.
9 See Fugard, Notebooks, pp. 128-9.
10 Cited in Vandenbroucke, Truths the hand can touch, p. 79.
11 Cited in O'Meara, Volkskapitalisme, p. 108.
12 Cited in de Klerk, The puritans in Africa, p. 294.
13 Moodie, T. Dunbar, The rise of Afrikanerdom, Berkeley and Los Angeles: University of California Press, 1975, p. ix.
14 Vološinov, Marxism and the philosophy of language, p. 87.
15 Gramsci, Antonio, Selections from the prison notebooks of Antonio Gramsci, ed. and trans. Hoare, Quinton, and Smith, Geoffrey Nowell, London: Lawrence and Wishart, 1982, p. 268.
16 Moodie, The rise of Afrikanerdom, pp. 14-15.
17 Moodie, The rise of Afrikanerdom, pp. 23-4.
18 Gramsci, Selections from the prison notebooks, pp. 265-6.
19 Fugard, Notebooks, p. 144.
20 Fugard, Athol, Statements, Oxford: Oxford University Press, 1978, Introduction, un-numbered pages.
21 Fugard, Notebooks, p. 172.
22 South African Research Service, South African review, same foundations, new façades, Johannesburg: Ravan, 1983, pp. 83, 95.
23 Cited in Platzky, Laurine, and Walker, Cherryl, The surplus people, Johannesburg, Ravan: 1985, p.100.
24 Cited in Platzky and Walker, The surplus people, p. 7.
25 The New Republic, 25 July 1970.
26 Eastern Province Herald, 11 July 1969.
27 Evening Post, 14 July 1969.
28 The Star, 4 November 1969.
29 Hauptfleish, Temple, 'Fugard's dramatic expression of the freedom concept in Boesman and Lena', in Gray, Athol Fugard, p. 182.
30 Vandenbroucke, Truths, p. 98.
31 The Financial Times, 10 July 1971.

6

Phela phela phela malanga

The early years of the 1970s saw an intensification of worker and trade union struggle and a growing mood of resistance together with the emergence of an increasingly problematic economy. 'Deep rooted grievances over housing, transport, influx control, liquor, crime corruption, and the complete denial of meaningful political rights'[1] finally led to a major explosion. Precipitated by a crisis in education, an angry, defiant and bloody uprising swept the country in 1976-77. This period also saw the beginning of a remarkable increase in oppressed class involvement in theatre which was to continue after the Uprising to the end of the 1980s. And this growth was all the more impressive because it occurred in conditions of continuing suppression and in the teeth of often ferocious active attempts by the government to stifle it. Theatre emanated from, amongst others, the Black Consciousness movement, from the collaborative efforts of Fugard, Kani and Ntshona, from Kente and from a multitude of university and fringe groups including, most significantly, Workshop 71.

Their plays often directly contested the entire apartheid system. If segregationist and then apartheid discourses have consistently provided sites for contestation in South African drama, Dhlomo and Butler, in their differing attempts to find identity within the periphery, engaged in part as well with the discourses of an imperialist and colonialist metropolis. Although lingering strands of colonialist assimilationist discourse sometimes survive in the collaborative multi-racial plays of the late1950s, theatre in the 1960s foregrounded ever more extensively issues or aspects of marginalised experience within the South Africa contemporary to the plays. But it is particularly in the first half of the 1970s, that dramas, located – partly as a result of the increased involve-ment of the oppressed classes and groups – in the urban spaces of the oppressed and attempting to represent their experiences,proliferated, while the imperial and colonial centre as partial locus for dramatic concern diminished further in importance. Emerging projects, working from multiple and often conflicting positions within oppressed classes and groups, endeavour now to displace the hegemony of a South African apartheid and ruling class centre.

I The state's punishment of transgression

The state's suppression of the drama of the oppressed classes and groups worked primarily through its continuing control of and restrictions in the use of township space. In the townships the almost complete absence of performance space and attendant difficult conditions for rehearsal and performance, to which Kente and others had been in the 1960s forced to adapt, remained. Soweto, for instance, which had a population approaching one million in the early 1970s, still had, towards the end of the decade only 'one established nightclub, one hotel, one cinema, a few discoes, Jabulani Amphitheatre and Orlando Stadium for outdoor concerts, and a small number of community halls'.[2] The lack of amenities, and often unwillingness to approach the 'Bantu administration' offices, meant too, as I indicated in the introductory chapter, performances of unscripted plays in hastily convened venues, little or no rehearsal time, with performances advertised on the day of performance on impromptu banners. How much of this kind of theatre existed and how much of it is now irrecoverably lost is, until future research may show us otherwise, a matter of conjecture. The lack of theatrical space in the townships continued until the end of the 1980s and remained for the state a primary significant *de facto* means of limiting and containing theatrical growth.

Furthermore, the state had indulged in multiple bannings of political parties in the 1960s, and was therefore well versed by the early 1970s in its practices of detention, house arrests and worse, remaining determined throughout the decade to maintain its grip on the media and on education, and to implement its severe censorship laws. As its hold on the social order, despite its power, seemed to become at times less firm, the government found itself increasingly unable to tolerate the interrogation of apartheid which theatre practitioners were in different ways undertaking. Drama performance itself was to become for the state not only a site for overt repressive action but a theatre within which it might demonstrate its own power.

Thus the Black Consciousness movement of the late 1960s prompted the formation of several theatre groups, but these were, in turn, in the early and mid-1970s harassed and fairly swiftly destroyed by government action – just as government legislation, in the previous decade, had put paid to the activities of Union Artists.[3] The Theatre Council of Natal (TECON), which was founded in 1969, aborted in 1973 with the arrest of Saths Cooper, Ms Sam Moodley, and Strini Moodley, key Black Consciousness leaders active within it. The People's Experimental Theatre (PET), was formed in 1973, but again, as the introductory chapter notes, Mthuli Shezi, the author of its most well-known play *Shanti* (soon to be banned) was tragically killed at the end of 1973. PET disintegrated when several of its leaders were arrested in 1973 and charged with treason in 1975 while its newspaper was banned. Other theatre practitioners were harassed by the government as well. In 1975 'Port Elizabeth playwright Khayalethu Mquayisa's... *Confused Mhlaba* was banned just as its popularity began to grow in the townships.'[4] Located in the Eastern Cape, the Reverend Mzwandile Maqina – over the years intimidated, detained, and subjected to house arrest for extended periods – had his play *Give us this day*, which performed to full houses throughout 1974-75, together with another, *The Trial*, banned by the Publications Control Board.[5] Again, three months after the première of his play *How long* in February 1974 Gibson Kente was banned 'by the township superintendents of the East Rand and the Vaal Triangle from performing it in halls under their jurisdiction':

Kente interviewed Jannie Kruger, the chairman of the Publications Control Board, who assured him that the board would take no action against his play. The superintendant at Natalspruit nevertheless insisted on a letter from the censorship board. The Department of Bantu Education banned him from performing *How Long* at the Wilberforce Institute, a black teachers' training college under its jurisdiction. *I Believe*, Kente's next play, encountered similar problems, and in May Kente saw an official at the Department of Sport and Recreation. By June *How Long* was being banned in the Cape as well.[6]

Kente's *Too Late* was also banned, and he himself was detained by the police while trying to film his play *How long* at King Williamstown during the 1976-77 Uprising.[7] Despite the fact that *Too Late* was subsequently allowed performances by Ministerial permission, township superintendents continued to ban performances of it.

Even Fugard, working with John Kani and Winston Ntshona, was afraid of censorship, refusing to commit either *Sizwe Bansi is dead* or *The island* to script form until it had been performed abroad. He had good reason, for, as Brian Astbury, the director of The Space in Cape Town describes, the first night of the play in 1972 did not go off without incident:

On the opening day the police visited us and informed us that we would not be allowed to open. This at 4.30 in the afternoon. We took hurried legal opinion. At 8.00 o'clock – with a full-house audience clamouring at the doors – we were told that we would all end up in jail. We cancelled...We re-opened the following night to be confronted by two plain-clothes policemen who, after trying to buy seats without membership [The Space was run as a club to circumvent apartheid legislation] identified themselves to me and tried to stop the show. I refused on the grounds of our legal opinion. They asked to see the director and cast. Athol, John, Winston and I gathered in the office and were warned that we would be charged if we went on with the performance. The other three decided that if I, as management, was prepared to go on, so were they. The policemen repeated their warning, and then asked to see the performance. They very obviously enjoyed the first half and then left. We were never charged.[8]

Subsequently, however, all scheduled performances of the play in Port Elizabeth were stopped, and when, in 1973, Sizwe Bansi opened in Johannesburg at the Box Theatre, University of the Witwatersrand, security police interrupted the performance and attempted to arrest the cast and members of the audience by chasing them across the university lawns. In 1975, on the other hand, the first performances of Survival at The Space and at the University of the Witwatersrand were not interfered with and the play left shortly after for an extended tour abroad. But 'when Survival ...began to tour...in the townships in 1978, it was promptly banned'.[9] The entire acting cast of Survival, together with the director, now live abroad in voluntary exile.

Such measures by the government were most certainly intimidatory in intention. Through such acts, particularly those repeatedly carried out against Black Consciousness Theatre, the government might dramatise its own ruthless opposition to any transgression of prevailing apartheid discourse. Theatre in the 1970s nevertheless repeatedly showed itself determined to interrogate what the state sought to suppress.

II Stand united, fight united: Shanti

Black Consciousness and the emergent theatre of Black Consciousness tried, in the early 1970s, to construct a new kind of subjectivity for the oppressed class subject. For instance, prevailing discourse in South Africa has worked over the years to present the oppressed subject, amongst other things, as both defeated and submissive, thus marginalising as much as possible any evidence of contestation and struggle. Indeed, such production of the oppressed persists, in a variety of ways, until the present day. It is evident, for instance, amongst much else, in the annual ritual celebration of what was originally called 'Dingaan's Day'. This has since transmogrified into the Day of the Covenant and, more recently, into the Day of the Vow and it is meant to celebrate the vow taken by a number of trekkers to avenge the killing of Piet Retief and his party by Dingane the Zulu chief. The Battle of Blood River which followed, breaking Zulu power, is thought to manifest intervention by the Calvinist deity. For certain groups within the ruling classes, the annual ritual has always been taken as celebrating not only this event but the images of victory and defeat it recalls, perpetuating the allegedly divine sanction thus given to the trekkers' descendants for continuing domination.

It was against such positionings of the subordinate classes, as well as against the often blatant strands of prevailing racist and apartheid discourse in South Africa that the Black Consciousness Movement reacted.[10] Its own beginnings may be traced to the Extension of University Education Act, which, passed in 1959, destroyed the last vestiges of academic freedom at tertiary level and created a number of ethnically based 'tribal' colleges. A few years later a number of black students including Steve Biko and Barney Pityana broke away from the National Union of South African Students, mainly white-run and white-dominated, and formed the South African Students Organisation (SASO) in 1969 at the Turfloop tribal college north of Pietersburg. Black Consciousness first and foremost emphasised the need to resist what it saw as the psychological domination of the white ruling classes, which fixed blacks permanently into positions of inferiority and subordinacy. Its adherents drew upon, amongst others, Fanon and the Black Power Movement in the United States, as well as Freire and the liberation movements in South America. It was also opposed to any connections with white liberals who did not, it believed, have black interests at heart. But its concept of black unity did incorporate Indians and 'coloureds', in this way attempting to oppose the government use of ethnicity to create divisions amongst the oppressed.

Although primarily a student organisation, not aiming itself to become a political party,[11] and a movement that embraced various conflicting positions and arguments, Black Consciousness nevertheless became a major force in the 1970s until it was banned by the government. Its objective of consciousness-raising amongst the oppressed very soon permeated literary practices, producing, for instance, a new aggressive and more assertive poetic style – 'didactic, exhortatory and overtly political'[12] – in the work of writers such as James Matthews, Don Mattera, A. N. C. Kumalo and Oswald Mtshali. Contemporary poetry organisations such as Medupe (eventually to be banned in 1977) performed in schools and public halls in Soweto where the oral dimension to their performances was particularly significant, for 'in terms of the Black Consciousness Movement...while reading is largely an individual occupation, recitation of poems within the oral framework has to involve a group, or audience, and this sort of structure is more conducive to feelings of group solidarity'.[13]

Black Consciousness theatre too drew directly on this didacticism and search for group solidarity in its work. Thus the writer and poet M. Pascal Gwala, discussing optimistically the hoped for emergence of a national theatre, emphasised the need for plays to conscientise their audiences:

the entire moral and intellectual bearing of our black artists revolves around their social circumstances. There are those playwrights, writers, artists who can claim to be committed to black consciousness...Through the conscientisation process of Black Consciousness blacks begin to feel they are part of the human race; that their black heritage is rich with deeply human attributes; that they are not and never were – savage or barbaric outside the context of primitive culture.[14]

His last remark in these observations, published in 1973, provides yet further evidence of the marked extent to which older assimilationist ideological discursive formations still flowed through the social order, and confirms the extent to which the Black Consciousness Movement's emphasis upon black pride was in impulse at least partly reactive and corrective.

From the beginning, Black Consciousness drama groups performed plays from the metropolitan centres as well as from other parts of Africa. The Music Drama Arts and Literature Institute (MDALI) was among the first of the radical theatre groups to attempt to operate in the townships. An offshoot of Union Artists and Phoenix Players, formed in 1972, it sought, typically, to 'promote self determination, self realisation and self support in theatre arts', rejecting 'white artistic leadership, criticism, financial sponsorship and inter racial front organisations'.[15] Together with the Mhloti Black Theatre, it performed *Marat-Sade* and West African plays which had 'little impact on township theatre or theatregoers' (p. 223). PET, formed in 1973 in the Indian

location of Lenasia outside Johannesburg, flourished only for a brief
period before its leaders were banned, but it participated in plays,
poetry readings, and mixtures of poetry, music and readings from
Black revolutionary writings.[16] Black Consciousness theatre practitioners were clearly influenced by the didactic thrust in oral poetry
performance as well as by the interaction between poet/performer and
audience. TECON, founded in 1969, also began with productions of
a string of European plays, including The caretaker and Look back in anger.
But in 1971 it staged Antigone in '71 which stressed the theme of
resistance while in 1973 it became an all-black group, creating its own
works including Black images, a collage of music, poetry and dialogue.
However, as I have indicated, by the end of 1973 all three leaders of
TECON were banned.

One of the few – and perhaps the only – Black Consciousness plays
to survive in published form from this period is Mthuli Shezi's Shanti,
produced by PET.[17] Kavanagh writes that it was

first performed some time before September 1973. In November 1973 it was
in Soweto. On 27 November it was reported that the police had raided a
performance of the play in the 'Coloured' residential area of
Coronationville...Other performances were given in November and December near Pretoria...PET had [also] presented Shanti in Natal under the auspices
of TECON.[18]

In a series of brief sequences, Shanti depicts the love of a young
African student Thabo for Shanti, a young Indian woman, his unjust
imprisonment, and his escape to join a resistance movement in pre-
independent Mozambique where he dies. The play draws on central
tenets in Black Consciousness thinking, attempting in the context of
the (white) apartheid system to construct blacks as unified subjects of
history. Koos, a 'coloured' in the play, addresses the audience in a
significant speech at one point to argue of Indians, 'coloureds' and
blacks, 'Are we three not the components of Blacks?/Are we not all
Black, who shouldn't only be proud/but who should also guard
against contamination by induced inferiority complex?' (p. 72). Many
of the sequences in the play are designed in this way to attack defeatism
and continuing psychological subjection to prevailing discourse. Thus
Shanti maintains to Thabo, who has confessed as a result of police
harassment to an impulse to give up his activism, that his manhood
depends upon his readiness to demand 'your rights in a legal or
recognised method' (p. 73) and his readiness, not to 'wait for the
crumbs falling from the master's table' (p. 74) but to negotiate with

the white oppressor as an equal. In his writings Steve Biko had called for 'a very strong grass-roots build up of black consciousness such that blacks can learn to assert themselves and stake their rightful claim', and condemned the liberals whose protests, he observed, 'are directed at and appeal to white conscience, everything they do is directed at finally convincing the white electorate that the black man is also a man and that at some future date he should be given a place at the white man's table'.[19] Developing similar notions in a prison scene, a prisoner exclaims 'My Black brothers, have pride in yourself! Fight what afflicts you! Stem our racism, improve your lot! Go to the whiteman's table, discuss as equals, but take not their silver – for then you shall have dug a pit of suffering for all Blacks' (p. 77).

Certain critics have nevertheless pointed out that the appeal for black unity in the language of Shanti fails to take into account social and economic differences in the various black groups it sought to unite.[20] Again, Thabo, who has been unjustly imprisoned, escapes and leaves South Africa to fight in the liberation struggle in Mozambique, and the second half of the play stresses the need for armed insurgency. But when it was written and performed, attempts by organisations such as the ANC to infiltrate South Africa in alliance with the Zimbabwe African People's Union had collapsed.[21] From this point of view, it may be argued that taken literally the presentation in Shanti of Thabo's response to his situation is, as Kavanagh maintains, pure fantasy[22] – a consequence of PET's own class-bound petit-bourgeois vision. Members of PET were drawn from a student and professional elite: Shezi was president of the SRC at the University of Zululand, Sadicque Variava was a teacher and Vusi Khumalo was a journalist.

Nevertheless, it must be remembered that the liberation struggle in Angola and Mozambique was a source of inspiration and encouragement within South Africa. SASO and the BPC called for Viva Frelimo rallies in September 1974 to celebrate Machel's victory in Mozambique, despite government banning orders. Moreover, as Shava has observed, the play was powerfully contentious in raising a revolutionary situation at all, although he acknowledges that the spectre of state censorship must have resulted in the suppression of any direct reference to a South African revolution.[23] From this point of view, if Shanti moves from, in the first half of the play, concern with some of the psychological and linguistic mechanisms of oppression in South Africa to, in the second half of the play, a more metaphoric and symbolic use of the image of resistance, it continues to contest by means of this shift the images of defeat and passivity imposed upon the oppressed classes within prevailing discourse. And what has been alleged in other respects to be its *petit-bourgeois* position should at the same time be set against Tom Lodge's observation about Black Consciousness that 'merely because its exponents and identifiable followers were relatively socially privileged and hence unrepresentative of the black community as a whole did not mean they were not popularly influential...student advocates of Black Consciousness were to become school teachers, priests and journalists, and its basic themes were taken up in the popular press, in township cultural events, and even, though at a later stage, in African consumer-oriented advertising'.[24]

In its theatrical techniques, too, *Shanti* worked to construct a more aggressive and non-conforming version of the oppressed subject. Amongst its other objectives, PET was concerned to disrupt traditional South African theatre convention.Thus although *Shanti* may be said to adhere in many of its scenes to conventional realism, in the traditions of performances of Black Consciousness poetry and audience participation it mingles such scenes frequently with forms of song and poetic address that express viewpoints directly to the audience. Indeed many of the moments of conventional realism in the play prove to be only token or strategic, providing the opportunity for the activation of a different kind of dramatic encounter. Lacking concern for any extended examination of interiority they are aimed at swiftly positioning the audience so that they may perceive the significance of the experiences presented on stage predominantly in terms of Black Consciousness.

Such frequent breaks with the conventions of realism were consciously perceived by these practitioners as a means of rejecting what they saw as the staid techniques of a white theatre for a more revolutionary kind of drama. Their style of address at such moments is accordingly sometimes that of the slogan, or the direct statement. For instance, a central prison scene offers an extended ritualised critique of the social order during which one prisoner strongly counteridentifies white ruling-class discourse, as well as its practice, directly to the audience, and all the prisoners argue for resistance:

SECOND PRISONER: In all seriousness, whites are thugs, knaves, criminals. How can they justify their methods of exploitation? How can they justify their having used us in mines, industries and roads, to build the proud cities of this land? And then kick us out to go and start afresh in the Bantustans? To the whiteman, the Blacks are nothing but tools. The Blacks are used as tools, they are used as hard as tools, they are broken as tools and later thrown about like toys…How can the whites expect us to love them when we have turned both cheeks and at each turn they have slapped us.

ALL: Stand united, fight united, bring sense to the oppressor! (p. 78)

As Kavanagh points out, the directness of what often reads as simple sloganeering on the written page should not be taken as a sign of dramatic ineffectuality. When uttered to an audience in ways that locate them, together with the actors, within an oppressive social order and in ways that also contest the discourse and actions of the dominant classes, such language itself contributes to a conflict in which the South African state becomes one of the primary participants, and against which the language of dramatic characters and actors addressing the audience thrust.

The influence of the Black Consciousness movement in theatre as well as in poetry and the new modes of performance poetry exploring it, contributed to the recognition particularly amongst other theatre practitioners, that theatre space might be recovered by the oppressed classes for their own use in political struggle. This led TECON in 1973 to bar all whites from attending its performances, and together with other Black Consciousness theatre groups to rule out all collaboration with whites. Such actions were one manifestation of a continuing battle in South Africa to wrest theatre back from the control of the ruling classes.

III Representing apartheid: *Sizwe Bansi is dead* and *The island*

In *Boesman and Lena*, the old black man does not speak. His death in an open field suggests the extreme indifference of the apartheid system towards its victims. But Fugard recognised that the silences and absences denoted by his presence in the play needed to be filled. The completion of *Boesman and Lena* was followed in the early 1970s by his collaboration with John Kani and Winston Ntshona, members of the Serpent Players, the company with whom he worked throughout the 1960s. Together, the three produced *Sizwe Bansi is dead* in 1972 and *The island* in 1973.[25] *Sizwe Bansi is dead* made an enormous impact upon its audiences and was itself influential in encouraging the realisation that theatre space might be used to present oppressed class subjects and experience. Kani and Ntshona also provided continual demonstration of oppressed class empowerment within the theatre, something Kente had in other ways achieved in the late 1960s, and something which adherents of Black Consciousness in their own particular way, were urging.

Both Sizwe Bansi is dead and The island are powerfully concerned to show in what ways the oppressed subject is structured and constructed by the apartheid state. Sizwe Bansi is dead explored, in the increasingly fluid context of the early 1970s, the problem of the pass laws while The island, one of many plays that then and since has focused significantly in one way or another on the South African penal institution, examined aspects of the judicial and prison systems in South Africa. These were endeavours to comprehend – again in Philip Fisher's phrase[26] – 'nearly ungraspable' processes involving labour and involving government by means of arrest and detention.

The collaboration of Kani, Ntshona and Fugard, which itself transgressed apartheid laws insisting on segregation in theatre, was to provide a new impetus to South African theatre, showing the value of group improvisation and workshop for South African theatre practitioners coming from different spaces and classes and isolated from one another through apartheid legislation. The workshop situation helped to remove barriers to knowledge and understanding about that social order which they were trying to represent on stage. As important, in Sizwe, and in much that was to follow it, the traditional reliance on the South African stage upon techniques of naturalism and realism, the dependence upon the proscenium arch so crucial, in Boal's terms, to bourgeois theatre, was disrupted. As Fugard's diaries show, he was, together with his collaborators and others, consciously seeking new modes of theatre, and particularly concerned with the need to address the audience more directly. In June 1970 he notes:

For the Group. We have reached an impasse, a reality which has only got the two-dimensions of an 'idea', of the intellect. The reality of a truly living moment in theatre (actors in front of an audience) must involve the whole actor, be a whole act in order to involve them wholly…We have been illustrating an idea – not creating a new, uniquely theatrical reality…Addressing the audience – arrogance? Pride. How, sincerely, do we want to 'talk' to them.[27]

In Sizwe, Styles's initial improvised sequence, usually with repeated reference to a newspaper published on the day of each performance, broke down this barrier immediately, one further disrupted by the narratives he proceeds to offer directly to the audience about his past, and again, significantly undermined by the occasional use of the actors' own names during the dramatisation of the exploitation of workers. Such direct communication with the audience links the enacted drama to actors and audience, and situates all, in turn, directly within processes within which they are lodged in common. Similarly, in *The island*, in the play's final moments when Wilson uses his role as Antigone to address the putative audience of prisoners and warders directly – who are also the theatre audience – the step he takes towards the audience breaks the realism and naturalism upon which until then this particular play has largely relied. Moving away from metaphoric use of the Antigone story, this technique helps the play to point towards – even if it does not fully analyse – the state's actual practice within the social order which audience and actors/devisors of the play inhabit.

In September 1970 Fugard again addressed the attempt to find an awareness of a new kind of theatre:

First real 'move' came out of talking to Y. We were discussing Grotowski's idea in *Towards a poor theatre* of the actor/spectator relationship in space being special and unique for each of his productions ... Parallel with our exploration ... Y and I embarked on a long dialogue as to why she as an actress and myself as writer and director were turning our backs on the securities and orthodoxies of our past work...The issue on my side was simply this: Did the sort of play I had been writing with its central dependence on logical and chronological sequence (mechanical linkage) give me a chance of communicating my sense of self and the world as experienced by that self. Was I experiencing the world in the fashion and logic of an alphabet (A followed by B followed by C followed by D...followed by Z full stop) or was I experiencing self and the world rather like somebody spinning the dial on the short-wave band of a transistorised radio...not just a question of efficiency either but of a new 'mode', a new 'way' of getting information across to someone else.[28]

The departure from the technique of realism that results from the swift change of roles all played by the same actor, in *Sizwe*, to accord – again against traditional stage conventions – with swift changes in stage narrative, enables the presentation of a variety of characters situated within conditions of oppression, exploitation or struggle. This technique, complemented by the image of Buntu and Sizwe working together for survival, evokes a sense of a common bond against the apartheid process amongst the members of the oppressed classes.

Through the narrative and enacted reminiscences of the photographer Styles and then Sizwe Bansi, who comes to have his photograph taken, *Sizwe* dramatises aspects of the black struggle to survive within the apartheid system. The discovery of a dead body enables Sizwe Bansi, using the dead man's pass, to find employment, support his rural dependants, and avoid endorsement out of his urban area. But at the same time the extent to which the apartheid state constructs the labouring subject in terms of absence is demonstrated in a brutal decoding of the traditional 'Jim comes to Joburg' theme.[29] In a series of extended dramatised narratives, sharpened by satirical point and humour, Styles conveys the filthy working conditions of the Ford factory, the lack of safety regulations, and exploitative labour hours. The play goes on to recognise the way in which labour is controlled through the use of labour bureaux and elaborate procedures (which often impede the acquisition of valid permits), the use of hostels and the fragmentation of families. Buntu's enactment of the funeral oration of Outa Jacob (pp. 27-8), presents at length a tale of migrancy, landlessness and vulnerability that points, moreover, to the underlying structures created by legislation such as the Land Act of 1913 and the Hertzog Bills of 1936, determining Outa Jacob's situation, of which too, Sizwe Bansi himself, with his family in King Williamstown, are further casualties.

Dramatisation of the dehumanisation in the structuring of the apartheid subject comes to chilling climax in the scene where Sizwe has to memorise the number in Robert Zwelinzima's passbook, the new 'identity' that will give him the ability to work in the city. This foregrounds the extent to which his significance for the apartheid state resides solely in his body as unit of labour and source of exploitable energy, to be registered, with disregard for his family, and with crucial indifference to what the play shows are to the state interchangeable subjects, identifiable by their pass numbers alone.

Against this process, the text draws sporadically upon essentialist notions of the subject, in an apparent attempt to argue some means of recuperation from the processes of dehumanisation it dramatises. Thus, discovering the dead body of Robert Zwelinzima abandoned in the open, Sizwe Bansi strips himself and, in language recalling that of Shylock in *The merchant of Venice*, cries:

Would you leave me lying there, wet with your piss? I wish I was dead because I don't care a damn about anything any more. [*Turning away from Buntu to the audience*] What's happening in this world, good people? Who cares for who in this world? Who wants who? Who wants me, friend? What's wrong with me? I'm a man. I've got eyes to see. I've got ears to listen when people talk. I've got a head to think good things. What's wrong with me? (pp. 34-5)

Such language draws on many liberal and humanist assumptions, pursued in part in South African Liberal Party discourse which gave the individual supreme importance and stressed the same basic human rights for all without regard to race, culture, sex or creed, freedom of thought and conscience, speech and press, movement, association, and education.[30] But when *Sizwe* opened the liberal cause had been powerfully denigrated by the government and liberal politics largely suppressed. The small Liberal Party, which had been formed in 1953, and the small Progressive Party, formed in 1959, both of which championed the liberal cause during the 1960s, were obstructed by the Political Interference Act of 1968 which prohibited racially mixed political parties. While the Liberal Party had no choice but to disband, the Progressive Party decided to fight on as a single race party, but at the cost of compromising on some of its liberal principles (p. 56).

The concern in *Sizwe* to represent aspects of actual relations and material conditions within the social order may be seen as attempts at counteridentification of the claims and more usually the omissions in prevailing discourse dealing with bureaucracy, labour and land. Moreover, *Sizwe* does evidence tendencies towards militancy which were no doubt held in check for fear of censorship. Thus the play's title suggests the meaning 'the people are strong' and possibly points as well to Umkhonto we Sizwe, the armed resistance wing of the African National Congress.[31] Anger is articulated in comments such as that about Outa Jacob at his funeral, 'No matter how hard arsed the boer on this farm wants to be, he cannot remove Outa Jacob. He has reached Home' (p. 28). It is acknowledged too in the motif of exploitation and robbery, suggested not only in the description of worker conditions (pp. 3-9) but in the bitterness of Style's account of the meagre reward his father was given for serving in the South African army during the Second World War (pp.16-17), and especially in Sizwe's bitterness at the robbery involved in the creation of 'independent' homelands. These were established in the least developed and most overcrowded parts of South Africa, making altogether only a tiny percentage of the total land mass of the country:[32]

I'm telling you friend...put a man in a pondok [decrepit hut] and call that Independence? My good friend, let me tell you...Ciskeian Independence is shit! (p. 31)

Such anger culminates finally in Buntu's outburst ending, 'be a real ghost, if that is what they want, what they've turned us into. Spook them to hell, man!' (p. 38).

The island also in some senses strives for a militant counter-identification of apartheid claims to justice. It was based upon the experiences which the group had described to it by ex-political prisoners who had been imprisoned on Robben Island and the earliest versions alluded to a warder on the island directly.[33] Initially produced for limited audiences at The Space in Cape Town in 1973 before being taken abroad, it is concerned to explore the suffering of two prisoners, again, significantly called John and Winston, their rehearsals for a performance of *Antigone* to be put on before the warders and other prisoners, their reactions to the news that John is shortly to be freed, and, finally, performance of part of their version of *Antigone* itself.

It is true that in *The island's* construction of the subject, under pressure, in terms of existentialist discourse the play contributes to prison literature applicable anywhere. This discourse, which uses the bleakness of prison life metaphorically culminates in the *angst* of Winston's cry, together with his plea for witness and for support, when he realises John is to be released:

Why am I here? I'm jealous of your freedom, John. I also want to count. God also gave me ten fingers, but what do I count? My life? How do I count it, John? One...One...another day comes...one...Help me, John!...Another day....one...one...Help me, brother!...one.... (p. 72)

But, like *Sizwe*, the play manifests other tendencies that suggest a militancy against the South African social order – most evident perhaps in the appeal that Winston makes to John to help him which leads to John's reply, '*Nyana we Sizwe!*' (p. 72), the Xhosa rallying cry meaning 'son of the land' or 'people'. This relocates the two within a more specifically South African prison context and confirms that the judicial system is being used as an instrument by the ruling classes to suppress all contestatory interrogation, and all opposition. Moreover, the image of the island itself points to the real island in Table Bay. Behind Winston, and the portrayal of Antigone in the final scene, the imprisonment of Nelson Mandela and other opponents of the state is suggested. Such resonances frame Winston's movement away from his despair in the latter part of the play when in the face of his interminable sentence he still agrees to play Antigone.

But despite this, even as they attempt to counteridentify aspects of the social order evident in prevailing discourse, both *Sizwe* and *The island* are contained by tendencies to absence and avoidance, to which *Shanti* in a highly censorious and intimidatory climate, as Shava notes,[34] may also be said to be partly subject. Thus the concern in *Sizwe* with influx control, and in its early moments with poor industrial worker conditions, came, it should be noted, during a period which saw the beginnings of renewed worker struggle within the worsening economic situation. In December 1971 Ovambo workers in Namibia went on strike and 'brought the economic life of the territory to a standstill'.[35] By January over 13,000 men were out on strike. When it was over, marginal improvements in wages and improvements in some conditions – despite subsequent reverses – showed South African workers that 'strike action was possible and that concessions could be forced out of the ruling class' (p. 133). In Johannesburg a highly successful strike of bus drivers took place in June 1972. After *Sizwe Bansi is dead* opened, from October strikes spread throughout the country and over 200,000 black workers struck work during the period from January 1973 to mid-1976 (p. 133).[36]

Such developments have prompted certain critics to argue that, while Styles registers dissatisfaction with the system, *Sizwe Bansi is dead* reveals a level of consciousness about the social order that does little more than remind 'guilty liberal consciences, especially outside South Africa, that the Pass Law system is inhuman, unworkable, and absurd'.[37] Seymour maintains that 'statements on racism which ignore its class basis are not in essence radical' (p. 275) and sees Styles's decision to leave the Ford factory and to work as a photographer in his own business as an assertion of individual and petit bourgeois aspiration. This has not been the only criticism about the play. There is also no overt acknowledgement in it of the interests the pass laws served, and, from another perspective, the play's mood of anger, as the Nigerian Abiodun Jeyifous has commented, does not extend to any overt recognition of the need for resistance:

[*Sizwe Bansi is dead*] does attack certain social themes: the problem of pass carrying, the question of the extremity of economic hardships, the inequality of work conditions in South Africa, but it leaves the social situation as given without transcending it.[38]

It is, finally, undeniably true that the play's contestatory thrust is at the same time contained: if Buntu calls for opposition to the white man's racism he adds, '*Ag kak!* we're bluffing ourselves' (p. 43), when he talks of assertion of pride he continues 'If that is what you call pride, then shit on it! Take mine and give me food for my children' (p. 43), and, if he expresses anger, he also does not, in the last analysis, seem to move beyond the statement 'A black man stay out of trouble? Impossible, Buntu. Our skin is trouble' (p. 43).

But such incidents of containment and the strictures that have been levelled against the play should not diminish the important impact it had at the moment of its appearance, and the extent to which its techniques as well as its transgressive counteridentification of prevailing discourse were, for many other theatre practitioners at the time, inspiratory. Moreover, they should be set against the fact that most plays in the 1970s, although powerfully subversive were still in different ways themselves also subject to containment by powerful state hegemonic processes.

Indeed, the attempt to represent the prison system as well as the system of justice in *The island* was if anything even more difficult. *The island* draws, for the most part, on an implied assertion of a 'universal' and 'absolute' morality – in the name of which state law is condemned – that remains unexplained in social, political or material terms. Censorship may be seen to be operative here and ensures that the political position of prisoners cannot be identified and that the part played by prisons within the larger apartheid system remains unacknowledged. Legislation forbids any real discussion or representation of police and prison conditions in South Africa. But if the history of police action both in controlling the subject in South Africa and within the prisons, has been circumscribed or suppressed as much as possible by the state, it is well known that the majority of the population, for most of the twentieth century – and certainly after 1948 with the intensification of pass law legislation and labour control – have been subject at some stage in their lives to arrest, and often prosecution and a prison sentence for 'infringement' of the 'law'. For instance, bearing in mind that *The island*, was first performed in 1973, the statistics for the year 1972-73 show that an average of 1,413 trials for pass law offences took place *every day*, including Sundays.[39] Moreover, this figure represents a significant *decrease* on figures for previous years. It is well known too that, in addition to controlling the subject by means of frequent arrests consequent upon the system of influx control, the use of arrest, detention without trial and worse has become habitual practice in South Africa in the case of political opponents of the state. This tactic was frequently used and sharpened in the 1960s with the passing of several laws steadily increasing the period a detainee might be held in solitary confinement without trial.

Some attempt was made within South Africa by the *Rand Daily Mail* in the 1960s to break the silence about prison conditions – a difficult project because of legislation inhibiting any such endeavour. For instance, 'when the Prisons Department denies access to its records or unilaterally refutes the sworn testimony of prisoners or warders, newspapers can be prosecuted for publishing false or unproven material'.[40] The accounts of their prison experiences in the sixties by Ruth First, Albie Sachs and Dennis Brutus, all published in London, were banned by the South African government.[41] In 1973 the Minister of Justice, questioned in the Assembly about people detained under the Security laws said that sixteen people were detained during 1972 under the Criminal Procedure Act (which contains the 180 day clause). But, when asked about detentions under the Terrorism Act 'the Minister replied, "Except to confirm that a number of persons were arrested...during 1972, I consider it not to be in the public interest to disclose the required information."'[42] The Minister also found it necessary to add that none had died in detention.

The island attempts to imply the reality of prison conditions in the mimed opening sequence portraying the brutal daily treatment meted out to the prisoners by their warders. But the warders remain significantly absent. Such imagery, together with later references in the dialogue is the closest the text comes to an actuality that may not be admitted on stage. To take, by contrast, one random example, *The survey of race relations* in recording information about prisons for 1973 notes that on 7 October five prison warders were found guilty of assault on two prisoners 'with intent to do grievous bodily harm'. This was at a trial following the death of one of the prisoners, Mr Lucas Khoaripe:

In his summing up the judge, Mr Justice Hiemstra, said that one of the warders had accused Mr Khoaripe of having stolen some money. In an endeavour to extract a confession, warders had him dumped in a bath of water, his head being pushed under several times. Lieutenant S .L. Potgieter was present. Next day Mr. Khoaripe and a fellow-prisoner were assaulted in what the judge termed a barbaric, cruel and inhuman way, and Mr Khoaripe died as a result. After this event, Lieutenant Potgieter had been promoted to the rank of captain. The judge said, 'This exposes a cynicism on the part of the prison authorities which I cannot condemn strongly enough'...No one was so naive, he said, as to believe that these assaults were an isolated instance. Had the prisoner not died, nothing would have been disclosed outside the prison walls. Three of the warders were jailed for 18 months each, the others being given suspended sentences...Replying to questions in the Assembly on 15 October, the Minister of Justice said that at the time when Captain Potgieter was promoted, no adverse information about him had been known. A letter had been sent to all commanding officers, he stated, strongly condemning assaults and unworthy behaviour in general, and drawing attention to standing orders and previous circulars on these subjects...Between 1 January and 30 September...there had been 230 departmental investigations into allegations of assault by warders. Of these, 117 were deemed unfounded, 11 cases were referred to the police and the rest had been or were being dealt with by the department. Forty people had thus far been found guilty and 15 acquitted. Members of the Opposition called for a judicial inquiry into prison conditions, but the Minister said that such an inquiry would take at least six years to complete, during which time the whole question of jails would be sub judice.[43]

This is to note nothing of the terrible psychological as well as physical dangers to which political prisoners have been and continue to be subject in South Africa. And over the history and present functioning of state policing and state prisons in South Africa, the shadow of Steve Biko and the scores of other political prisoners who have died in prison will always fall. As recently as two weeks after the release of Nelson Mandela from prison the newspapers were full of reports of the testimony of prisoners as to the torture and death of a young boy in prison. And The Weekly Mail noted on 23 February 1990 that six people had died in police custody in the previous month.[44]

IV Subversion and containment in Not his pride

Some of the strictures offered by certain critics about Sizwe may be recalled in the context of another play appearing a year later, this time by Makwedini Julius Mtsaka, a member of the oppressed classes who was born in 1944 to working parents in Duncan Village a township near East London. In his play Not his pride, too, the difficulties in contesting prevailing discourse are suggested.[45] The legislation on the homelands of the 1970s a further feature of government policy, about which Sizwe Bansi is so caustic, included the assertion that every black was a citizen of the new proposed bantustans.[46] With the legislated independence of each bantustan – organised on ethnic lines to maximise the chances of dissension within the black population – the blacks concerned would cease to be citizens of South Africa. This encouraged the illusion that there would eventually be no black South Africans only migrant labourers (with little or no rights) from other 'countries'. As part of this project the policy of removals, noted in the last chapter, was implemented, involving the resettlement of large numbers of the population from what were deemed 'black spots' in white areas to undeveloped areas in the homelands as well as elsewhere.

Mtsaka's birthplace Duncan Village, like many other parts of South Africa was subject to this policy. Platzky and Walker, writing in 1985 note that 'over the past twenty years the government...has moved 80,000 people out of Duncan Village...to Mdantsane'.[47] Not his pride confronts the audience with a partly demolished township, one, in other words, situated within this process. The main concern of the play is to explore Meko's claims for compensation for one of the houses still standing. In the course of the play he discovers that he was born out of wedlock. Despite the promised support his father's brother Palamente gives him in return for a bribe, he loses his claim to any inheritance to the woman Noqwashu whom his father, after he was born, went on to marry. At the end of the play all Meko receives is his father's empty scoff tin which he compares to the emptiness of the 'gift' of Transkei homeland independence to blacks.

Not his pride attempts to suggest the way in which government policies have broken family life. It portrays the three dramatic characters moreover, not only as victims of these policies but, as well, shows how their predicament in no way protects them from their own self-seeking behaviour. Thus Noqwashu resorts to cheating in the play and Palamente, perhaps intended to anticipate or suggest at times in his behaviour the expedience of those blacks who co-operated with the homelands policy, follows his own vested interest in both giving and withdrawing allegiance.The language of the play is frequently characterised by a measure of sarcasm and irony about the process to which the protagonists, – and their people – are subject.

But, at the same time, the text reveals itself at least as subject to pressures towards containment as Sizwe. Apart from the power of censorship, this may result from the fact that Mtsaka, after failing to find the capital to produce a musical version of his play for the townships, wrote Not his pride for performance in front of largely white audiences on English-speaking campuses throughout the country – although it did in the end have two township performances. The play is concerned primarily with mere description of and information about those processes to which its dramatic characters are subject. Indeed, as in the case of The Kimberley train, it depends upon the simple revelation of plot for its momentum – upon the uncovering of details of family history. Furthermore, the expression of bitterness at the details and conditions registered in this play is, like *Sizwe Bansi is dead*, not accompanied by any movement into overt acknowledgement of the need for resistance. And perhaps most interesting is the extent to which the protagonist's search for identity is conceived of in familial terms and as a means to the inheritance of compensation for confiscated property, an emphasis repeated in the recognition of self-interest in the other characters. In this, it might be argued, again from the perspective of more radical forms of discourse, the play presents or constructs the subject in a way that is complementary to the emphasis in prevailing discourse upon divisive and ethnic structurations which encourage doctrines of privatisation – all the while discouraging any current arguments stressing the need for unified action.

A similar presentation of the subject may, finally, be found in Fugard's other play written during this period, *Statements after an arrest under the immorality act*, performed first in London in 1974, although earlier versions of it had been attempted within South Africa.[48] While it is not concerned extensively with prison life, it does explore the policing of the body within the South African social formation, a concern first raised in *The blood knot*. The play presents a relationship that defies government legislation about sexual behaviour, and in its second half the state's discovery of the naked lovers and its persecution of them is enacted on stage. Their dehumanisation is suggested in the projection on stage, too, of photographs of their exposed bodies, the statements they are forced to give to their interrogators and the way in which the police, in turn, define them. But the text seeks more determinedly essentialist and existentialist discourse here; instead of the sense of commonality in struggle which perhaps Kani and Ntshona had brought to *The island*, both lovers are, under the relentless policing of the state, presented as in an alien prison world, separated, alone and broken. Still, *Statements*, together with *Sizwe* and *The island* may be said powerfully to foreground examples of ways in which the state, in its bid to construct submissive, dehumanised subjects of apartheid laws, ruthlessly works to constrict the possibility of multiple subjectivities and endeavours to suppress or incarcerate all difference.

V Representing resistance in the townships: *Too late*

The brief period in the townships when the theatre of Black Consciousness struggled against state harassment and suppression to find space for itself, was not of course the only kind of theatre to be found in township space in the early 1970s. Indeed, as chapter 4 indicated and as Coplan notes, from the 1960s on

an autonomous, community-based black show business again began to flourish in the very teeth of apartheid. Its medium was musical theatre, and its exponents made it a major cultural force in the 1970s...[Kente] kept admission prices and expenses low, establishing a circuit of seemingly endless one-night appearances in township halls all over the country. By 1974 he had three travelling companies and was paying actors between 25 and 50 [pounds] a week.[49]

Sam Mhangwane and Solly Meko were other exponents of this genre. Kente himself, in the early 1970s, began to respond to the growing politicisation of theatre by trying in his new plays to represent current power relations and the impulse to resistance. In this he was partly inspired too by the work of Fugard, Kani, and Ntshona. He produced How long, I believe and Too late, 'a series of political melodramas between 1974 and 1976... that squarely placed the blame for the suffering and squalor of the townships on apartheid, while compassionately heroising the resilience, vitality and essential humanity of their people'.[50] Of these three plays, the one with the greatest populist appeal was Too late – the only one to date to have been published.[51] Immensely successful with township audiences, despite its conclusion – again, perhaps, with an eye upon state censorship – in a 'moderate' plea for reform, it was perceived by the authorities as sufficiently contestatory in performance to warrant its banning. It juxtaposes images of ordinary everyday township life with frequent enactments of police harassment that in almost every scene repeatedly interrupt and impede the dramatic action. Images of police violence – the murder of a young courageous crippled girl who tries to resist police brutality – counter-identify the state's claims that the police presence in the township ensures order, and encourage an impulse to resistance which is not only voiced but, innovatively for the South African stage, enacted several times in the play. Furthermore, the episodes of prayer, song and dancing, which interrupt, accompany and complement the dramatic action – often in content interrogative of the status quo, of qualities of patience and endurance in the face of the system's violence – repeatedly reinforce the assertion of an energetic township unity and commonality in the face of repression.

Significantly, Kente, particularly in his dramatisation of police violence and episodes of resistance, and despite his moderate position, seems to have won much greater township support than either the work of Black Consciousness theatre practitioners, or Fugard, Kani and Ntshona. Thus David Coplan, recording some of the objections which he encountered from blacks to *Sizwe*, notes

Black playgoers...complain that despite the high quality of *Sizwe* and the strength of its protest against homeland policy, influx control, and the pass laws, it is too complex in structure and expression, too 'talky', and too unmusical – in short, too Western in form – to be worth seeing more than once. As one theatrical promoter in Port Elizabeth told me, Africans might return any number of times to Kente's *How Long*, but *Sizwe* is not 'a renewable experience'.[52]

VI Attempting an alternative discourse: *Survival*

Numerous other theatrical projects were undertaken in the early 1970s including Sol Rachilo's *The township wife* (1972) and Sidney Sepamla's *Cry yesterday* (1972).[53] The Shah Theatre Academy formed in Durban in the 1960s by Ronnie Govender, Muthal Naidoo and Bennie Bersee, continued to stage plays including some of Ronnie Govender's own works, up to the 1980s (p. 79). Again, as had already been the case in earlier decades, a number of plays drew upon black traditions. In 1973 Workshop 71 performed Credo Mutwa's *uNosimela* which explores the odyssey of its central character from her pre-mythical birth, and traditional way of life to her life as a prostitute in Hillbrow, Johannesburg (pp. 83-5). Three years earlier, Welcome Msomi, collaborating with Elizabeth Sneddon director of the Theatre Workshop Company in Durban and Peter Scholz produced *Umabatha*, a Zulu version of *Macbeth* which was performed both in South Africa and at the World Theatre Season in London in 1972 (p. 78). Elliot Mkhonto, in Cape Town in 1972 with *Alukho ndlela mbini* and later Elliot Ngubane in Durban in 1979 with *Isanusi* also tried to develop dramas showing the clash between traditional cultures and urbanisation (pp. 81-2). Of such attempts the most exploitative and notorious was *Ipi-tombi*, devised by Bertha Egnos, which first appeared in 1974 and eventually supported three touring companies abroad. Its popularity was not affected by its gross misrepresentations of the cultures and processes it presented, but despite its commercial success, black participants in the venture were continually underpaid and exploited.[54]

Coplan notes that 'the real spirit of *King Kong*, of interracial artistic collaboration... has lived on in the productions of a "fringe circuit" of university and "off-Broadway" companies and theatres in Johannesburg, Cape Town and other cities' (p. 219). He notes the endeavours of Dorkay House's Phoenix Players to produce Phiri, an African jazz musical which placed Ben Jonson's *Volpone* in a township setting (pp. 219-20). Workshop 71 made a similar attempt with their first play *Crossroads* which also presented *Everyman* in township terms. Because of the closing of the Bantu Men's Social centre, Phiri opened at Witwatersrand University but it was not well received. Phoenix Players also in 1972 sponsored Corney Mabaso's *Black and Blue, Isuntu* – 'a "traditional" stage musical that later toured Japan as *Meropa* and London as *KwaZulu*'(p. 220) – and promoted the first Johannesburg performances of *Sizwe Bansi is dead* (p. 220). But the disappointment over Phiri as well as other factors led to its eventual demise together with cessation of theatrical activities at Dorkay House. Nevertheless, other inter-racial ventures were undertaken. The Inkhwezi Players, 'a Black theatre group founded in Grahamstown in 1974, was recruited by Don Maclennan, a white lecturer at Rhodes', and The Imitha Players were 'founded in East London in 1970 by Skhala Xinwa and Rob Amato'.[55] These groups staged European works as well as works by Soyinka.

Some of these collaborative groupings, emerging and functioning in the early 1970s may be said to recall in some respects Freire's description of periods of transition, although these refer to the colonial situation in South America and the practice of colonial power elites:

once the cracks in the structure begin to appear, and once societies enter the period of transition, immediately, the first movements of emergence of the hitherto submerged and silent masses begin to manifest themselves...In the transitional process, the predominantly static character of the 'closed society' gradually yields to a dynamism in all dimensions of social life. Contradictions come to the surface, provoking conflicts in which the popular consciousness becomes more and more demanding...groups of intellectuals and students who themselves belong to the privileged elite, seek to become engaged in social reality, tending to reject imported schemes and prefabricated solutions. The arts gradually cease to be the mere expression of the easy life of the affluent bourgeoisie, and begin to find their inspiration in the hard life of the people.[56]

At the same time, however, it is interesting to note Nolotshungu's observations on the extent to which attempts at counter-discourses in South Africa at this time did not allow for the possible exploration of alternative socialist discourses. He argues that in South Africa 'the character of the state conditions not only the terms of domination and submission but also the ideologies and political behaviour that challenge and reject it'.[57] In the context of Black Consciousness, for instance, Nolutshungu suggests that, especially in the early years, although the 'desire to restore the black person to a fuller humanity also testified to a radical unease with capitalism... there was no reference to Marxist ... ideas.in any but a very few cases' (p. 155-6). The alternative to capitalism was envisaged variously as entailing some kind of 'pristine African communalism', only for some 'a euphemism for socialism' (p. 156). Thus the constitution of the subject in Black Consciousness thinking entailed the amalgamation of a variety of notions which included an 'intuitive naturalism' recalling 'natural right and the light of reason which for those who were religious, was, in a quite Thomist way, also a mirror of the will of God', the existentialism of writers such as Sartre and Jaspers, and, in some cases, an interest in Black Theology (p. 156). Nolutshungu also argues that the 'poor showing of Marxism' results from the 'suppression of communism' in South Africa, preventing awareness of communist publications, what was permitted circulation in tribal colleges dominated by 'the more cerebral products of the Afrikaans universities' and the isolation of the early Black Consciousness movement from the 'extremely small pockets of neo-Marxism that continued to exist among some white intellectuals who had better access to books and publications and ideas that were forbidden in South Africa' (pp. 157-8). The rejection of apartheid capitalism in such thinking involved, then, a concentration on essences and values rather than any movement into socialist modes of discourse.

While this may be true, to some extent an attempt was made, although again, arguably contained by conditions of repression, by one of the several groups that grew out of university and fringe situations, involving a measure of collaboration, Workshop 71. In its construction of the subject, their play, *Survival*, works towards disidentification with prevailing discourse.[58] Thus the subject is constructed in ways that point towards an awareness of class and worker unity, and, although the various forms of materialist discourse to which this may relate are not openly indicated, they remain implicit in the play's argument. Again, unlike the urge in Black Consciousness to construct a unified black subjectivity, *Survival* attempts to advocate unity in struggle through the recognition of differing subjectivities. And while it also attempts to develop a discourse of resistance it argues more deliberately than either *Shanti* or *Too late* that resistance depends upon an analytic awareness of the structural mechanisms that perpetuate apartheid.

Like so many plays in the last two decades, *Survival* contributes, in its focus upon a group of prisoners in jail, to prison literature. It was produced by Robert Kavanagh/Maclaren/Mshengu, together with Dan Maredi, David Kekana, Themba Ntinga and Seth Sibanda, who were all recruited from their jobs as city workers. As I have already noted, all of these theatre practitioners now live abroad; since his voluntary exile Kavanagh, erstwhile lecturer on the English Department of Witwatersrand University for a brief period, and author of *Theatre and cultural struggle in South Africa*, has studied at Leeds, worked in Ethiopia and, at the time of writing, works in Zimbabwe. Workshop 71 devised several other significant works in the short time it operated including *Crossroads* (1971) and *uHlanga* (1975). *Survival*, produced like its predecessors in workshop, was commissioned by the Space Theatre. It opened there in May 1976, subsequently playing successfully in what was a very tense period, before large black as well as white audiences in townships and cities throughout South Africa, before leaving for a tour abroad.

Survival is built round four 'reports', presented by means of theatrical techniques first evident in *Sizwe Bansi is dead*, together with the use of song – the actors enter the theatre as themselves to introduce the roles they will assume in the narrating and enactment of the four 'reports'. While the first two work, often through sharp humour and remarkably swift subversive verbal play to expose and satirise the workings of the judicial and prison systems, as well as the alleged attempts at 'reform' allegedly undertaken by the government in the early 1970s, the final two reports more aggressively and seriously present the prison as metaphor for the South Africa of apartheid. It juxtaposes the partly narrated and partly dramatised autobiographies of two young men, Leroi Williams and Edward Nkosi. Williams, an intellectual, describes to the audience how as a result of his studies and his experiences he began to see that the small petty injustices and frustrations within the social order – many of which have been satirised in the first two reports – 'were in fact just parts of something bigger – a system':

Suddenly at obstinate moments…circumstances come together and trap a human being so tightly that for one moment the parts become the whole. Injuries in mines. No phones. No electricity. Unreasonable traffic cops. All parts – then suddenly…a whole. (p. 160)

Nkosi's story shows that it is the violation of his mother's and his own integrity, that has produced his anger, one which is, for the drama of this period, pursued innovatively – even further than the similar impulse glimpsed in Too late – to the overt expression on stage of a desire not only for resistance but for retribution. The final sequence of his tale traces, after a motor accident, his rescue of the black driver but his refusal to help the trapped white ruling-class occupants who are left to burn to death.

Having established the lawless criminality of the apartheid system itself, the dramatic dynamic of the play – its developing consciousness – moves explicitly to the need for overt resistance. At the conclusion of the third report the four prisoners address the audience directly, asserting that they are not 'criminals' as they originally proclaimed but that they are all 'against a system not of our making…Under laws not of our framing' (p. 166), offering a final angry image: 'As they move slowly forward towards the audience they utter a low, slowly rising scream of hatred' (p. 167).

If, in this dramatisation of developing consciousness about the totality of the apartheid structure, the play argues for a more analytic approach to the social order, in the final report it seems to point through the enactment of a prison hunger strike to forms of worker-determined resistance. And the portrayal of the weakening of Vusi during the strike, probes the difficulties in achieving unified action, and recognises the existence of differing and conflicting subject positions within the struggle:

This time the pressure was too much for him. He was weak. Give him your strength and he too will be heroic.

The prisoners turn their heads to the audience and sing 'Phela phela phela malanga'[let there be an end to these days]. The cell door opens. Food is brought. The ritual of rejection. Each prisoner takes the plate and tips the contents onto the floor. He clutches his stomach in pain – hunger and beatings – and falls to the ground. Vusi too rejects the food. For a short while there is silence. The prisoners lie on the floor of their cell weakly. Then there is the quiet sound of tears. One by one they cry. (p. 168)

Importantly, in all four reports, while interiority is not denied to the speakers, their identity as well as their past is presented as socially dependent: what they 'report' to one another is offered, within the framework of the play, for communal evaluation and discussion. In the final moments of the play the actors step out of their roles again and, in their own capacities, discuss the parts they have played, communicating their personal attitudes to the narratives they have enacted for

the audience. By these means, as well as in its awareness of the social
context of language and action, the play's links with its audience is
underlined. And in this constitution of the subject as socially
positioned rather than privatised, also, Survival determinedly seeks
disidentification:

THEMBA: A people survive by grimly holding on. But at the same time they
achieve what their oppressors cannot help envying them for. The strength lies
with the people, who carry with them in their lives the justification for the
struggle – the victory that is...
ALL: SURVIVAL! (p. 170)

Nevertheless, it should finally be added that if Survival seems, remarkably and in some respects innovatively, to encourage the
construction of the subject not only in terms of a discourse of
resistance, but in ways that at least hint at the need for class analysis,
worker unity, industrial action, it still works with the jail strike as
metaphor to imply this. This strategy may itself suggest the difficulties
of transgression, the effects of the continuing grip on the country of
censorship, which, as Albert Gerard even as recently as 1981 argued,
seems still to be such 'that no writer can possibly permit himself to
deal with either the principles or the realities of South African society
in a spirit of serious, not to mention critical, analysis'.[59]

VII Emerging syncretisms

Coplan, writing on the township style of drama, notes that 'despite the
widespread use of tsotsitaal and urban dialects of Zulu, Sotho and Xhosa
in the townships, playwrights almost always write in English,
interlarded with jokes, exclamations, song texts and throwaway lines
in a variety of African languages and polyglot slang'.[60] He comments
also on the emergent syncretism evident in some of the dramatic
productions of the 1970s: 'The township performance aesthetic
...blended with European modes of theatrical expression and techniques as in Sizwe Bansi is dead and...Survival to gain acceptance outside
the townships' (pp. 214-15). While attempts have been made by
critics to privilege one or other stream of theatre activity in the 1970s
as key to subsequent development, beyond recognising in this way that
a rich syncretism appeared to be emerging during this period, lack of
evidence makes further theorising largely speculative. For instance, the

didactic powers of Black Consciousness theatre were an important source of inspiration, but apart from our knowledge that Tecon, Pet and Mdali, operated, and apart from well-trodden paths in scholarship recounting their activities, almost no script, except for *Shanti* has been published. Moreover the constitution of their audiences, and their numbers, remain uncertain. State suppression of Black Consciousness theatre most certainly marginalised further what might otherwise have perhaps won greater exposure and had even greater influence. Again, the immense success of Kani, Fugard and Ntshona and their indubitably important development of workshop techniques must be set against the scepticism of some township voices regarding aspects of their work. And Kente's township theatre continued to win larger audiences than anyone else, despite its exaggerated melodrama, and sporadic tendencies to 'moderation'. Furthermore, Workshop 71's *Survival*, combining the techniques of workshop, the didactic thrust of Black Consciousness theatre, and elements of township theatre was itself a highly important moment in South African theatre. Shezi, Kente, Fugard, Kani, Ntshona, and Workshop 71 all struggled, in the context of the heightened awarenesses and increasingly courageous movement into open confrontation with the state unfolding in the social order in the 1970s, to transgress significantly pressures to silence and conformity. But, as I have tried to suggest, none of these theatrical practitioners seems to have been entirely immune from the state's determined and often violent bid for hegemony, manifest in one or other way in occasional avoidances or apparent absences in each text. And, as I have indicated, determined ever more brutally to repress all opposition and difference, the state was not to tolerate, without interference, much of their work for very long.

Notes

1 Brickhill, J. and Brooks, A., *Whirlwind before the storm: the origins and development of the uprising in Soweto and the rest of South Africa, June-December, 1976*, London: International Defence and Aid Fund for South Africa, 1980, p. 274.
2 Coplan, *In township tonight!*, p.184.
3 For what follows see Coplan, *In township tonight!*, p.224 and the account in Kavanagh, *Theatre and cultural struggle*.
4 Coplan, *In township tonight!*, p.224.
5 Steadman, 'Drama and social consciousness', pp. 463-5.
6 Kavanagh, *Theatre and cultural struggle*, pp. 121-2.
7 Larlham, *Black theatre, dance and ritual*, p. 66; Coplan, *In township tonight!*, p. 211.

8 Astbury, Brian, The space/Die ruimte/Indawo, March 1972-September 1979, Cape Town: Brian Astbury, 1979, unnumbered pages under account Sizwe Banzi is dead.

9 Coplan, In township tonight!, p. 215.

10 Accounts of Black Consciousness, on which the following is based, may be found in Kavanagh, Theatre and cultural struggle, Lodge, Black politics, and in Hirson, Baruch, Year of fire year of ash, London: Zed, 1979.

11 Nolutshungu, Sam C., Changing South Africa, Cape Town: David Philip, 1983, p. 149.

12 Shava, A people's voice, p. 98.

13 Emmet, Tony, 'Oral, political and communal aspects of township poetry in the mid-seventies', in Chapman, Michael, Soweto poetry, Johannesburg: McGraw-Hill, 1982, p. 177.

14 Gwala, M. Pascal, 'Towards a national theatre', South African Outlook, CIII, 1227, 1973, pp. 132-3.

15 Coplan, In township tonight!, p. 223.

16 Larlham, Black theatre, dance and ritual, p. 76 from which these and the following details are taken.

17 Shezi, Mthuli, Shanti, in Kavanagh, Robert Mshengu, South African people's plays, London: Heinemann, 1981.

18 Kavanagh, Theatre and cultural struggle, p.170.

19 Biko, Steve, I write what I like, London: Bowerdean Press, 1978, pp. 21-2.

20 The importance of such differences is argued by writers such as Kavanagh and Hirson.

21 See Lodge, Black politics, p. 297ff.

22 Kavanagh, Theatre and cultural struggle, p. 172ff.

23 Shava, A People's voice, pp. 140-2.

24 Lodge, Black politics, p. 324.

25 Fugard, Athol, Sizwe Bansi is dead and The island, in Statements: three plays, Oxford: Oxford University Press, 1978.

26 Fisher, Hard Facts, p.3.

27 Fugard, Notebooks, p. 186.

28 Fugard, Notebooks, pp. 188-90.

29 See Shava, A people's voice, pp. 132-6; the point is also helpfully made in an unpublished article by Pechey, Graham, 'Fire with your pen: cultural struggle in South Africa 1906-1976'.

30 See Leatt, James, Kneifel, Theo, Nurnberger, Klaus, Contending ideologies in South Africa, Cape Town: David Philip, 1986, pp. 53-4.

31 See Cosmo Pieterse in a panel discussion in Lindfors, Berth, Contemporary black South African literature: a symposium, Proceedings of the First Annual Meeting of the African Literature Association, 20-22 March 1975, The University of Texas, Washington: Three Continents Press, 1985, p. 119.

32 See Platzky and Walker, The surplus people, p. 16, 37.

33 See Walder, Dennis, Athol Fugard, London: Macmillan, 1984, p. 77ff., 87ff.

34 Shava, A people's voice, p. 142,

35 Hirson, Year of fire, year of ash, p. 130.

36 see also Kavanagh, Theatre and cultural struggle, p. 35.

37 Seymour, Hilary, 'Sizwe Bansi is dead: a study of artistic ambivalence', Race and class, XXI, 3, 1980, p. 284.

38 Lindfors, Contemporary black South African literature, p. 132.

39 Horrell, Muriel, Horner, Dudley and Hudson, Jane, eds., A survey of race relations, 1974 (SRR), Johannesburg: South African Institute of Race Relations, 1975, p. 171.

40 Vandenbroucke, Truths the hand can touch, p. 173; see SRR, 1974, p. 78.

41 For an account of these writers see February, Vernon, And bid him sing: essays in literature and cultural domination, London: Kegan Paul International, 1988.

42 Horrell, Muriel, Horner, Dudley, A survey of race relations in South Africa, 1973, Johan-

nesburg: South African Institute of Race Relations, 1974, p. 78.

43 Horrell, Horner and Hudson, SRR 1974, pp. 86-7.

44 The Weekly Mail, VI: 6, 23 February 1990, p. 1.

45 Mtsaka, Makwedini, Julius, Not his pride, Johannesburg, Ravan, 1978.

46 For this and what follows see Platzky and Walker, The surplus people, especially pp. 7, 16, 22, 57.

47 Platzky and Walker, The surplus people, p. 57.

48 Fugard, Athol, Statements after an arrest under the immorality act, in Fugard, Statements: three plays.

49 Coplan, In township tonight!, p. 210.

50 Coplan, In township tonight!, p. 211.

51 Kente, Gibson, Too late, in Kavanagh,ed., South African people's plays.

52 Coplan, In township tonight!, p. 215.

53 Larlham, Black theatre, dance and ritual, p. 81.

54 Coplan, In township tonight!, pp.217-19.

55 Larlham, Black theatre, dance and ritual, p. 77.

56 Freire, Paulo, The politics of education, London: Macmillan, 1985, pp. 76, 78.

57 Nolutshungu, Changing South Africa, p. 147.

58 Workshop 71, Survival, in Kavanagh, ed., South African People's plays.

59 Gerard, Albert S., African language literatures, Washington: Three Continents Press, 1981, p. 209.

60 Coplan, In township tonight!, p. 213.

7

Khalo

If, given the events of 1976-77, some of the members of Workshop 71 found it preferable, after their tour with Survival abroad, not to return to South Africa, other theatrical practitioners, some from dissenting members of the ruling classes and others from the oppressed classes, had been and were continuing on their own, or in collaboration, to produce new work. This work too attempted to contest prevailing apartheid discourse by presenting particularly ruling class subjects as lodged in conditions of extreme anxiety and uncertainty. The 1976 Uprising, a 'watershed' in South African history, had presented a new landscape to all South Africans.[1] Beginning on 16 June 1976 as a student demonstration it spread to an estimated 200 black communities throughout the country and only subsided gradually by early 1977. At its peak:

Tens of thousands of men, women and children, students, parents and workers in the black townships and ghettos... clashed regularly and ferociously with heavily-armed police... used fire to damage or destroy government buildings and vehicles. They burned down beerhalls, liquor stores, and post offices. They boycotted schools, staged massive demonstrations and marches, and organised three stay-away strikes. They closed down state-affiliated structures such as the Soweto Urban Black Councils. They attacked the homes and property of black policemen and others considered to be collaborating with the white authorities. The pinnacle of the 'June Events' was reached in the September 1976 'stay-at-home'; an enormous country- wide stoppage.[2]

The ruling classes were confronted, through these events, with a new and unprecedented image of black militancy, anger and the will to resist. Cramped and poverty-ridden but hitherto relatively submissive townships had suddenly exploded into terrains of urban violence, contestation, warfare – but for heavy police and military presence, always threatening to spill over into the privileged and white-owned suburbs of the cities. Caught off-balance, the state responded with massive arrests, detentions and military force. In addition to detaining numerous community activists and church leaders, it banned eighteen major black community, political and religious organisations in October 1977.[3] The fact that in 1977, as I indicated in chapter 6, most if not all Black Consciousness-affiliated organisations, were banned, leaders were harassed, detained or worse, together with 'the murder of Steve Biko while in police detention [all] underscored the perceived threat that Black Consciousness posed to the white authorities'.[4] Like any discourse contesting prevailing discourse within the South African social order, the phenomenon of Black Consciousness was dimly understood by most members of the ruling classes while the media tended to emphasise only its apparently racist tendencies. In the period leading up to 1976 as well as after, ruling class uncertainty was further aggravated by fears of the 'swart gevaar' or 'black danger', the anxiety about 'swamping' that decades before obsessed segregationists, and that over the years was always skilfully exploited by the Nationalists in elections – to say nothing of secret fears of retribution which the upheavals in the townships seemed to herald for the heavily-guarded and protected white urban suburbs a short distance away.

A number of plays emerging shortly before, during and after the Uprising from dissident members of the ruling classes focus primarily upon the interiority of various ruling class subjects depicted in conditions of guilt, withdrawal and impotence – well captured in the title of one play performed at the time, The fantastical history of a useless man. These plays often evidence concern about the social order, but eschew any attempt to dramatise or represent material conditions amongst the oppressed classes, who remain largely marginalised or ignored. At the same time, however, a theatre group, whose members came from both ruling and subordinate classes, the Junction Avenue Theatre Company, began to explore in its work the potentials of Brechtian epic theatre. The subsequently diverging directions taken by different members of this particular group were to lead to differing attempts in the late 1970s and throughout the 1980s to construct the subject in terms of materialist discourse and to develop what each offshoot conceived of in its own way to be contributions to the emergence of a popular and a non-racial national theatre.

I Dramas of interiority

Commercial and State subsidised theatre in 1976-77 and after, despite the explosion of indigenous theatre from the early 1970s on, remained largely indifferent to new South African work. In 1976 for instance, the only possibly contestatory South African play to be performed by the Performing Arts Council of the Transvaal (PACT) was Adam Small's *Kanna hy ko huistoe*, perhaps because it was written in Afrikaans, while in 1977 PACT risked a production of Fugard's 1965 play *Hello and goodbye*. On the other hand PACT performed in addition to Small's work eleven other Afrikaans plays, some indigenous and some in translation, while their productions in English during 1976-77 included *Boeing-Boeing*, *Our town*, *A flea in her ear*, *Scapino*, *Joseph and the amazing technicolor dreamcoat*, *Lee Harvey Oswald*, *Butley*, *London assurance*, *Blithe spirit*, *Charlie and the chocolate factory*.[5] Their record was hardly to change throughout the 1970s, or in the 1980s, although recently, token attempt has been made to provide space for more indigenous attempts, which has not, however, led to any work of note at all. Moreover, Performing Arts Councils throughout the country as well as commercial theatre continued to adhere to the segregation laws.

One of the spaces where new kinds of theatre could be attempted in the mid-1970s, as earlier, was the University of the Witwatersrand which afforded for non-racial audiences not only its Great Hall, but also a smaller theatre in the Students' Union Building called The Box, where *Sizwe Bansi is dead* first opened and The Nunnery, where the first performance of *The fantastical history of a useless man* was given in 1976. Theatre by dissident white dramatists was considerably enabled and encouraged too because of the existence of The Space in Cape Town since 1972, which also pursued a policy of non-racialism.[6] It functioned until 1979, after which Rob Amato continued to run it as The People's Space. Apart from producing Western and other plays, it promoted in the 1970s the new work of Pieter-Dirk Uys (*Selle ou storie*, *God's forgotten*, *Karnaval*) and Athol Fugard (*Dimetos*) and produced also new plays by Geraldine Aron (*Bar and ger*) and Barney Simon (*Miss South Africa*). Again, Fatima Dike's play, *The sacrifice of Kreli* was first performed at The Space – with the help of dissident members of the ruling classes, although it drew on Black Consciousness themes. *The first South African* and *Glasshouse*, her subsequent plays, were also produced there. During the 1970s, The Space made it much easier for many theatre practitioners as well as groups such as Workshop 71 to perform their work.

Other attempts to provide venues for new theatre were less successful. In Durban Kessie Govender the playwright founded The Stable Theatre which 'served as a focus for Black theatre...between 1977 and 1979'[7] and produced *The last generation* (1978) by Mobongeni Ngema and two of Govender's own plays, *Working class hero* (1979) and

The shack (1979). Larlham also notes the brief existence of the Upstairs Theatre Company in 1981 which presented *Woza Albert!*, by Ngema, Mtwa and Simon, *Vuka* by Matsemala Manaka, and *We three kings*, by Muthal Naidoo (p. 79).

At this time, one of the plays to appear by dissident members of the ruling classes was *Dimetos*.[8] Working again on his own Athol Fugard premièred it at the University of the Witwatersrand Great Hall in 1975. The play was subsequently produced at The Space as well as in Edinburgh and London. About an engineer who has withdrawn from a city, that is now in trouble and that needs him, it was highly metaphoric and allegorical and thus moves away from the concerns with the social order that Fugard's work with Kani and Ntshona particularly, had manifested. It meditates in allegorical and metaphoric vein on the significance of human creativity, understood in individualist and essentialist terms. In its concern with the need, through the act of creation, to discover a means to defy a time which 'stinks' and to seek for the creative subject, in terms of its essentialist perspective, generosity and a capacity to give without demands, obsessions, evident in *Hello and goodbye* return. Concern with Calvinism within the family unit is evident in the guilt in Dimetos's love for his daughter, in his relationship with his wife and in the need, too, for an authoritarian presence or strength within the subject – located, it is suggested, with again strong Calvinist resonances, in a mortal and corrupted world, one in which 'the smell of decay has itself started to decay' (p. 47). Although manifestly concerned to register or construct subjects full of guilt and unease, the play's allegorical context inevitably excluded any direct reference to either the oppressed classes in South Africa or the increasing ferment within the social order from which the play, in 1975, came.

By contrast, in *God's forgotten*, also produced in 1975, a play by Pieter-Dirk Uys – a writer of Afrikaans origins who studied in England before returning – which opened at the Space theatre in Cape Town, some recognition of the oppressed classes is made.[9] But, located in a futuristic, beleaguered racist state facing its own imminent collapse, Uys's play also works primarily through the allegorical and its central concern lies with the interiority of its characters – their reactions to what they perceive to be their own decline. It presents concerned subjects who express repeatedly their sense of guilt as well as culpability for what remains acknowledged only in generalised terms, to be a racist and exploitative system. The play, particularly powerful in its satirical counteridentification of ruling class attitudes – registered as evidence of blindness and hypocrisy – dramatises the responses and growing sense of private disillusion, despair and helplessness of two sisters as they confront their sense that 'we're the sad figments of our own sick imaginations' (p. 155). Uys's next play, performed first in 1977 at the Rhodes Theatre in Grahamstown after which it played in both Cape Town and Johannesburg, *Paradise is closing down*, examined the reactions to their individual predicaments after the 1976 Uprising of four white women.[10] As in the case of his earlier work, the play endeavours by means of satiric focus upon character, to chart boredom, the 'national disease' of whites and their sense that 'we're the last of the Great Blind...Nothings'(pp. 169, 161). In both plays, often sharply, Uys strives to counteridentify through this presentation of ennui and emptiness, many of the assertions made by a state that is presided over by, as one character has it, 'the Great White God on his segregated Cloud to celebrate the triumph of the Great South African Dream!'[11] *Paradise is closing down* endeavours at the same time to move, to a degree, towards recognition of material conditions – the home in which the four gather is located in what was District Six, now made available for white ownership. At the conclusion of the play a young man interrupts the gathering to ask if he may view what was in fact, before the removal, his old home. And the fact of struggle currently under way in the social order is registered briefly in heavily ironic exchanges such as :

MOLLY: What do you do for a living?
YOUNG MAN: I'm a terrorist among the high school kids.
MOLLY: You mean you...eh...go to bed with them all?
YOUNG MAN: No, I teach them to make bombs.
Molly laughs, not quite convinced
MOLLY: Yes, and the junior school kids you learn how to throw grenades.
YOUNG MAN: Stones. (p. 173)

But despite this, as in the case of his lack of a name, little else is identified in the play about this visitor, who is received by the four women with a mixture of fascination and fear that clearly points to the stereotype, deriving in part from colonialist discourse, of threatening, destructive and proto-savage presence. Although the play is aware of this stereotyping its own avoidance of, if not lack of awareness about what it presents as, to the woman, a slightly threatening but attractive, intelligently ironic presence, tends in this respect to leave the stereotype largely unchallenged.

   Paradise is closing down played at the recently opened Market Theatre in Johannesburg. This was the brainchild of Barney Simon and Mannie Manim, both devotees of the theatre who had worked with the state-subsidised Performing Arts Council of the Transvaal as well as with a variety of theatre groups including Leonard Schach's The Cockpit Players and the Phoenix Players at Dorkay House, before forming The Company in 1974. The Company was intended to be 'an independent company committed to non-racial theatre'[12] and initially it produced what were considered avant-garde plays from abroad. With the support of amongst others the Johannesburg City Council, Murray McLean, the head of the engineering group Abercom, Ian Haggie, Chairman of Haggie Rand, and John Wall, Chairman and Managing Director of Ryan Nigel, together with numerous members of the professional and business sectors of the ruling classes, the Market Theatre Complex came into being in 1976. At first its policy of an integrated theatre space contravened the Group Areas Act, but after some uncertainty the board of trustees agreed that it would from the start be a multi-racial venue. It was very soon to become not only the most well-known complex in South Africa, consisting eventually of the main Market Theatre, the Theatre Upstairs, the Laager and the Warehouse, but host to the work of innumerable South African theatre practitioners from the subordinate as well as from the ruling classes. A point of intersection for enlightened capital, ruling and subordinate class participation, offering sometimes militant and contestatory drama and sometimes more traditional Western fare – the Market Theatre provided a non-racial space to which audience and theatre practitioners might come, indeed, to which many of them might cling within an increasingly turbulent and divisive apartheid order. Whatever the contradictions that informed and inform the Market Theatre's existence – some of which I note in Chapter 8 – the kind of space it provided from the start, remains rare, one of the few places where people have been able, to an extent at least, to share a non-apartheid space and to glimpse within the space of the theatre itself, intimations of an alternative South Africa.

In 1978 Fugard's allegory of intellectual withdrawal and search for meaning in essentialist terms in *Dimetos* was paralleled by a portrait of political withdrawal in *A Lesson from aloes*, one of the many new South African plays now opening at the Market.[13] It portrays the decision of a number of activists to retire from what seems a useless struggle: although set in the early 1960s and begun then, it is significant that Fugard felt able to finish it only in the post-1976 period. Fugard's

interest in language and the privileging of literature as a means of con-
stituting identity, as well as traces of Calvinism recur in the way in
which the strongly authoritarian survivor Piet Bezuidenhout chooses
to constitute his sense of self in what is presented as a repressive world.
His concern with language is also pursued further in the exploration
of the breakdown of Bezuidenhout's wife Gladys, threatened both by
her husband's patriarchal insularity and the violent invasion of her
identity perpetrated by the state police, who have seized and read her
private diaries.

If such constructions of the subject tend to privilege essentialist and
liberal discourse in their presentation of processes of decay and decline,
this is evident too in the work of Barney Simon. His play *Cincinnati*, opening
in 1979 at the Market, is structured by a series of monologues and
vignettes delivered to the audience in the style of *Kennedy's children*, which
had been produced some years earlier also at the Market.[14] It depicts
the reactions of a number of characters from the ruling and the
subordinate classes to the closing down of a multi-racial nightclub.
They deliver the minutiae of their personal experiences as well as their
responses to the closing of the club, communicating a generalised
sense of unease, and emerge largely as passive recipients of a process
not fully understood – best suggested in the closing words of the play:
'What can we do, but see what we can, understand what we can and
follow the courage that we feel in our hearts' (p. 235).

In his later work in the 1980s Fugard continues to draw on liberal,
essentialist and existentialist discourse as a means to counteridentify
prevailing apartheid discourse, which even in Afrikaner churches up
to 1986 posited the ethical correctness of segregation. While the social
order was moving more seriously and decisively into a long, protracted
and fierce struggle, Fugard's base was becoming more and more
international and he was spending much time away from South Africa,
with access to theatres such as that at Yale, for the opening of his plays,
together with, to date, the certainty of performance not only on
Broadway but by the English National Theatre (contrasting, it is worth
noting, with the continuing unwillingness of state-subsidised theatre
in South Africa to take on South African plays in English). Nevertheless,
Fugard's own sense of place in these plays does not disappear, although
it becomes narrower in focus, directed more specifically at his own
childhood in Port Elizabeth in '*Master Harold' and the boys*, and at rural
Calvinist pressures in *The road To Mecca*.[15] While it does not marginalise
the oppressed classes, it still foregrounds and explores the interiority

of its central characters. Thus 'Master Harold' ventures into territory not often explored by white dramatists: the master/mistress-servant relationship within the domestic environment. But the dramatic characterisation of the two men who work as servants for Hal's family in the play, is presented mainly in terms of an interest in ballroom dancing and, for the most part, they prove to be a function of Hal's own growth and development, although the ballroom dancing motif is used powerfully as a metaphor as well, to point to the difficulty of survival, of dancing through the apartheid world. This is underlined in the play's poignant final image of the two men dancing with one another and achieving a moment of grace denied to them by their social context. It is denied also by the racism Hally draws upon in fear, in his anger against his own father, to exploit them. His interpellation with racist discourse, under the pressures of personal insecurity even as he struggles with different kinds of language to constitute an identity, is the focus of the play.

Fugard's interest in interiority and his privileging of art and literature as a means of self-identity within a social order through which flows the mostly repressive thrust of Afrikaner Calvinism, becomes even more prominent in *The road to Mecca*, while his recent play, *A Place with the pigs* opts again for a highly allegorical context.[16] Set in Russia after the Second World War it explores the fears of a deserter, Pavel, believed dead by his village and converted into a hero, who has been hiding in a pigsty for years. Its dramatic struggle, in Calvinist fashion, centres on Pavel's self hatred. He manages at last to leave the pigsty in which he has been hiding all this while to confront his village (and himself) with the truth, dramatising an existential struggle, that unlike the ending of *Hello and goodbye*, culminates in a hint of optimism about the individual's chance for self-redemption. Interpreted as in part an allegory of the struggle against alcoholism – the play takes Fugard the furthest away, since *Dimetos*, from the South African place, to which he endeavours to return in his most recent work, *My children, my Africa!*

II Seeking Brecht: *The fantastical history of a useless man and Randlords and rotgut*

The activity of theatrical practitioners from a variety of contexts working together in workshop to produce plays, popular in the period leading up to the 1976 Uprising, was notably pursued after 1976 by the Junction Avenue Theatre Workshop. Their first venture, however, was restricted to the participation of middle-class white dissident students and intellectuals from the University of the Witwatersrand who had begun the group. Although the title of their play *The fantastical history of a useless man* suggests, as I indicated, a response common to several other plays of the time, and although it too acknowledges a sense of impotence – 'my upbringing has taught me to avoid violence at all costs…I cannot truly comprehend the daily lives of people who constantly live in the midst of violence…the most I can do is be the least obstruction', says the young white man at the end of the play[17] – the text nevertheless develops some of the techniques and tendencies evident in the plays of Workshop 71. Also produced in workshop conditions under the direction of Malcolm Purkey, who, in the early 1970s had, significantly, been associated with Workshop 71, it was first performed in September 1976 at the Witwatersrand University Nunnery Theatre in Johannesburg. It played too in Cape Town and won support mainly from dissident white audiences who clearly identified not only with the mood it expressed but with the attempt to examine the dissident white predicament in the immediate context of the Uprising. First published in 1978, the play ran to two impressions, has been revived in performances several times and is at present out of print – unusual for a published playtext in South Africa.

The Junction Avenue Theatre Company, began a process in this play that would in their later work, draw more consciously upon various materialist and Marxist modes of discourse. Unlike the predilection for a focus upon interiority in other plays from dissident members of the ruling classes, the *Fantastical history* strives to present and explore the subject in South Africa – from Brechtian and epic perspectives – as primarily located within and affected by process. Partly using techniques suggesting the review, pastiche and the undergraduate skit, in a mood of anarchic irreverence itself unusual in the context of the ruling class's reverent and fanatical treatments of selected moments in South African history, the play charts in the first Act several crucial historical episodes culminating in a parodic lecture by an insensitive white woman at the International 'Azalea' Flower show, on the employment of gardeners. This was a rare attempt in South African drama to satirise master/mistress-servant relationships, which the Junction Avenue Theatre Company had the courage to explore more fully, in satiric vein again, in their play produced at the Market in 1980

Dikitsheneng. While Dikitsheneng was not always successful and has not been published to date, its importance as an attempt to explore, more boldly than in 'Master Harold' and the Boys, a crucial aspect of the apartheid mechanism, and the many moments of satiric potential and acuity it evidenced were missed by hostile reviewers, who were unable to stomach sarcastic and critical treatment of an aspect of middle-class South Africa for the most part suppressed in prevailing discourse.

In the second half of the Fantastical history, the play attempts more closely to explore the typical growth and education of young white South Africans. Although a concern with the inadequacy of education appears often in Kente's work such as Too late, which shows the extent to which apartheid education, designed to qualify young people for a subordinate position, has led to the disillusion of the young men in the play who have become majietas (young rebels of the townships), the Junction Avenue Theatre Company, in its desire to analyse the production of disabled and submissive white subjects in South Africa, crossed on stage into hitherto unexplored territory.

It is true that, despite the company's Brechtian aspirations, their achievement in the play is only partially successful. Most of the individual scenes do not penetrate beyond caricature to analyse, from perspectives in materialist discourse, not only the master/mistress-servant relationship in greater depth, but socio-economic elements in the production of these submissive middle class subjects. Nevertheless the directions chosen in this play proved highly significant and were pursued further in the Company's later work. After the departure of Survival abroad in 1976, Workshop 71 was forced to dissolve and several black members of the company joined the Junction Avenue Theatre Workshop, giving it a dimension and awareness which the kind of educative and cultural system within which the white members were lodged – and which their first play was so concerned to identify – prevented. Amongst other work, the group went on to devise Randlords and rotgut, largely based upon the historian Charles Van Onselen's study of the social and economic history of the Witwatersrand at the turn of the century and concerned particularly with 'the relationship between labour and liquor on the goldmines'.[18] The play, as in all Junction Avenue productions, produced in workshop, was commissioned by the first History Workshop to be held at the Witwatersrand University in February 1978, and performed in the Nunnery Theatre. It was revived, by the Witwatersrand University drama school, only in 1989-90. Randlords and rotgut, reveals a firmer grasp of the materialist discourses that underlie Brechtian devices. It presents in different scenes ruling class and working class attitudes and experience, drawing on the style of music hall as well as on epic techniques to suggest some of the ways in which social being determines consciousness. Thus the miners sing 'When we cross the river/To the white man's mine/ We assume another blanket/All that we are is left behind' (p. 82) and different episodes in the play, based upon the experiences of some of the new participants in the company, depict the way in which the miners' lives are determined by harsh working conditions and the exploitation of alcohol – as the 'Ruling Class' at one point sing 'We will lay them flat with liquor/And we'll lash them to the mines' (p. 70). Furthermore, the second act suggests that understanding of this process, for the miners becomes enabling. Against an essentialist focus on interiority and the concern in conventional bourgeois theatre with the hero, the miners in *Randlords and rotgut*, eschew individualism as a mode of consciousness and resistance and advocate instead a sense of class unity, observing 'When one man shouts they laugh. They crush a single man' (p. 102) to assert 'Together we'll win victories... Together we will stand...We will find the word that unites us, we'll discover our communal song' (p. 102) And the play ends in Brechtian fashion with a song directed at the audience to work for a shift in their consciousness as well.

III Towards a 'worker' theatre

The 1980s saw 'a growing awareness of the resilience and importance of black working class culture':

groups such as Savuka and Abafana Bomoya...spread Zulu migrant music to a white and international audience; short stories, autobiographies and poems by black workers such as Bheki Maseko, Petrus Tom and Makhulu wa Ledwaba [were] published, choirs such as Ladysmith Black Mambazo, who...always had a big reputation, [increased] their following; and no longer [were] *mbaqanga* musicians, *isishameni* dance troups, *isicathamiya* choirs and the like treated with... scorn.[19]

Perhaps complementing this process, in the late 1970s, partly out of the Junction Avenue Theatre Workshop movement a new endeavour, side by side with the growing power of the trade union movement, began which, in the course of the 1980s, attempted to constitute on stage a working-class subject in terms of materialist and Marxist discourses, one that might facilitate and enable confrontation with prevailing discourse and state. At The Space in Cape Town in 1978, Imfuduso, produced by the women of Crossroads to dramatise their predicament in a squatter township under great pressure, was particularly well received. Brian Astbury describes his encounter with it:

We were told of 'Imfuduso' by Sue Williamson of the Women for Peace Movement. A play that had grown spontaneously from a community with no previous theatrical experience or urge…they staged six performances at The Space. It was very exciting and very moving. Not so much because of its quality as a piece of 'theatre' but rather because of its very existence – because the community had decided that theatre was the best means of conveying its message to the world.[20]

Playing again at the Market in 1979, it was an important but relatively isolated incident in community if not specifically working-class theatre. But in 1979 the Junction Avenue company was asked to produce a short play entitled Security to raise money in support of a strike by the Food and Canning Workers Union. Then the following year, during a strike at the Rely Precision Foundry on the East Rand, the assistance of Halton Cheadle, a lawyer, was sought to help defend some of the arrested strikers most of whom, migrant workers from KwaZulu, belonged to the Metal and Allied Workers Union.[21] Cheadle, 'found it absolutely impossible to take statements', and, in his own account:

Each of the 55 arrested workers had a different version of what took place…I set up a role play and cast one of the workers as the manager. The manager would come in and no sooner than he opened his mouth, one of the 'workers' said: 'No he didn't say that. Remember he said this…' And what happened was that they collectively reconstructed the incident…We also re-enacted the strike itself. They acted out the dancing and what actually happened when the Department of Labour arrived and tried to speak to the workers. I didn't realise what they had done. No-one had told me of this incident in their statement. Then we acted out the strike because I wanted to know what the Department of Labour had said and how the workers had responded. (p. 23)

Cheadle with a transcript of his role-plays approached a member of the Junction Avenue Theatre Club, Ari Sitas and together they formed a workshop with some of the dismissed foundry workers:

To give you an idea of who these labourers were: they were migrant workers; they were illiterate and one of them said he had never seen a play in his life. Later he recalled that he had indeed seen one, but this turned out to be a slide show ... He mixed up slides, film, theatre. He had never been to any form of what we might call Western entertainment, and yet he acted absolutely amazingly...We structured the play together, myself, Ari and five workers.(pp. 24-5)

Other members of the Junction Avenue Workshop assisted and *Ilanga lizophumela abasebenzi* (*The sun will rise for the workers*) was performed both to worker audiences and subsequently at the University of the Witwatersrand.

Two members of Junction Avenue, Sitas, who was the son of Greek immigrants and Astrid von Kotze, the daughter of German immigrants, moved to Durban where their experience in the production of *Ilanga* led to a decision by Metal and Allied Workers Union (MAWU) to workshop what eventually became known as *The Dunlop play*. The committee of shop stewards decided to go ahead with the play in order to 'unite the workers and at the same time tell people how things at Dunlop go, what management is doing to us'.[22] Showing the story of a worker's life from the moment of his employment at the Dunlop Factory to the party twenty-five years later held to honour him and exploring his responses to important moments in the labour movement and the political issues of the time,[23] it premiered in Durban at the Annual General Meeting of MAWU. The play, like those that followed it, was directly concerned to foreground its links with its audience, which was encouraged to interrupt and discuss issues which affected them as well as the performers, as they saw fit. Moreover the fact that the performers worked often in their own African languages, then and in other plays since, not only made their work immediately accessible to their worker audiences but to a degree protected the play, not as easily accessible to those government agents, at least, who spoke only English and Afrikaans.

This movement, beset by many difficulties and frustrations was not only to survive but to make an impression within the trade unions. Sitas and von Kotze were joined by several workers, including the shop steward A. T. Qabula, who first encountered plays at mission school and Naftal Matiwane who knew nothing about drama until he joined rehearsals for *The Dunlop play*, both of the Dunlop Factory, and Nise Malange of the Transport and General Workers Union. As a group within the Federation of South African Trade Unions (FOSATU) they met in the Durban Gale Street Union offices and workshopped a new play. Despite problems they began to attract increasing interest.[24] Mi Hlatshwayo, an *imbongi* (praise singer) who worked at Dunlop, had heard Qabula perform his 'Praise Song To FOSATU', and was inspired to write his own poetry and to join MAWU after which he himself became a major contributor to the Worker play movement 'by drawing on his life experiences, his knowledge of traditions and his imagination'.[25]

In 1985 the attempt to appropriate drama in the trade union struggle for liberation intensified. The Durban Workers Cultural Local (DWCL) was created to link activities within the movement and over fifty-four activists prepared for the FOSATU Education Workshop to be held in July. They formulated a number of principles for cultural struggle which Hlatshwayo was to deliver as a keynote speech.[26] This document amongst other things asserted that 'we are a movement which announces a real democracy on this land – where people like you and me can control for the first time our productive and creative power' (p. 10).

Despite troubles between different factions in the townships from 1985 on, the group's activities continued to increase, including assisting Sarmcol strikers to develop a play at Howick/Mpophomeni in Natal, and organising a cultural festival to celebrate the victory of the Dunlop strikers. MAWU and several other union organisations gave the DWCL a factory floor in Clairwood to develop a trade union and cultural centre, the local appointed Hlatshwayo as a full time cultural organiser and by 1986 Cultural locals began to spring up throughout Natal, including Ladysmith, Hammarsdale, Howick, Port Shepstone, Pinetown and Newcastle. Activities of all kinds multiplied. This phenomenon, complementing the robust development of trade unionism in the 1980s, has led to the creation by the powerful Congress of South African Trade Unions (COSATU) of a full-time National Cultural Co-ordinator. Hlatshwayo, who occupies this position, describes in an interview the generation and evolution of one of these plays, in an extended account worth quoting at some length:

In many cases…a play will be based on the facts surrounding a specific form of labour action, for instance a strike. The material of the play is drawn from the results of collective bargaining. In the process of producing the play, the members of the union will discuss details, such as who wants to, and who will, participate in the play. The group which emerges from such a discussion is given the mandate to work out the content and theme of the production. This is done in a workshop method which once again draws on the contribution of everyone in the group…Before the play is put on publicly, it is presented to everyone concerned, so that workers have the opportunity to decide whether the play presents their strike or not. If it is found that the play does not represent the history and issues of the strike or other forms of labour action accurately, this is conveyed to the production group and the necessary corrections are made. This, I must stress, does not mean that when a person or group creates something, that it will be rejected out of hand. If the work represents the feelings of the majority, it is welcomed. If, however, the majority have a problem then discussion is initiated with the comrade or the group concerned. This happens when the feeling arises that a particular production is detrimental to the cause of the workers. We recently had a case when a member from one of our unions presented a very exciting script for the May Day Celebrations...Unfortunately there were some things which contradicted the principles of COSATU and the Mass Democratic Movement... he was called in by a group of shop stewards... and they related this problem to him. He responded by saying that since he created the play independently, he wished to retain his freedom as a writer and dramatist. The comrades responded by telling him they respected his position and perhaps he was right. They did not threaten him with expulsion from the union but tried to point out some of the dangers in his position, like the possibility of him ending up in isolation from other workers as well as the democratic movement and its allies... the central principles and goals of COSATU and the Mass Democratic Movement are the creation of a united, democratic, non-racial society... Regarding the case in question, the play contained strong racial and tribal elements. These were displayed in a rather crude, unanalytical and negative manner. The attitudes adopted towards other population groups were such that they tended to foster unacceptable forms of prejudice towards these groups. The workers pointed out to the comrade that while the culture of oppression in this country promotes notions of individualism, tribalism and racism, these ideas were not in accordance with the culture of liberation. The comrade eventually came to understand this as well as the dangers it possesses. He decided to consider these objections and to re-work his play. This is not, as you can see, a form of censorship, or an example of someone being threatened. It is an educative process which takes place in an atmosphere of tolerant discussion from which all can benefit. It is also an example of the problem which often arises in the production of committed culture, namely how to balance the relationship between politics and the demands of a particular art form in terms of the freedom of the cultural worker to decide as he or she sees fit.[27]

During the period 1983-87 von Kotze notes the generation and subsequent performance of no less than thirteen plays, many of which played in several parts of the country while The long march has also been performed in England. Sitas recently provided the following account of another more recent play which has since its first appearance toured England:

Bambatha's Children, created by SAWCO is a significant extension of their highly-regarded first play, The Long March. It is simultaneously, a historical reconstruction of their communities' struggles against dispossession, it is a statement about their struggles against BTR Sarmcol, and it is, in its own right, a continuous oral spectacle: they have managed to combine playful, and humorous enthusiasm with memorable song and dance sequences. And, through that, they wove narrative after narrative of their epic stories: it speaks of the land dispossession after Bambatha's resistance, it speaks of the struggle to find new roots through labour-tenancy, on 'white' farms; it also shows the final dispossession towards strict wage-labour. Such broad themes are woven together via the stories of a family of the Zondi people.[28]

Sitas's account of the growth of this movement in which he has been so involved, confirms its attempts to explore the worker's 'experience in alienation'[29] and to constitute the working-class subject in Marxist terms. Stressing the extent to which 'the worker is "annexed for life by a limited function"... a mere "appendage" to the factory's giant mechanisms' (p. 87), Sitas argues also that

in so far as alienation is an irreducible pressure of modern life so are responses to it...workers respond by attempting to control their condition of life, through defensive combinations, through normative communities and cultural formations...[and] the experience of production, captured in the Zulu word khalo, which means pain but also grievance, which is lamentation but also complaint, which is tears but also a 'wrong', is handled through unique cultural formations. (pp.87-8)

At the same time, Sitas registers that 'the nature of accumulation and class formation in South Africa has created tremendous obstacles against genuine grassroots self-expression' (p. 88). Such expression has to 'subsist under the most limiting material conditions' while 'from segregation to apartheid, racial domination and separation have worked against genuine cross-colour or in many instances cross-"ethnic" homogeneity' (pp.88-9). Because there is so 'little space for institutional and/or popular cultural reproduction in South Africa' the aims of those in the DWCL include therefore the 'imperative to situate the physical spaces of cultural reproduction amongst South Africa's workers' (p. 89). And Sitas delineates various problems his group has encountered in the endeavour to constitute a working class subject on stage and to dramatise and communicate ' khalo about exploitation' (p. 94).

Critical responses to this phenomenon have varied. The concern with 'issues crucial to the experience and struggles of the industrial working class' such as 'strikes, scabbing, accidents in the workplace, health hazards, hostel conditions, boss-worker relationships, the situation of foremen, overtime, the desirability of factory as against other types of work... liaison committees, the need for unions and a mandated union leadership, retrenchment and the difficulties the workers have in understanding the bosses' English and Afrikaans'[30] rare in South African drama, in class-based analyses prompts in some critics and theatre practitioners the privileging of these plays above others.[31] But contradictions seem to extend everywhere in theatre and theatre studies in South Africa. For instance, as intellectuals attached to the ruling classes, van Kotze and Sitas remain interventionists, confirming, even in an overwhelmingly workerist constituency, an element of contradiction. Moreover, to date, what we know of such attempts at a workers' theatre apart from the performances themselves, results mainly from their own mediation in reports, papers, published articles and a book. By contrast, in Kavanagh's work, as I indicated in chapter 6, the petit bourgeois nature of aspects of some Black Consciousness participants, who have deliberately attempted to exclude all intervention by dissident members of the ruling classes, has been argued. Yet again, if, from another point of view, the involvement of intellectuals and sociologists in worker plays has been interrogated, these criticisms come, it is worth noting, from critics themselves not members of the working class[32] – contradictions inevitably inform the positions of critics too! Such contradictions will always complicate any attempt to develop a rigidly theoretical model for the study of drama, particularly drama emerging predominantly, if not exclusively from the oppressed classes. This is often complicated even further, as I have already repeatedly remarked, by continuing lack of evidence and research into conditions of production, constitution of audiences, even the availability of scripts themselves. There is, for instance, to date no script of *Bambatha's children* available, only a number of discussions and video recordings of it.[33]

But while the use of worker plays by the trade unions remains experimental, and while critics differ on how they should be categorised, interpreted and validated, there is no doubt that this has been a highly important theatrical phenomenon. From within materialist discourse, the Marxist argument that 'the working class is important because it is one of the two major contending classes in capitalist society with access to the means of production, and the only one structurally in a position to alter the relations of production'[34] seems pertinent here. In terms of this discourse Sitas and von Kotze have been remarkable facilitators, making possible predominantly working-class exploration and expression of their own experience.

There is no doubt that within the trade union movement, the plays have served the function of helping to mobilise members and also to increase awareness.

It may be true that the drama practised currently in Christian churches in South Africa, itself still in need of much research, also aims at the mobilisation of its members and their increase in awareness. But this surface similarity should not be used to hide the fact that the working-class in South Africa has been undermined and suppressed in ways that make the recovery of working-class expression or the facilitation of it no easy task – a matter of continual struggle and assertion. On the one hand factors such as migrant labour, poor living conditions and the continual construction of or reinforcement of 'ethnicity' by the ruling class have worked against working-class identity and solidarity. But on the other hand, 'a common experience of workplace conditions, and subservience to wage labour', the task of surviving and adapting and the development of activities including 'homeboy clubs, shebeens, self-help societies, Zionist churches... sport, songs, music and dancing' (p. 75) – all, as I suggested in the Introduction, also in need of further research – have helped to maintain and develop working-class identity despite the factors which work to suppress it. 'Worker' theatre appears to be potentially important in facilitating this process, enabling the articulation by workers of their own experience in ways that contest their marginalisation in prevailing discourse. Although in one sense these plays lie beyond the parameters of this study because they are sometimes not performed, for the most part, in English but in the African languages of the people who make, perform and also watch them, and because they are mostly not yet published, they nevertheless provide powerful evidence of the possibilities of transgression in theatre in South Africa, of achieving disidentification through the use of, in performance, alternative discourse.[35]

IV Recovering a 'national past': *Sophiatown*

In the endeavour to construct the subject within the South African social order, contestatory theatre practitioners, particularly in the late 1970s and 1980s – although in other respects drawing on different discourses – often increasingly promulgated versions of a 'national liberation culture'. This, as one commentator argues, seeks 'to build up a national popular consciousness among South Africans which will construct and legitimate a broad South African identity in opposition to apartheid and its divisions'.[36] Thus the chorus in Matsemela Manaka's play Pula sing, 'In the name of the people,/ let peace prevail/ amongst all people and all parties.../ let us not allow our differences/ to stand against our national aspirations'.[37] The DWCL document, again, states that 'we discovered that we had to overcome our hatreds for each other: amakholwa against traditionalist; Christian of the official churches against Zionist; Muslim against Hindu; Pondo against Zulu; Zulu royalist against Zibhebhu's offspring; migrant against urban; Zulu against Indian; black against this is difficult, very difficult in South Africa – black against white. We discovered that our fate as workers and our needs as human beings bound us together, but language, cultural chauvinism and divisions tore us apart'.[38] And Malcolm Purkey, in his preface to the Junction Avenue Theatre Company's most recent work, Sophiatown, defines their 'obsession to reclaim and popularise the hidden history of struggle in our country' as the company's 'self-appointed task'[39] arguing that:

This history has been wiped off the map by the State in its oppression of the majority of South Africans. The powerful flourishing of the contemporary theatre in South Africa, against all the odds, indicates the hunger that all South Africans have, to have their world interpreted. We need an informed and articulate new generation, steeped in the past and carefully theorising about the future, who have shaken off the blanket of silence and are committed in the deepest way to liberation. We believe that one of the most effective ways to communicate ideas, information and feelings is through the living theatrical encounter. (p. x)

Sophiatown, which is perhaps amongst the most successful of the post-1976 plays produced by a number of dissident ruling-class as well as oppressed subjects in workshop provides us with an example of the endeavour, in seeking such articulations of a national culture, to construct or recover what might be called a people's history and myth about its past.

Sophiatown was workshopped in late 1985 and it opened in the Market Theatre in February 1986. Since then it has had several runs in both Cape Town and Johannesburg and has played in North America and at the Hampstead Theatre in London. It tries, by drawing on oral narratives, documents and other accounts of Sophiatown – destroyed by government edict, as I noted in chapter 2 (and converted into the white suburb of Triomf) – to represent and construct a 'reality' that disappeared more than two decades before. The representation it strives for, moreover, contrasts with that evident in the township plays of the fifties which, written when Sophiatown was still in existence, are mostly unable to move beyond the parameters permitted by prevailing discourse.

Thus the play presents Mingus, member of the Americans, one of the Sophiatown gangs, as the delinquent son of Mamariti the Shebeen Queen, owner of the house in which the play is set, who reveals as much insecurity as he does bravado or occasional violence and who supports his mother if he also steals – when he can, if preferable, from whites in the city. His sister at school with her growing awareness of the inadequacy of her education, Jakes the journalist who endeavours to gain success in his career, and Ruth Golden, based on a newspaper report taken from the period, telling of a Jewish girl who lived for a time in a Sophiatown home, provide, amongst others, equally significant contributions to the evocation of Sophiatown life.

Sophiatown suggests consciousness of its reliance upon narrative in order to construct its world. It comes at a time when the novel, from the mid-1970s on, was itself increasingly being used as a strategy to disrupt the apartheid gaze, in the works of diverse writers including Serote, Sepamla, Gordimer and Coetzee. The act of writing to create 'reality' forms a repeated motif in the play. Thus Jakes evokes aspects of the milieu of Sophiatown in the 1950s directly to the audience in his descriptive speech at the beginning and, as journalist, evokes too the many journalists whose writings now provide part of the record of Sophiatown life. His reported endeavours during the play to write about his world for Drum magazine and his short stories are parallelled by the schoolgirl Lulu's attempt to write about her home and the people close to her in her school essay. The scenes that, after Ruth Golden's arrival, explore the way she learns about Sophiatown life, tsotsitaal – the argot spoken in Sophiatown and meticulously re-searched by the Company – and even the language of the gambling system, fahfee, are further means whereby the text suggests its own strategy of representation, partly through such dramatisations of the acquisition of language patterns as well as attempts by the characters on stage to create their world through narratives of one or other kind. Thus Mingus, the delinquent gangster in the play, is shown to live sporadically through his fictions about his own life based upon American gangster movies, while Fahfee, the man who takes the illegal bets from the people of the township willing to play, interprets his world through the meanings attributed to each number in the fahfee system.

These readings of experience indicate the play's reflexivity about its fictive endeavour. During an account of her essay in one scene, Lulu says of Jakes's short stories, 'Everywhere in this house it's just fiction, fiction, fiction' and a moment later asserts 'Fiction! I want the truth!' (p. 32). The play's dramatic concern is to move by means of the making of these fictions of different kinds towards an understanding of some kind of 'truth' about Sophiatown. And in this, although Jakes and Ruth are attracted to one another, the play avoids romanticising their relationship – a focus on personal love and the body much favoured in the plays of the 1950s – in any sensationalist way which might foreground such personal involvement at the expense of the play's central thrust. Thus Jakes asserts towards the play's end when the occupants of the house are forced by government edict to leave:

I'm not letting some white girl put her hands around my heart when she feels like it. You want to ride over me like a bulldozer and leave me here for dust...We lost what little chance we had... We let the Boere drive a wedge between us. Who gives a damn whether a black journalist and a white storyteller can or can't meet? When the war comes, as it will, it will be fought in the barren ground between us, and it will be so large as to make us invisible. (p. 70)

Instead the play's central conflict comes from the evocation – through various kinds of fiction and language, through a predominant reliance on realism for most of Act 1 interspersed by song as well as a measure of narrative to the audience – of a lost world whose 'truth' is that it was destroyed. It resides now only in stories similar to the Drum story about the Mamariti household Jakes manages to have published, discussed in the final scene of Act 1, as well as in the play Sophiatown itself. The government's edict, announced by Fahfee who asks 'will Drum tell this story? It's the end for us' (p. 35) initiates the major movement of the play into conflict and contestation. Christopher Hill's focus, in a different context, on the lives of those without power, the 'various groups of the common people'[40] and their attempts to find solutions to the problems of their time, may be recalled here, as Jakes recognises that all he can do is to 'write the story' (p. 35), as Fahfee argues, in a way not pursued in the 1950s' plays, for political resistance: 'Congress says we mustn't move. We must resist, like in the Defiance Campaign. Congress calls for five thousand volunteers. We've got a plan' (p. 35), and as he cries:

What am I going to do in this Meadowlands? How am I going to put bread in my mouth? What's going to happen to my business with the Chinaman, the Gong? Where's he gonna be when they move Sophia? And the Indians? And the caureds [Coloureds]? Where's the jazz? Where's the life? Where's the situations? Where's the teachers? Where's the life? Where's the Fahfee? Where's the life? It's just dust and blood and dust!' (pp.36-7)

As the second act unfolds, scenes of confrontation between Mingus and Princess, Mingus and Ruth and then Jakes and Ruth are replaced by that between the state and these ordinary inhabitants of Sophiatown. This is represented partly by an increasingly emptying stage as the realistic detail of the Mamariti home is replaced by the visual image of packed boxes on a bare stage. In contrast to the presentation of crime in the late 1950s' plays, at one moment in a challenge to Mingus, the play argues directly for united resistance against material exploitation:

FAHFEE: We need you Mingus. We need the Americans to fight. We need the numbers, man. We need fighters. We need planners. We need the Berliners and the Americans and the Vultures and the school children, and the journalists to fight. Can't you see what's going on?

JAKES: What's going on? Hundreds of people living in shacks, paying rents so home-owners can get rich − that's what's going on. Nobody's going to stop them moving. They're going to get houses.

FAHFEE: Where? Twenty miles from town. So Verwoerd has a clean white city. (p. 55)

This argument contributes to what, in the second Act, which mingles strands of realism more deliberately with songs of militance and direct narrative to the audience, emerges as an attempt to constitute or develop views of the oppressed subject that draw on, as I indicated, not only a discourse of resistance but one that posits a national culture of liberation. This has been anticipated already in Act 1 in the presentation of Ruth Golden's sense of the complexities of her identity, of the different strands contributing to it, as well as in Jakes's recognition of a similar mixture, 'God is One, and God is Three, and the ancestors are many, and I speak Zulu and Xhosa and Tswana and English and Afrikaans and Tsotsitaal, and if I'm lucky Ruth will teach me Hebrew, and the Boere and the U.P. and the Congress fight it out, and this Softown is filled with Coloured and Indian and Chinese and Zulus...'(p. 44). It is worth noting in this context the emergence in

the early 1980s to oppose the government, of the United Democratic
Front (UDF) which represented 'the re-emergence of Congress Alliance
politics',[41] resembled 'a multi-class popular front' (p. 229) and

advocated 'the creation of a true democracy in which all South Africans will
participate in the government of the country', subscribed to a vision of 'a
single non-racial, unfragmented South Africa... free of Bantustans and Group
Areas', and... proposed the unity of 'all community, worker, student,
women, religious, sporting and other organisations under the banner of the
United Democratic Front' to 'unite in action against the evils of *apartheid*. (p.
229)

This movement, in the years to come was to form a focal point of
resistance in South Africa, until its leaders were arrested and charged
with treason and in due course the movement itself severely restricted.
Sophiatown, in its attempt to argue for a multi-cultural people may be
seen to suggest, as in the case of some of the statements by those
involved in the worker play movement, aspects of UDF discourse. And
in the second Act of the play, again in contrast to township plays of
the 1950s, a tradition of resistance is recalled, including the miners'
strike of 1946 and the 1949 tram boycotts, leaders active in the
Sophiatown attempts at resistance, named, while a future of resistance
– 'Fahfee disappeared. Some say he was recruited – joined Umkhonto
We Sizwe' (p. 74) – glimpsed. The final sequence of the play, providing directly to the audience a narrative of the removals, expresses
not only lament and anger but a call for liberation:

This bitterness inside me wells up and chokes. We lost, and Sophiatown is
rubble. The visions of the mad Boere smashed this hope, turned it to rubble.
And out of this dust, like a carefully planned joke, Triomf rises. What triumph
is this? Triumph over music? Triumph over meeting? Triumph over the
future? Sophiatown was a cancer on a pure white city, moved out at gunpoint
by madmen. With its going, the last common ground is gone. The war has been
declared, the battle sides are drawn... I hope the dust of that triumph settles
deep in the lungs like a disease and covers these purified suburbs with ash.
Memory is a weapon. Only a long rain will clean away these tears.(pp.73, 74).

V Speculating on censorship

In drawing in such ways upon narrative fictions to recover what
becomes the myth of Sophiatown, and in those elements in the text
that appear to suggest the articulation of a national culture of

liberation, *Sophiatown* may be said largely to counteridentify prevailing discourse which, in the name of difference and tribalism, breaks down calls to unity and commonality and erases memories of a non-racial past. It responds to the literal *absence* of a world destroyed by the ruthless system of removals with fictive constructions of it, thus attempting to recover a sense of *presence*, although its reflexivity continually admits that much of what it deals with is fiction, that the very presence it attempts to re-enact is lost. From this, it is true, it does infer the need for resistance, but it might be argued that this does not move beyond basic assertion into, to any marked degree, an alternative discourse. The imagined possibilities provided within the limits of the play – either text or time span of its performance – balance those potentials, that might encourage a more interrogative awareness of cause and effect, with evocation of a past that ends, inevitably again, with the absence of the world it has evoked and thus, perhaps, with a sense of defeat (although used in part, as I have just argued, to inspire a mood of resistance). This may encourage the speculation that, despite moments of contestation within the play, and despite its success, it was not perceived as threateningly subversive by the dominant order. And it is true that, in comparison with its earlier work, the Junction Avenue Theatre Company, in its evocation of a lost world and the articulation of a national culture of liberation does not draw on alternative discourses to the same degree, preferring instead to explore and investigate memory, the magic of fiction, the construction of myth.

It is worth noting that other plays of this period sometimes draw more equivocally even if inadvertently on images of defeat. Thus *District Six: the musical* (sic) offers a protest against the government destruction of the famous 'coloured' suburb District Six in Cape Town, providing a tribute to and lament for the community uprooted and displaced by the heinous government policy of group removals. Devised primarily by Taliep Peterson, a former inhabitant of District Six together with the Afrikaans cult singer David Kramer, it opened in 1986 at the Baxter Theatre in Cape Town.[42] Its popularity with huge 'coloured' audiences then and in subsequent runs, may be explained by the language of anger in the play as well as by the attempt to reconstruct a world that, since its disappearance, has also been marginalised as much as possible. At the same time white middle-class audiences in large numbers also patronised its run at the Market Theatre in Johannesburg. For them the protest in the play was most certainly contained by the fact that, despite an appeal to 'the children' that they remember *in the future* what was done to District Six, the play concludes with its focus fixed firmly on images of defeat. Significantly, the call for some kind of contestatory awareness is made by a 'gangster' stereotype, thus presenting the attempt to articulate a discourse of resistance within a socio-pathological context. And the final song of the play foregrounds permanent loss. The 'curse' of the famous Seven Steps, thought to be the heart of the once 'coloured' suburb, is recalled but only to stress that even 'they too have been broken/And scattered like the bricks/ The stones cement and concrete/That once was District Six' (p. 97). Again, another play, *Saturday night at the palace*, enormously successful amongst white audiences at the Market, first performed in 1982 and ostensibly directed at exposing racism, ends with a black man as completely controlled victim, chained to one of his tormentor's motorbikes.[43] Such images of the oppressed – against which Black Consciousness fought so vigorously – despite other tendencies in these plays towards contestation, finally fix them, as is the case in *The dam*, in positions that reproduce the negativity of defeat (tinged sometimes, as I noted in chapter 2, with associations of social pathology).

It is, however, difficult after 1976-77 to account for the way in which the state reacted to the emerging South African theatre. A number of other reasons might account for the fact that *Sophiatown* and other post-1976 plays have been tolerated. The relevant section of the Publications Act of 1974 provides that public entertainment is to be deemed undesirable when amongst other things it:

brings any section of the inhabitants of the Republic into ridicule or contempt…is harmful to the relations between any sections of the inhabitants of the Republic…is prejudicial to the safety of the state, the general welfare or the peace and good order.[44]

But in 1978 the legislature amended the Publications act, introducing a committee of experts whose function is 'to advise the Publications Act Board on the literary and/or artistic merit of a work' (p. 9) and since the late 1970s increased flexibility has been evident in practice in the decisions made by the Publications Control Board, while the government also abolished segregation in theatres in 1977.

Such developments may at least in part be understood in the light, firstly, of comments made by the Board's chairperson:

Control in the field of state security has…become more realistic. This is a consequence of the realisation that the Act is applicable only when the potential harm is real; much has been learnt from the American 'clear and present danger' doctrine. The board has also realised – as has been substantiated by various reports by experts – that an absolutist approach in this field is likely to be counterproductive, and that the expression of grievances often acts as a safety valve for pent-up feelings. (p. 11)

He also remarks that 'over-reaction by adjudicators may itself pose a threat to security...the security of the state is not so fragile that the slightest ripple in the sea of political debate and rhetoric will be prejudicial to it' (p. 106).

These comments suggest that the new policy of flexibility – like 'reform' in the wider sense – was at least partially designed to maintain the status quo as far as possible. And we may recall here that, writing from a related context, but drawing on materialist discourse, Freire has argued that

the emergence of the popular consciousness implies, if not the overcoming of the culture of silence, at least the presence of the masses in the historical process applying pressure on the elite...Just as there is a moment of surprise among the masses when they begin to see what they did not see before, there is a corresponding surprise among the elites in power when they find themselves unmasked by the masses...The elites are anxious to maintain the status quo by allowing only superficial transformations designed to prevent any real change... the phenomenon of the emerging masses forces the power elites to experiment with new forms of maintaining the masses in silence, since structural changes that provoke the emergence of the masses also qualitatively alter their...consciousness.[45]

Furthermore, still viewed cynically, the apparent shift in attitude of the censors and government may have been facilitated by the decline in the late 1970s and beyond of theatrical activity in the townships. The opening of theatres to all audiences must, too, in part at least have been prompted by concern for the government's image in view of the increasing opprobrium which apartheid South Africa earned abroad in the 1980s.

On occasion, theatre coming from dissident white dramatists in the late 1970s and 1980s did encounter hostility, mostly for offending notions of sexual and religious propriety. An attempt in 1979 to stage *Holy moses and all that jazz*, 'a colourful romp through six Old Testament stories set to music'[46] was opposed by the Directorate of Publications although the Publications Appeal Board decided after a legal hearing to permit performances of the show. Then in 1988 *Sunrise city* at the Warehouse within the Market complex, a not very successful attempt to satirise the Sun City Holiday Complex in Bophutatswana, was banned by a committee of the Publications Board:

Naked female breasts, 'simulated copulation', hints of a lesbian relationship and the fact that evil triumphed over good and there was no corrective message were among the committee's complaints. An immediate appeal by the producers resulted in the Chairman and members of the Publications Appeal Board attending a public performance and suspending the ban pending an official hearing before the Board. An age restriction of 2 to 18 was imposed during the period of suspension and, ultimately, the Board upheld the appeal, imposed no cuts and raised the age limit to 19.[47]

However, most plays by dissident dramatists from the ruling classes, while in their own ways contestatory, did not arouse irritation in or provoke action from the state. This contrasts starkly with the state's responses to the pre-1976 plays that were attempting to dramatise and construct oppressed class subjects within the township environment as well as with the suppression of township drama throughout the 1980s. Yet, as well as Sophiatown, the worker plays discussed in this chapter, perhaps because confined to a particular constituency, were not overtly interfered with by the state either. But, yet again, as the next chapter will show, this is not true for all contestatory theatre with dominant subordinate-class involvement in the cities, nor has the worker theatre movement in Natal gone completely unscathed. Internal contradictions in the ruling classes and particularly the Nationalist Party government, in the decade after 1976-77, in some respects at least, were also beginning to fragment monolithic attitudes towards theatre so evident in the state of the previous two and a half decades.

Notes

1 See Swilling, Mark, 'Introduction: the politics of stalemate', in Frankel, Philip, Pines, Noam, Swilling, Mark, State, resistance and change in South Africa, Johannesburg: Southern, 1988, p. 1.
2 Murray, Martin, South Africa, time of agony, time of destiny, London: Verso, 1987, pp.200-1.
3 See Murray, South Africa, p. 201, from which these details come.
4 Murray, South Africa, p. 224.
5 Details taken from brochure of the Performing Arts Council of the Transvaal entitled Decade 2, undated, unnumbered pages.
6 See Astbury, The space, from which the following details are taken.
7 Larlham, Black theatre, dance and ritual, p. 78.
8 Fugard, Athol, Dimetos and two early plays, Oxford: Oxford University Press, 1977.
9 Uys, Pieter-Dirk, God's forgotten, in Gray, Stephen, ed.,Theatre two, Johannesburg: Donker, 1981.

10 Uys, Pieter-Dirk, *Paradise is closing down*, in Gray, *Theatre one*, Johannesburg: Donker, 1978, pp. 169, 161.

11 Uys, God's forgotten, p. 143.

12 See Schwartz, Pat, *The best of company*, Johannesburg, Donker: 1988, p. 19ff., from which the details following are also taken.

13 Fugard, *A lesson from aloes*, Oxford: Oxford University Press, 1981.

14 Simon, Barney and The Company, *Cincinnati*, in Hauptfleisch, T. and Steadman, I., ed., *South African theatre: four plays and an introduction*, Pretoria: HAUM Educational Publishers, 1984.

15 Fugard, Athol, '*Master Harold'and the boys*, Oxford: Oxford University Press, 1983; Fugard, Athol, *The road to Mecca*, London: Faber and Faber, 1985.

16 Fugard, Athol, *A place with the pigs*, London: Faber and Faber, 1988.

17 Junction Avenue Theatre Company, *The fantastical history of a useless man*, Johannesburg: Ravan, 1978, p. 51.

18 Purkey, Malcolm, 'Introduction to "Sophiatown"', in Junction Avenue Theatre Company, *Sophiatown*, Cape Town: David Philip, 1988, pp. ix-x; see Junction Avenue Theatre Company, *Randlords and rotgut* in Gray, Stephen, ed., *Theatre two*, Johannesburg: Donker, 1981.

19 Sole, K., Review of *Organise and act*, *Staffrider*, VIII, 3/4, 1989, pp. 204-5.

20 Astbury, *The space*, unnumbered pages.

21 See Tomaselli, Keyan G.,'The semiotics of alternative theatre in South Africa', *Critical arts*, II, 1, 1981, pp. 14-33.

22 Von Kotze, Astrid, *Organise and act*, Natal: Culture and Working Life Publications, University of Natal, 1988, p. 21. Much of the information in this section is drawn from von Kotze's work.

23 Von Kotze,*Organise and act*, p. 30.

24 Sitas, Ari, 'The flight of the gwala-gwala bird: ethnicity, populism and worker culture in Natal's labour movement', unpublished paper delivered to the History Workshop, University of the Witwatersrand, February 1986, pp. 8-9.

25 Von Kotze, *Organise and act*, p.52.

26 Sitas, 'The flight of the gwala gwala bird', p. 10.

27 Hlatshwayo, Mi, 'Culture and organisation in the labour movement', interview given to *Staffrider*, VIII, 3/4, 1989, pp. 40-2.

28 Sitas, 'The voice and gesture in South Africa's revolution', p. 11.

29 Sitas, Ari, 'Culture and production: the contradictions of working class theatre in South Africa', *Africa perspective*, New Series I, 1&2, 1986, p. 87.

30 Sole, Kelwyn, 'Identities and priorities in recent black literature and performance: A preliminary investigation', *South African theatre journal*, I, 1, 1987, p. 76.

31 See, for example, von Kotze, *Organise and act*, pp. 13-14, Sole, Kelwyn, 'Black literature and performance: some notes on class and populism', *South African labour bulletin*, IX, 8, 1984.

32 See Sole, 'Identities and priorities' and 'Black literature and performance', and Tomaselli, Keyan G. and Muller, Johan, 'Class race and oppression: metaphor and metonymy in "black" South African theatre', *Critical arts*, IV, 3, 1987, pp. 40-58. Related and other aspects of problems involved in characterising or evaluating 'worker' theatre, are explored in Tomaselli, 'The semiotics of alternative theatre in South Africa'; Sole, Kelwyn, 'Black literature and performance: some notes on class and populism'; Naledi Writers Unit/Medu Art Ensemble, 'Working class culture and popular struggle', *South African labour bulletin*, X, 5, 1985, pp. 21-30; Sole, Kelwyn, 'Politics and working class culture: a response', *South African labour bulletin*, X, 7, 1985, pp. 43-56; interview with the Durban Fosatu Local, 'Culture and the workers' struggle', *South African labour bulletin*, X, 8, 1985, pp. 67-74; Spiegel, A. D., 'Transforming tradition or transforming society: Sitas, Hlatswayo and performative literature', *Transformation 6*, 1988, pp. 52-6.

33 Sitas, 'The voice and gesture in South Africa's revolution', pp. 15-16.

34 Sole, 'Identities and priorities', p. 87

35 Three short plays mostly in English by Mi Hlatshwayo and the Clairwood Trade Union and Cultural Centre, by Rankoa Molefe and by Victor Shingwenyana, have been published in *Staffrider* VIII, 3/4, 1989.

36 Sole, 'Identities and priorities', p. 90.

37 Manaka, Matsemela, *Pula*, in Gray, Stephen, ed., *Market plays*, Johannesburg: Donker, 1986, p. 67.

38 von Kotze, *Organise and act*, pp. 65-6.

39 Purkey, Malcolm, 'Introduction to *Sophiatown*, p. x.

40 Hill, Christopher, *The world turned upside down*, London: Temple Smith, 1972, p. 11.

41 Murray, *South Africa*, p. 215.

42 I am grateful to David Kramer and Taliep Peterson for very kindly providing me with an unpublished script of *District Six: the musical*.

43 Slabolepszy, Paul, *Saturday night at the palace*, Johannesburg: Donker, 1985.

44 van Rooyen, J. C. W., *Censorship in South Africa*, Cape Town: Juta, 1987, p. 7.

45 Freire, *The politics of education*, pp. 76, 77-8.

46 Schwartz, *The best of company*, p. 110.

47 Schwartz, *The best of company*, p. 124.

8

Elamanqamu namhlanje

The post-1976 period in South Africa saw an attempt by the ruling classes to initiate a measure of reform in order to widen if possible the consensus on which they depended. But in the 1980s levels of resistance were to rise to unprecedented new heights of sustained struggle, leading to the declaration of a state of emergency which even in early 1990 remained in force – amidst promises that it was to be lifted. Despite continuing difficulties, theatre from predominantly or exclusively oppressed class practitioners was produced more and more frequently. This theatre was far more militantly and aggressively positioned against the state than ever before. It also implicitly or explicitly sought to enunciate or dramatise a national culture. But the attempt to enunciate such a culture inevitably came from practitioners drawing on different and often contradictory discourses. For instance, in a paper which he gave to the Cultural Festival in Amsterdam in 1987, Robert Kavanagh offers the following version of a national theatre:

theatre for national liberation involves…a programme of revolutionary cultural action among the masses, in the working class movement, among the armed fighters and in countries all over the world to mobilise, conscientise and win support for our struggle… while writing and acting material relevant to the struggle for national liberation, we should be reflecting a social consciousness and more and more demonstrating that only economic liberation in the form of socialism can make the struggle for national liberation truly meaningful for the broad majority of our people.[1]

But attempts at developing a national theatre in the late 1970s and 1980s draw just as readily on non-socialist forms of discourse, or offer a mixture of socialist and essentialist discourses, or, again, in their construction of the subject, foreground the search for an essence and a strength – that might defy and withstand the continuing onslaught of apartheid – that is rooted in interiority. Thus Matsemela Manaka and Maishe Maponya, amongst others in this period, draw with an urgent militancy on the Black Consciousness movement while the work of Mbongeni Ngema and Percy Mtwa suggests affinities with emerging Black Theology. Often too, in their attempts to address the social order, many of the plays of this period find or provide evidence of the imminent approach of what is posited as the millennium, the moment of liberation itself. Still, it should be emphasised that, whatever they foreground, most plays address more determinedly than previously, current power relations as well as the fact of continuing and often heroic struggle within the oppressed classes. And in this regard it is worth, finally, noting Nolutshungu's argument that

the colonial state, because of the role it gives to national and racial domination and oppression, calls forth in opposition to itself and to the economy it would defend alignments among the subject population that are focused primarily on the terms of political domination rather than those of exploitation. In time, however, such movements may acquire a more definite economic character (responding in part to the economic strategies which the state adopts in self-defence). While nationalist movements are to be distinguished from class movements, they may and often do provide the medium in which class struggles can develop, and can, in their own right, severely weaken the ideological and political supports of the order of class exploitation.[2]

I Township and city theatre in the late 1970s and 1980s

After 1976 some forms of township theatre continued to function. Gibson Kente, working with his usual system of one night stands throughout the country followed by an extended run in Soweto, produced *Can you take it* (1977) with a 'single thematic focus on the urban black generation gap' and *La duma* (1978) which depicted 'direct confrontation between radical political organisation and family and community solidarity', while *Mama and the load* (1980), which played also at The Market Theatre, pursued the themes of 'poverty and family disintegration, the decline of adult morality and guidance, and the need for renewed kinship and community among urban blacks'.[3] Sam Mhangwane, dealing with similar problems, produced *Thembi* in 1978 and *Ma-in-law* in 1979.[4]

Despite such activity, more politically concerned theatre declined in the late 1970s and in the 1980s in the townships for a number of reasons, some of which I touched on in chapter 7. Most important, if the state built the Nico Malan Theatre in Cape Town on the tenth anniversary of the Republic and the Pretoria State Theatre to celebrate the Republic's second decade, townships remained without any proper theatre venue of their own. One of the few (if not the only) spaces that could be used primarily for theatre was the Experimental Space at the Funda Centre just outside Soweto. Furthermore, despite its apparent leanings towards reform, the state persisted in its attempts to control access to venues for theatre in the townships:

In Soweto the West Rand Administration Board (WRAB) set up its own Cultural Section in 1975. Duties of the Cultural Section included the collection, reading and viewing of scripts and plays before they were cleared for performance in WRAB controlled venues. The head of the Cultural Section, H. Pieterse, even attempted to stage a production of SHAKA, written and directed by himself. Plays which were performed at church-owned venues were still subject to the controls of legislation, censorship laws, and from 1985, emergency regulations.[5]

Again, with the widespread detention and arrests of many of those directly involved in the 1976 Uprising and the fact that many activists chose to leave the country to continue their struggle from abroad, theatrical activity in the townships dwindled. Conditions for theatre in the townships, always bad, worsened in the late 1970s and during the 1980s. The absence of theatres and the reluctance of white capital to build any, meant that rehearsing in very difficult conditions and performing 'in YMCAs, church halls, schools and garages' remained the norm.[6]

These problems were certainly exacerbated by the increasing police presence in the townships together with, in the 1980s the presence sometimes of South African troops – a ferocious form of suppression so far as possibilities for theatre were concerned. Theatre practitioners and audiences in the townships responded in two ways. Perhaps the more significant was use of the political arena as site for theatrical activity, one description of which is provided by Kavanagh in 1987:

In the people's movement there is a kind of theatre that takes place side by side with the mass protests and demonstrations which have made large parts of our country ungovernable. Peter Makhari's 'guerilla theatre', as reported by A. Osipov of Novost Press Agency, is an example. In a street in Orlando under a tree, an episode in the people's constant confrontation with the police is acted out. The police are forced to retreat. The people sing ANC songs and the return of the political prisoners is acted out, singing 'We are free but what about thousands like us who still languish in racist prisons? What have you done for their liberation, to abolish the shame of the country – apartheid? Power to the people!' Then dramatically the real police arrive on the scene. Word of the performance has reached the police station. Armoured cars disperse the audience. The actors melt into the passages of Orlando to emerge elsewhere to re-enact the same drama of defiance.[7]

Plays or short scenes prepared in the townships were performed in the 1980s during political rallies where they contributed to cultural spectacle and rhetoric. This move of drama into political sites of contestation countered the state's own dramatisation of its power by using the army as well as the police in townships to arrest and silence as much opposition as it could. Including political meetings and trade union activity, to say nothing of the drama of political funerals – all activities hardly yet charted – it may be seen, amongst much else, as itself a means of challenging the state's attempt to silence theatre within township life.

The second way in which the crisis for theatre in the townships had perforce to be handled was the steady move by the oppressed classes to theatres in the cities. I noted in chapter 7 that in 1977 the state, as part of its new strategy of reform, finally lifted the ban on multi-racial theatre companies and abolished segregation in theatres. In consequence, the new Baxter Theatre built by Cape Town University in Rondebosch and, particularly, The Market in Johannesburg were able to provide a less transitory and contested alternative to the continuing dangerous as well as difficult township conditions. But this necessity entailed its own problems. The playwright Maishe Maponya commented in the 1980s on the need for capital to enable the production of plays in city theatres:

most money that is donated comes from white capitalist concerns with their own interests. For obvious reasons the black community does not have that kind of capital, and those black businessmen and individuals who are well-to-do just don't concern themselves with theatre…economic necessity forces me to write, direct and often act in my own shows. I am also responsible for funding, publicity and public relations.[8]

Performers from the oppressed classes were furthermore 'too despised to be regularly reviewed by the white dailies' and were also 'underremunerated and compelled to maintain daytime jobs in factories, schools and offices'.[9] The difficulty of funding actors paralleled the practical difficulties in travelling to rehearsals and performances. Women, who were not always easily mobile, tended to be underused. And the absorption into the system since the advent of black television, strictly state controlled, of black theatre practitioners contributed further to the drastic reduction of theatre activity in the townships. Sponsorship for black actors and productions, as compared with the subsidies which the state regularly doles out to the Performing Arts Councils, remained non-existent. The cost of travel for theatregoers from the townships into the city in turn reduced the potential size of the township theatre-going public. In view of the extensive involvement of ruling class capital in the Market, an attempt was made by Benjy Francis to establish and run a black-controlled theatre, The Dhlomo Theatre, in central Johannesburg but it was closed in 1983 as a fire hazard. The contradictions which they found in the constitution of the Market complex still provided a problem for practitioners such as Francis, who argued that, although the theatre had a meaningful role, and although they still used it, 'what the Market is doing comes from the will to do good, not from an historic organic experience and the only way it can have that is if it is run by black folk and not just any black folk – people with a vision'.[10] Kavanagh, taking into account the international recognition won by a number of Market productions, made related points more strongly:

The weakness of the Market Theatre and other similar cultural organisations is that they tend to function to siphon the creativity and talent of the masses out of the community into products which, brilliant as they may be, even at times quite hard-hitting in their political content and presentation, are then marketed for the consumption of petit-bourgeois audiences in South Africa and various Western countries. In a sense, especially when these plays are performed abroad or televised in these countries, such plays perform an important role in this period of struggle when we need to mobilise as many audiences as we can to support or at least not to oppose our struggle. However, the real audience for some of these plays, the most *politically effective performance*, is an audience not to be found at the Market theatre…The fact is our plays are sent invariably to the established theatres in western countries – the very ones, in fact, that uphold and support the apartheid regime in our country. While we may influence our audiences with the anti-apartheid material of our plays, the commercial theatres and their personnel influence us with their methods, their money and their ideology. It is no accident that many of our actors who started in community-based theatre in South Africa, change after such foreign exposure. The people no longer see them. They abandon principled political action for the exploitation of politics for money.[11]

However, spaces such as the Market remained – and until conditions in the townships are radically altered, continue to be – vital. It is here that much of the work of theatre practitioners from the oppressed classes has been able to find its first space for performance.

II Overt state intimidation and suppression of theatre in the late 1970s and 1980s

Despite the state's alleged policy of reform, township theatre practitioners working mostly in the cities often continued in the late 1970s and 1980s to be openly harassed while their work was sometimes suppressed. Matsemela Manaka's *Egoli*, for instance, was banned although the play had been performed widely in South Africa as well as abroad. Another Black Consciousness dramatist, the Reverend Julius Maqina from the Eastern Cape, whose unpublished work, as I indicated in chapter 6, was popular in the townships during the period of the 1976 Uprising and after, was subject to harassment, detention and house arrest. He has tried to arrange for performances of his plays to white audiences but, as he himself commented on one occasion, the security police 'are doing everything possible to see to it that I don't put any of my ideas on the stage or even on paper...they have seen to it that I don't even get the Township Halls, let alone those in the city'.[12] Zakes Mda is the author of a number of plays including *We shall sing for the fatherland* and *Dead end*, both of which were produced by Benjy Francis for the Federation of Black Arts in 1979 at the Diepkloof Hall in Soweto.[13] They then ran at the Market and, later in the year, *We shall sing for the fatherland* was produced with another of his plays, *Dark voices ring* at The Space. When Ravan Press published a collection of his works the volume was at first banned by the Publications Board because of the inclusion of *Dark voices ring*, which is concerned in part with blacks who co-operate with the apartheid system and which implicitly suggests to the young that they leave to join resistance movements abroad. However, a subsequent appeal against the banning was upheld by a committee who, it has been argued, failed to read the play accurately (pp. 33-4). Maishe Maponya too has been detained and interrogated by the security police and his play, *Gangsters*, earned its author a restriction order which effectively prevented him from producing it in township halls and cinemas:

The directive from the director of publications in Cape Town stated that, under section 30 of the Publications Act of 1974, the following ruling should apply: 'In regard to the play "Gangsters" – a.) it may only be performed in small intimate four-wall theatres, of the experimental or avant guard (sic) type; b.) a request for approval of any future venue for the performance of the play must be directed via the Directorate of Publications; c.) The Laager

Theatre in the Market Theatre complex in Johannesburg is an approved venue'.[14]

Finally, it should be noted that, if, apart from chronic difficulties, theatrical activity in the townships has steadily decreased because of overt police harassment and interference with audience and actors, as well as the increasing uncertainty that results from repeated incidents of struggle and resistance, suppression also comes in other forms. For instance, those involved in workers' theatre have sometimes been tragically involved in strife-torn Natal: 'Simon Ngubane [one of the actors in The long march]...was murdered by politically motivated assailants in 1986;...prominent COSATU activist, poet and actor, Alfred Temba Qabula, was forced to go into hiding during the ongoing UDF-Inkatha clashes in Natal after receiving death threats.'[15] Again, Woza Albert! and Asinamali! contain sharp criticism of the homeland leaders, who are generally thought to be 'tied to Pretoria's platforms and [who] march to the tune of their white advisors'.[16] These include Gatsha Buthulezi, the Chief Minister of Kwazulu, who is also head of Inkatha, which in Natal has been instrumental in the formation of groups of vigilantes which have 'participated' in current upheavals in the townships. Most analysts claim that Inkatha, 'accommodationist in substance if not in tone', 'has been largely responsible for extinguishing the flames of unrest in Natal' (p. 284), and more recently, at least partly responsible for the continuing violence there. Performing in a Natal township, Ngema's company was on one occasion visited by a group of vigilantes who, mistaking the road manager at the front door for, it is believed, Ngema, murdered him. Since then Ngema has produced his plays within South Africa, only at the Market Theatre.

III Spaces of exploitation: Egoli, The hungry earth, Gangsters

Matsemela Manaka and Maishe Maponya, two dramatists who draw on Black Consciousness, like Dhlomo and Butler before them endeavour to construct the subject in terms of the South African landscape, but for them it is most powerfully a landscape of industrial exploitation and human oppression. Born and educated in Soweto, Manaka worked for a time with Ravan Publishers in Johannesburg, editing Staffrider magazine. He is a founder of the Soyikwa Theatre Group and has written and produced a number of plays including Egoli (1979), Imbumba (1979), which was staged at Diepkloof in Soweto in 1980,

Vuka (1980), *Pula* (1982) and *Children of Asazi* (1984). Maponya was born in Alexandra Township, but his family was forcibly removed to Diepkloof in Soweto when he was eleven years old.[17] Working as an insurance clerk for a period, he is a founder member of a group of Black Consciousness performance poets and the Bahumutsi Drama Group, and has written and produced several plays including *The cry* (1976), *Peace and forgive* (1978), *The hungry earth* (1978), *Umongikazi* (1983) about apartheid in hospitals, and *Gangsters* (1984).

Joining John Ledwaba and Hamilton Silwane, two actors from the townships, Manaka devised *Egoli* in workshop.[18] It was performed in 1979 at the Space Theatre, attracting audiences totalling 5,000 by the end of the run, before it played in Langa Township and at the Market, and then at various cities in West Germany (after being invited to the Erlangen Festival in 1980). *Egoli*, which means 'city of gold', presents the South African landscape as a place of human as well as mineral exploitation and was written in a period when the price of gold rocketed, bringing massive increases to state income. It endeavours to suggest how the mining industry, in extracting the mineral strategically crucial to the continuing function of the South African economy, remains indifferent to the migrant labourers who are forced to serve it. In presenting the lives of migrant workers separated from their families, it counteridentifies any claim in prevailing discourse to a just economic order. The play dramatises the interaction between two miners in their compound room, forced as they are to live in single-sex compounds, and exposed to highly dangerous as well as exploitative conditions. At the same time, as in the case of *Shanti* in the 1970s, the play endeavours to conscientise its audience, and to do so it employs a great deal of mimed action and visual stage imagery together with the use of song as the dramatic characters recall their mutual pasts, or later enact their working life. Thus the two are ex-prisoners who, although they have escaped, yet remain imprisoned – 'We run...We go back to the women and children. We watch them starve. We come back again to breathe dust for them' (p. 5). In a central dream sequence, the actors mime their escape from prison and the breaking of the chain which binds them, providing a metaphor for the struggle for liberation. Steadman suggests that the chain signifies that 'the men are chained in bondage to the economic system', chained together 'as partners against the forces of oppression' and that their goal and that of all workers is to break these chains.[19] Here, the militant essentialist and nationalist aspects in some strands of Black Consciousness discourse become particularly evident. As the men struggle to break the steel rings around their necks with a rock, their language posits an idealised past seeking through this as well as symbolic imagery and the constitution of a partly essentialist version of the subject, release:

John: Egoli, wearing chains on our brains. Egoli. The place where our people have lost a sense of respect for their own culture. They mock their beliefs. They curse their customs. They forget all about their traditions. Egoli, city of misery. City of hate.

THEY SING:

Thina sibanjelwe amahala	We have been caught for nothing
Singenzanga lutho	We have committed no sin
Tixo somandla	God almighty we ask from you
Sibuza kuwe, senzeni na?	What have we done?
Kule lizwe lenhlupeko	In this country of poverty
Sikhulule somandla	Set us free, Almighty
Nguwena kuphela Owaziyo	You are the only one who knows
Ukuthi iqiniso liyaphilisa	That the truth heals
Sicela kuwe, Somandla	We ask from you almighty
Suza izitha	Chase away our enemies,
Siza iSizwe, Esimnyama	Help the black nation.[20]

At the conclusion of the play, after one of the miners has heard that his son has been killed in a mining accident below ground and has given vent to his grief, the two actors kneel to give the dead young man a 'spiritual burial' with language that also, in the attempt to construct a sense of national potency, militance and resistance, recalls metaphors used by Dhlomo decades earlier:

For justice, freedom and peace to prevail in the country of our forefathers, we shall all have to stand up and face the enemy without fear. We shall all have to worship the spear and drink blood from the calabash until we all sing the same song – Uhuru –-
> Azania
> Uhuru
> Azania (p. 28)

Despite its attempts at reform, such contestatory counteridentification proved intolerable to the government which, although *Egoli* had had widespread exposure, was driven, as I have noted, to banning the play.

Maponya encountered Brecht's *The measures taken*, while he was in Britain on a British Council scholarship and this influenced his writing of *The hungry earth*.[21] One of the few plays that has been produced independently of white managements, it was first performed in May

1979 in Soweto, and reworked a number of times before being taken on tour of Europe in 1981. The urge to conscientise, evident in Manaka's work, is even more powerfully present in The hungry earth, which is structured consciously on Brechtian lines as a lecture demonstration consisting of a prologue and five scenes designed to present, as in Egoli, a landscape characterised by human as well as industrial exploitation.

In scenes entitled 'The hostel', 'The plantation', 'The train', 'The mine' and 'The compound' The hungry earth counteridentifies the claim to a Christian social formation made by the prevailing apartheid order. It depicts aspects of the lives of migrant and child labourers, poor working conditions in the mining industry, the ruthless quelling of a strike and the destruction of family life. The characters are named according to the qualities they represent – Shield, Loin Cloth, Sufferings and Imbecile and instead of a focus upon interiority, the text presents the subject as crucially shaped and controlled by the processes within which s/he is located. In a manner reminiscent not only of the medieval morality play but of traditional African drama with its concern to identify and ritualise for its community what it perceives to be important truths, the play, even more than Egoli, endeavours by means of song and direct address to the audience as well as semi-realistic dramatic sequences to conscientise. Throughout the play, Maponya's interest is continually directed against prevailing discourse – which defines such processes differently – in the world of audience as well as actors. Thus in the first scene, Matlhoko tells of a dream he has had. This briefly expresses the discourse of colonialism, beginning with the white man's arrival and how 'We gave him shelter. We adopted his ideas and his teachings. Then he told of a God and all Black faces were full of smiles' (p. 153) He then registers some of the material processes accompanying this 'Christianisation':

we grumbled inwardly, smiled and listened hard as he was quoting from the Holy Book…and whilst we were still smiling, he set up laws, organised an army, and started digging up the gold and diamonds; and by the time our poor fore-fathers opened their eyes… he had moved to Europe. He has left his army behind to 'take care of the unruly elements that may provoke a revolution'. (p. 153)

The ensuing dialogue repeatedly juxtaposes colonialist and Black Consciousness modes of discourse in ways that imply and argue for the reconstitution of the subject in terms of militance and resistance:

Umlungu deserves to die. Let us set out to catch him and when we catch him we will hang him from the nearest tree. His servants must also be killed: they betrayed us. Let us kill the whole lot. (p. 153)

The text also resorts in this to the mystical evocation of 'Mother Africa', discovering an essential unity in the past, 'the days of ISANDLWANA and the days of UMGUNGUNDLOVU [the battle between the Zulus and the British in 1879 and the battle between the Zulus and the Boers in 1838]. The days when our forefathers fought hard for what was theirs, for mother Africa' (p. 155). It appeals aggressively to a divine force as well as to the assertion of black value and identity for inspiration. And as part of the attack upon prevailing discourse, Maponya also works through Zulu. If English is one of the two official languages in South Africa, the other being Afrikaans, as in other plays especially of this period, the text dislodges the potency of the apartheid centre by eschewing its official languages several times, particularly when expressing aggressively contestatory positions, thus disabling those members of the ruling classes in the audience who do not speak African languages.

Such merging of essentialism and nationalist references to the past, with attempts to address material conditions, in The hungry earth and in Egoli may partly have been influenced by developments in Black Consciousness itself. By 1974 some advocates becoming 'less hopeful about the urban middle class'[22] began to think more pointedly about the economy and many adherents of Black Consciousness who were driven into exile from 1974 on, explored Marxist texts, mostly of Chinese origin in Botswana.[23] Although overt Black Consciousness activity diminished because of state suppression, with the banning of the Black Consciousness Movement in 1977, the Azanian People's Organisation, formed in 1978, 'inherited the ideological mantle of Black Consciousness'.[24] It, as well as other organisations, particularly from the Cape, formed the National Forum in 1983 which pursued, as distinct from the broad-based popular United Democratic Front that also came into being in 1983, an 'avowedly class analysis and identification of the black working class as the primum mobile of genuine liberation'.[25] Nevertheless, it is important to add that despite 'its unambiguous commitment to building a socialist Azania', the National Forum remained 'a rather loose amalgamation of ideological currents from explicitly socialist to radical nationalist'.[26]

At least as significant, Manaka and Maponya worked in a period during which the government, after the crisis which the Uprising of 1976 signalled, had embarked on its policy of Total Strategy, particularly in the fields of industrial relations and urban policy. Through what were known as reformist policies the government attempted to regain control of the situation and maintain its own position – 'the Riekert Commission was mandated to investigate urban policy, the Wiehahn Commission was instructed to re-examine the industrial relations system'.[27] The one attempted 'to bolster the privileges of urban insiders at the expense of rural outsiders' by granting a measure of rights including the acquisition of property and local government to urban dwellers (while preserving the principle of national rights only through the bantustans); the other attempted to couple recognition of trade unions with 'the imposition of institutional checks and balances'.[28] But in the ensuing period, Total Strategy was opposed, notably by the trade unions who managed to obstruct 'the state's intention of excluding migrant workers from the trade unions'.[29] Migrant workers were thus able to 'organise and mobilise alongside urban insiders, thus undermining the Riekart strategy that attempted to divide the working classes along urban-rural lines'.[30] Protracted struggles to win recognition, wage increases and strike levels increased dramatically from 1979, side by side, over the next few years, with a growth in community organisations of all kinds.[31] It is perhaps not surprising therefore that plays such as The hungry earth and Egoli, endeavour to represent, explore and interrogate aspects of migrant labour, even if they do not register directly on stage, contemporary developments within industrial relations.

The Reverend Julius Maqina's work provides another example in this period of theatre which draws on aspects of Black Consciousness.[32] As I remarked, repeatedly subject to state harassment not only during the mid-1970s but after, he enjoyed popular support in the townships for work that, like Kente's, mixed political commitment with entertainment. Presenting all his plays in township venues on the Witwatersrand as well as in the Eastern Cape, Maqina, a former schoolteacher and President of the African Churches Association, based the next play he was able to turn to after five years of house arrest, Dry those tears (1983) upon the experience of a young man who, without the necessary documentation for work in the city, decides to commit suicide. The primary focus is upon the central character, his relationships and his search to find a place in his world, an essentialist preoccupation with identity that is paralleled by the Black Consciousness presentation of pre-colonial Africa in Utopian terms. But Maqina too investigates material conditions in his play, incorporating commentary on the legal system which controls black labour. The major theme song in the play is entitled 'We have the right to sell our labour', in, it is also asserted, 'this land of ours', (p. 466) and several other attacks upon modes of exploitation are delivered during the course of the play.

The more recent work of Manaka and Maponya shows an increased interest in the exploration of interiority in the attempt to assert a sense of identity and self against the erasures in apartheid discourse. Indeed, Manaka describes two recent plays directly as explorations of 'self'. Maponya's play, *Gangsters*, one of many plays that attempt to contest the silence of prevailing discourse about the penal system, was produced at the Laager in the Market Theatre complex in 1984.[33] Offering several times a critique of the policy of Total Strategy, the play focuses on the interaction between three characters: the poet Rasechaba, who expresses Black Consciousness and essentialist values, Whitebeard a white security officer and Jonathan a black security officer. Rasechaba is presented romantically – 'if the spirit of the nation moves within him, he will write about the nation. He will talk about man, he'll talk about pain and he'll talk about that which moves the people' (p. 64). The play's strongly essentialist predilection is evident, amongst much else, in the interspersion of the main narrative, which depicts the arrest and interrogation of Rasechaba, with sequences which show the dead Rasechaba on a cross while his two murderers discuss his death, and wonder how to conceal the fact of his murder.

IV Black theology and *Woza Albert!*

Mbongeni Ngema and Percy Mtwa, perhaps the most successful theatrical practitioners in recent decades with township as well as city audiences, suggest in their work, like Manaka and Maponya, just such a movement towards a sharpening of material consciousness, even if this falls short of the class awareness to which Nolutshungu as well as the even more determined Kavanagh point. Ngema and Mtwa met whilst working for Gibson Kente in his township musical *Mama and the load* and formed the Earth Players. Ngema, whose father was a policeman, was born in Natal and worked on jobs in Richards Bay and in various companies whilst he developed his expertise in music and with the guitar and slowly found work in theatre. Mtwa, who was born on the Witwatersrand, also became interested in music and theatre from an early age, and as a young man supported himself as a stores clerk in Dunlop Industries, whilst he worked as a dancer and singer. The two men devised an early version of *Woza Albert!*, whilst touring for Kente and then approached Barney Simon, to collaborate. As one of the founders of the Market theatre and producer of many plays he was a far more powerful figure in South African theatre than they. The play opened first at the Market Theatre in 1981 and was an instant success, subsequently playing throughout South Africa to black and white audiences as well as to audiences in many countries abroad.

Simon's liberal view of the subject, evident in his own work, must clearly have been excited by the interest in interiority which he found in the humanist concerns of *Woza Albert!*, in the actors' portrayal with superb miming and mimetic skills of different township inhabitants of different ages and sexes. The play suggests too the vitality and endurance of particular versions of Christian discourse in South Africa. Where in the case of Dhlomo, Christianity was used mainly as a means of counter-identifying the unChristian behaviour of the ruling classes, *Woza Albert!* operates in ways that suggest the inspirational Christianity and liberation theology which, especially since 1976, has increasingly influenced the practice of Christianity amongst members of the oppressed classes.

This version of Christianity developed partly from the Christian elements in Black Consciousness discourse, which argued that black Christians must, as Manas Buthulezi, a Lutheran theologian, declared, 'in delving into the immeasurable resources of the liberating gospel and exploiting that which God has implanted in their souls',[34] draw their resources not only from Christianity but from African culture, a connection developed too by Allan Boesak:

Black Consciousness may be described as the awareness of black people that their humanity is constituted by their blackness. It means that black people are no longer ashamed that they are black, that they have a black history and a black culture distinct from the history and culture of white people. It means that blacks are determined to be judged no longer by, and to adhere no longer to white values. It is an attitude, a way of life. Viewed thus, Black Consciousness is an integral part of Black Power. But Black Power is also a clear critique of and a force for fundamental change in systems and patterns in society which oppress or which give rise to the oppressions of black people. Black Theology is the reflection of black Christians on the situation in which they live and on their struggle for liberation. (cited in de Gruchy, p. 153)

Liberation theology grew in part too from the developing confrontation between many Christians and the state from the 1960s onwards. In 1968 the Christian Institute delivered a *Message to the people of South Africa* in which they asserted that apartheid could not be justified by an 'appeal to God's word'[35] to which the Prime Minister at the time John Vorster replied angrily:

I reject the insolence you display in attacking my Church as you do. This also applies to other Churches, ministers of the Gospel and confessing members of other Churches who do in fact believe in separate development...I again want to make a serious appeal to you to return to the essence of your preaching and to proclaim to your congregations the Word of God and the Gospel of Christ. (cited in de Grucy, p. 119).

Such views were not accepted by the black members of the Reformed Church movement to which Vorster claimed adherence. Dr Allan Boesak, moderator of that branch of the Reformed Church with 'coloured' members, which broke away from those Afrikaner Reformed Churches at the time still prepared to sanction apartheid, declared at the World Alliance of Reformed Churches in August 1982 at Ottawa, 'not only is South Africa the most blatantly racist country in the world, it is also the country where the church is most openly identified with the racism and oppression that exists in that society'.[36] He quoted a statement made by black participants in a South African Council of Churches Consultation on Racism in 1980, that 'the persistent cries of the black people that the Church is not consistent with the demands of the gospel of Jesus Christ have fallen on deaf ears' (cited on p. 2) asserting too that 'although this was said of *all* Churches in South Africa, it remains true that the white Dutch Reformed Churches must assume special responsibility for the situation' (p. 2). If it is in such contexts that liberation theology has developed in South Africa, its spirit may be glimpsed in the writing of the Reverend Frank Chikane, who at different periods of his life has been detained and tortured, forced to go underground, as well as spending time in exile from South Africa:

we need to thank God that Jesus rose again and He is alive. This assures us that in our death a new life will rise, a new society, a new heaven and a new earth (Rev 21). Philippians 1:20-21 became a reality for me on the fourth floor of Krugersdorp Police Station. I was tortured there and made to stand for 50 hours with teams of interrogators working eight hours per shift during my 1977-8 detention. When one of my torturers told me that I was 'going to die slowly but surely', I said to him that 'for me to live is Christ but to die is gain'. I told him that if he let me live I would still continue even more vehemently to proclaim the gospel and challenge the evil and satanic system of apartheid. But if they let me die then it would be gain for me, because I would be with the Lord. Because then, and now, as always, Christ will be honoured in my body whether by life or by death. Whichever way, their kingdom of apartheid will come to an end and Jesus will reign.[37]

The argument that Christ's sympathies lie exclusively with the oppressed in South Africa, or the image of the return of Christ to South Africa – both evident in *Woza Albert!* – is often put in this discourse. Boesak asserts that:

Behind the ideology of apartheid is the theology of apartheid. A theology has led Afrikaners to believe that they are the chosen people of God, that whites in some special way have a divine right to rule, and that their overprivileged position is somehow God's will...The truth of the gospel cuts through this propaganda. It is liberating for black South Africans to discover that the message of the Bible is that God is the God of the poor, that He is on the side of the oppressed. He is not on the side of the poor because they are black, but because they are poor and oppressed. His reign as king of kings means that this order of things shall be overturned. In the eyes of whites, black lives may count for nothing – as seen so vividly in the murder of Biko – but in His eyes the lives of the despised are precious.[38]

And the Director of the Commission on Justice and Reconciliation in the South African Council of Churches, Wolfram Kistner, developing such interpretations, asks:

In whose company do we encounter Christ in South Africa today? Which areas of the country are his preference areas? These areas...are the relocation areas, the areas of the marginalised and discarded people. Possibly the prison cells of the section 22 and section 6 detainees are his headquarters for many a night and many a day. Looking for him outside the gate we find him in resettlement camps and homelands where people are crowded together and economically deprived, abandoned to starvation, unemployment and the arbitrary rule of a political oligarchy supported by the South African government.[39]

Although it does not necessarily deliberately advocate such views, *Woza Albert!* is based upon 'a fantasy of a Second Coming to South Africa by Morena, the Saviour'[40] and portrays the dramatised reactions of a whole range of characters to this return. Inspirational and liberation Christianity is at the least complemented in the implicit hopes that underlie such a dramatic situation, and some of the tendencies evident within it. And from this point of view, too, the body which is in other respects important in the performance of the play signifies not only capacity for suffering but the capacity to stand up for principle and so resist – significations that clearly point to the agony of the Christ figure. *Woza Albert!* also expresses the certainty that when the Christian saviour comes, he will side with the oppressed. In one scene he advises the pass seekers at the Albert Street pass offices to throw away their passes and follow him to Soweto, and in another he encourages workers at the Coronation Brickyard to resist exploitation and to strike, so that Baas Kom, the white supervisor, phones the police, defining him in terms of prevailing discourse as a 'terrorist' (p. 51). Appropriately Christ is finally imprisoned on Robben island where he himself resists an attack – in words which parody the double speak of a 'government' announcer in the media seeking to deny events or recast them in terms of its own prevailing discourse:

Mrs Fatimah Mossop, domestic servant, Sea Point, a freak survivor of the calamity, insisted that the explosion emanated from a human figure walking across the bay from the Island, supporting the superstition that the nuclear-type explosion was an inevitable result of a bomb attack on Morena. The Prime Minister himself continues to deny any relationship between Morena and the agitator imprisoned on the island. Mrs Fatimah Mossop is still under observation by the state psychiatrists. (pp. 69-71)

These sequences reflect the notion of an active and militant Christianity rather than a passive one – as one of the speakers earlier in the play says to Morena to underline the point 'A man hits this cheek you give him the other. Aikhona Morena! They're calling the police to arrest you now!' (p. 52).

The play also manifests repeated concern with material conditions as when the brickworkers remind Morena that they live 'in a tin! Like sardine fish!' while the bricks they produce 'go to make a big house, six rooms for two people. A white man and his wife!' (p. 49). The return of Christ, it is imagined will entail his own interrogation of material as well as political conditions:

Morena will say… What place is this? This place where old people weep over the graves of children? How has it happened? How has it been permitted? I've passed people with burning mouths. People buying water in a rusty piece of tin…I see families torn apart… (p. 60).

If prevailing discourse works in part powerfully through the body itself, as I noted in discussing earlier plays – using the body and skin colour as signs either of worth and supremacy, or of lack of worth, impurity, and inferiority, *Woza Albert!* also works against this in its use of the body. Drawing on principles suggested in Grotowski, the actors appear on stage for the most part in track suit trousers, with bare torsos and their bodies become signifiers in performance of energy, wit, and intelligence, skill, the capacity for humour and humanity – all that is denied in prevailing discourse. In a swift sequence at the opening of the play the process whereby such bodies are dominated is quickly outlined. Firstly, the players impersonate an orchestra, and their virtuosity is followed by a satiric presentation of the stupidity of agents of the state as they demand those passes that control the movement and labour of these bodies, while the very next scene shows, by dramatising the physical examination of workers on stage, the way in which the ruling classes reduce these bodies into units of labour, subject at their whim to any kind of physical scrutiny.

And *Woza Albert!* also draws on and develops other techniques, used especially in *Sizwe Bansi is dead*, to intensify the play's metonymic thrust, such as the use of the actor's own names, the use of sarcasm and irony directed at existing relations and rapid interchange of roles to represent a variety of township inhabitants which, as I have already remarked, evokes not only the multiplicity of township life, but produces, in the intermingling of roles, effects of solidarity and commonality.

The dramatic conflict and contestation in the play comes from the presentation both of individuals and then the Christ figure himself, who are continually under pressure from a dominant and oppressive social order. They struggle to resist this pressure partly through this inspirational vision of the return of the forces of Christianity which is presented as militant, determined to contribute to the struggle for liberation and the millennium: 'and Morena will say, come to me, you who are divided from your families. Let us go to the cities where your husbands work. We will find houses where you can live together and we will talk to those who you fear! What country is this!' (p. 60). The final scene takes place in a graveyard in which some of the great past fighters of liberation, oppressed, banned suppressed, sometimes murdered, are resurrected, a metaphor for the recovery not only of a narrative of liberation to set against the denial of the role of such activists in history in prevailing discourse, but also for the intensifi-cation of the spirit of struggle which infused the lives and actions of those recalled. The ending entails also, in the image of resurrection, again desire for the millennium – in the discourse which this play often resonates, the resurrection of the body of the South African social order, in the spirit of the Christ in whom it believes.

V The days of reckoning: *Asinamali!* and *Bopha!*

The subsequent work of Ngema and Mtwa suggests a more urgent concern with material conditions in the social order, and a more aggressive stance against the state, expressed in their representation of the details of township struggle in the mid-1980s. Events in the late 1970s and early 1980s, included protracted labour struggles involving a series of strikes in the 1979-82 period in the Eastern and Western Cape, Natal, and the East Rand, the re-emergence of political organisations as I noted in the last chapter, such as the United Democratic Front (UDF) and National Forum (NF) in 1983, and uprisings, particularly in the Vaal triangle, against rent increases, producing 'rent boycotts, squatter camps, struggles and stayaways'.[41] These were to lead to levels of conflict between the state and the black communities 'unprecedented in South African history' (p. 11). The disintegration through successful boycotts of government attempts at administrative and constitutional reform in the townships as well as in the elections for the new constitution with its tricameral parliament in 1984 was followed in the coming years by 'widespread sustained popular rebellion, resulting in the collapse of civil government in many townships, a deepening recession... and the steady disintegration of civil society's social and ideological fabric as rising levels of violence, poverty and disillusionment [took] their toll' (p. 10). In the townships this included in the 1980s the continuing presence of the police, with their hippos, caspirs and sten guns, the use of stone throwing as a means of defiance, and for a period, in response to the problem of township informers and as a means of retribution, the use of necklacing. Since 1984

from the small rural villages of the northern and eastern Transvaal to the metropolitan agglomerations of the Witwatersrand, to the small towns and metropolises of the Cape, the communities, workplaces and schools have become the loci of black opposition and rebellion that has affected ever-widening layers of the black population. Workers through their trade unions, township residents in the civic associations, militant youths in the youth congresses, students in the student congresses and parents in the Parents Crisis Committee – all these constituencies have been organised and their efforts coalesced around a set of common demands frequently articulated by national organisations such as the United Democratic Front, National Education Crisis Committee and the major trade union federations. (p. 11)

Swilling notes that, in responding to this, the state detained over 50,000 people after 1984. Two states of emergency were imposed, countless meetings and demonstrations were broken up, the shooting of peaceful demonstrators, the banning and jailing of political leaders, and the ever increasing curtailment of press freedom followed.[42]

Asinamali! by Ngema opened in May 1985, at the Market Theatre in Johannesburg; in October 1985, *Bopha!* by Percy Mtwa also opened at the Market Theatre.[43] Both of these plays, paralleling or reflecting events within the social order portray the subject, while still recognising the exploitative and oppressive nature of existing relations from humanist perspectives, pivotally in the stance of continuing anger and readiness to resist. *Asinamali!*, meaning 'we have no money' presents five prisoners in a cell who relate their stories to one another. The most crucial of these involves the resistance which the people of Lamontville township in Natal near Durban have given to rent increases, part of the larger series of rent strikes and consumer boycotts that from mid-1985 swept townships throughout the country. *Bopha!* presents the story of a policeman who persuades his brother to join the force, but whose son participates in the resistance movement in the townships. In the course of the play both the father and his brother begin to understand the repressive system of which they are active agents, and by the end of it both change sides to join the activist son.

The plays interrogate the legal and police systems, utilising, in the school of *Woza Albert!*, satiric mockery, song, the playing of different roles by the same actor, together, particularly in *Asinamali!*, with direct address to the audience and at one point even direct interrogation. Often revealing hatred of police informers and betrayers, both plays also present the oppressed subject within a communal if not a class perspective. In *Asinamali!* as they recount their experience, the men interact with one another in ways reminiscent of *Survival. Bopha!*, which probes the interaction within a family, in the context of the larger movement to resistance, and which employs a greater measure of dramatic realism, portrays the need for growth in consciousness of at least political exploitation, an understanding that is in the course of the play achieved within the particular family in a way that argues for the importance of a unified stance within a situation of virtual civil war. Both plays thus tend to validate loyalty to community and to argue the value of socially based and considered perceptions. In neither play, by its end, is the subject presented in ways that seek or suggest positions of isolation or alienation.

Particularly in their readiness to confront the realities of current struggle in the townships and in their readiness to confront their audiences with the often harrowing incidents and events in the struggle, these plays transgress what until then had been explored on stage. Furthermore, the structure and techniques of such plays, especially Asinamali!, may be said to dislodge what in another context has been called the 'dominant specularity' of the audience, the sense that it has acquired 'a sure and centrally embracing view'.[44] The performance of plays such as Asinamali! in practice, in the shifting narratives delivered on stage, the continual movement from dramatic action into dance and then back again,the changing perspectives as first one and then another speaker addresses the audience, the movement from one enacted sequence into song, and then again into another enacted sequence, and the deliberate interrogation or provocation of the audience, work towards the recognition of discontinuity, con-tradiction, the fact of mobility in process, the impossibility of a sure and centrally embracing view. Traditional modes of dramatic realism or naturalism are constantly disrupted in ways that not only encourage an analytic stance but contest any construction of a smooth and continuous manageable dramatic action which might mirror or suggest a similar construction of the social order.

But what such plays, finally, resort to as dramatic means of containing the movement of the play from the space of the stage into the uncontrollable and disjunctive processes in that space within which the theatrical space is situated – as I have noted already in the case of several other plays – is again the reconstruction of a history of resistance, glimpses of retributive resolution, nationalism, the asser-tion of a culture of liberation, evocation of the millennium. Thus in Asinamali! the song

Winnie Mandela Hai!
Is our mother Hai (repeatedly)
Mrs Botha fuck you
Uzal'izinja [she gives birth to dogs]
Voetsek Voetsek.
Bishop Tutu Hai
Is our hero
Bishop Tutu is our father Hai (pp. 210-211)

is placed against the narrative

And then we buried my friend Bhekani. Like all our heroes, we carried his coffin on our shoulders. That was a funeral of courage... police moved in.

You know what they did? They shot women and kids inside the graveyard, and we, the men, they did not see us. We were hiding up there next to that informer's house. We just watched with nothing in our hands but stones. (p. 217)

This is placed also against another scene describing a police battle as well as the burning of an informer, and besides, as the play ends the actors' phalanx of resistance as they sing, in Zulu:

Elamanqamu namhlanje, namhlanje zinsizwa Elamanqamu, elamanqamu namhlanje Kwaphel'izinsizwa, kwasal'amavaka ayobaleka Elamanqamu, elamanqamu namhlanje. [(Today is the D-Day, today is the day) Gone are the brave men, only the cowards remain and they will run Because today is the day It is the day of Reckoning.] (p. 224)

VI Women in drama: Sarafina!

In Fugard's as well as in Uys's plays, contestation against prevailing discourse is almost always expressed through women and this in a social order the ruling class of which is dominated by strongly patriarchal and Afrikaner Calvinist discourse. And while there is no shortage of actresses, the number of dissident white women participating in the writing of or production of plays remains small. Although women of the oppressed classes experience exploitation, oppression and struggle in the same ways as men, in the vast majority of plays coming from the subordinate classes oppression, struggle and resistance is presented through the male figure. This is only partly explained by the practical and real difficulty theatrical practitioners experience in travelling great distances through sometimes hazardous conditions to audition, rehearse for and perform in plays.

In the 1970s, as I noted in chapter 7, the play Imfuduso was conceived and created by the women of Crossroads squatter camp to describe their experiences. Also in the 1970s, Fatimah Dike worked on two plays at the Space Theatre in Cape Town The sacrifice of Kreli, and The first South African – but while both her plays endeavour to engage with aspects of the social order current in the 1970s, both work predominantly through male dramatic characters.

In the 1980s, a few plays predominantly the work of women have emerged, most significantly in 1986 You strike the woman you strike the rock which, presenting women's perspectives on the struggle and the role

of black women in contemporary South Africa, was devised by
Nomvula Qosha, Thobeka Maqutyana and Poppy Tsira and directed by
Phyllis Klotz, a white woman from Cape Town, assisted by Xolani
September. To date not published, it has been performed in Cape
Town, Johannesburg and abroad. In 1985 the Market had held a six-
week Women's Festival of the Arts, during which several attempts at
drama were undertaken.[45] Other women from the ruling classes who
have written plays include Geraldine Aron, who eschews any overt
political concerns in her work, and more recently, Claire Stopford. And
a dissenting Afrikaans playwright Reza De Wet has won much praise
for her play in Afrikaans, *Diepe grond* which was followed by another
Nag generaal, also well received. Nevertheless, barring the work of Aron,
none of these writers have yet had their work published. *Have you seen
Zandile?*, a play which explores the life of a young teenager separated
from her mother, in profoundly personal terms, first performed at the
Market Theatre in Johannesburg in 1986, won the Fringefirst Award
at the Edinburgh Festival in the same year and subsequently played
elsewhere in both Europe and America.[46] Praised for its intimate and
personal perspectives in depicting a painful life of physical and
emotional deprivation, the play was devised by Gcina Mhlophe on
whose autobiography it is based, and Thembi Mtshali, both of whom
performed in it, together with Maralin Vanrenen a white theatre
practitioner who directed. And again, Else Joubert, an Afrikaans writer,
based a book on interviews she had with Poppie Nongena, recording
the black woman's experiences in both rural and urban contexts. Very
successful, it was turned into a play, and *Poppie* has since been produced
both in South Africa and abroad. In South Africa it was chosen for
performance by the government-subsidised PACT, virtually the only
play until then with partly black participation which it had undertaken.
The play, like *Have you seen Zandile?* is based on the woman's life presented
through narrative and enacted sequences that, in contrast to *Asinamali*,
construct a smooth and continuous narration of a personal history
albeit one full of suffering. While the audience's empathy is enlisted,
whatever subversive thrusts appear to inform the work are contained
– no interrogation that might prompt analysis of the relations of power
that underlie Poppie's suffering, and no hint of liberation from it
occurs. Thus a moment in the 1976 Uprising enacted in a brief scene,
is played, in darkness, suggesting through confused movement and
shouting, a sense of unarticulated fear and mindless violence. To a
degree like the numerous audiences who saw a different version of it

performed abroad, anxious for different reasons to find evidence of
their own sensibility, middle-class audiences filled the Alexander
Theatre in Johannesburg night after night. Presumably satisfied by such
evidence of their own compassion they were quite able to leave the
descriptions of suffering they had witnessed on stage behind them after
the performance.

The relative paucity of women's involvement in theatre made
Ngema's decision to concentrate on women in his presentation of
aspects of the 1976 Uprising in *Sarafina!* all the more significant. This
musical in the tradition of Gibson Kente's township musicals which
opened at the Market Theatre in 1986 has since become a hit musical
on Broadway, and its success enabled Ngema to open a second
company, which started its run at the Market in December 1988 and
was then taken on tour abroad in 1989. Ngema's Committed Artists,
which he formed after *Woza Albert!* and which, after the winning of a
number of awards and support from abroad for *Asinamali!* was able to
embark on the major musical, is an important organisation, affording
as it does increasing opportunity for acting and training to large
numbers of black actors who otherwise would not have the chance to
embark on careers in the theatre.

In addition to the opportunities for increased employment which
the success of *Sarafina!* has brought to black theatre practitioners, the
general level of expertise and ability in performance which the play
exhibits has in itself contestatory value; no other attempts in South
African theatre – and particularly not the shoddy offerings of the state-
subsidised Performing Arts Councils – have ever attained the same
standard.

Both of these practical factors should be born in mind when Ngema
is, as he has been, criticised by some commentators for an alleged
commercialism in his presentation of township struggle, or for his
apparent perpetuation of a focus upon the hero rather than upon
communal struggle. I suggest that more significant than this, however,
is his presentation in the play of woman. While accusations of sexism
have been levelled at, for instance, the presentation of the teacher in
the play, these should be set against the fact that it is the young teenager
Sarafina herself who emerges as the most committed activist. Mistress
the schoolteacher, moreover, contests what is insisted on in prevailing
discourse by teaching her pupils 'the history that is not in the books,
the history of our people' (pp. 1-12),[47] and sanctions, within the
school the student's production of not Shakespeare but 'a play about

this school and the children of Soweto' (pp. 1-14). And it is the story of Victoria Mxenge, the activist lawyer who was murdered by state assassins, that Sarafina tells her fellow students. In the final moment of the play she is the one who plays a freed Nelson Mandela addressing Soweto. The glimpse of the millennium and the discourse of a culture of resistance on which such theatre often draws, is, for once, presented on the South African stage by a young woman:

There will be millions of people, millions from all over the world in a big open field in Soweto. The whole place will be vibrating. Women will be ululating. *She ululates.* Dust will be rising to the skies. The air will be filled with the sounds of laughter. People will be rubbing shoulders with one voice, one thought, one colour. Everybody will be shouting…'My people today I am free'. And the people will say… We were released from prison because you never forgot us. You constantly demanded our release and carried on the struggle. We are here today not to revenge or destroy but to build the future. Where all of us, Black and White can come together and forget the past and work to liberate our land. We should remember that it is only when South Africa is free that all of Africa can be free. And the people will go wild! Today I see all my friends, brothers, sisters, our heroes. I feel the spirit of those that died for our liberation. The liberation of the *entire* African community in all corners of the world. The spirit of Steven Biko, Samora Machel, Martin Luther King, Kwame Nkrumah, Marcus Garvey, Robert Sobukwe, Malcolm X, Victoria Mxenge… Their spirit is right here with us today. They are here to celebrate what they believed and lived for and died for…The Day of Liberation! (pp. 2-28)

Notes

1 Kavanagh, Robert, 'Theatre and the struggle for national liberation', unpublished paper presented at CASA, Amsterdam, December 1987, p. 25.
2 Nolutshungu, *Changing South Africa*, p. 147.
3 Coplan, In township tonight!, pp. 211-12.
4 Coplan, In township tonight!, pp. 212-13; Larlham, *Black theatre, dance and ritual*, pp. 70-1.
5 Peterson, Bhekizizwe, 'Apartheid and the political imagination in black South African theatre', unpublished manuscript, p. 10.
6 Horn, 'South African theatre: ideology and rebellion', p. 212.
7 Kavanagh, 'Theatre and struggle for national liberation', p. 9.
8 Luther, Carola, and Maponya, Maishe, 'Problems and possibilities: a discussion on the making of alternative theatre in South Africa', *The English academy review*, II, 1984, pp. 19-21.
9 Horn, 'South African theatre: ideology and rebellion', p. 212.
10 Schwartz, *The best of company*, p. 162.
11 Kavanagh, 'Theatre and the struggle for national liberation', pp. 16-17.
12 Steadman, 'Drama and social consciousness', p. 468.

J

13 See Holloway, Myles, 'Social commentary and artistic mediation in Zakes Mda's early plays', *The English academy review*, VI, 1989, p. 28.

14 Larlham, *Black theatre, dance and ritual*, p. 91.

15 Sole, Review of *Organise and act*, p. 206.

16 Murray, *South Africa*, p. 107.

17 See Hauptfleisch and Steadman, ed, *South African theatre*, p. 150.

18 Manaka, Matsemela, *Egoli*, Johannesburg: Ravan, no publication date.

19 Steadman, 'Drama and social consciousness', p. 370.

20 Manaka, *Egoli*, pp. 19-20.

21 Maponya, Maishe, *The hungry earth*, in *South African theatre*, ed. Hauptfleisch and Steadman.

22 Nolutshungu, *Changing South Africa*, p. 155.

23 Nolutshungu, *Changing South Africa*, p. 159.

24 Murray, *South Africa*, p. 226.

25 Murray, *South Africa*, p. 228.

26 Murray, *South Africa*, p. 228.

27 Swilling, 'Introduction', p. 5.

28 Swilling, 'Introduction' p. 6.

29 Swilling, 'Introduction', p. 8.

30 Swilling, 'Introduction', p. 8.

31 See Swilling, 'Introduction', p. 9.

32 Steadman, 'Drama and social consciousness', pp. 463-8.

33 Maponya, Maisha, *Gangsters*, in Ndlovu, Duma, ed., *Woza Afrika!*, New York: George Braziller, 1986.

34 Cited in de Gruchy, John W., *The Church struggle in South Africa*, Claremont: David Philip, 1979, p. 153.

35 See de Gruchy, *The Church struggle in South Africa*, p. 118.

36 Boesak, Allan A., *If this is treason, I am guilty*, United States of America: William B. Eerdmans, 1987, p. 2.

37 Chikane, Frank, *No life of my own*, Johannesburg: Skotaville, 1988, pp. 6-7.

38 Boesak, Allan, 'Proclamation and protest: the lost sons', in Villa-Vicencio, Charles and de Gruchy, John W., *Resistance and hope: South African essays in honour of Beyers Naude*, Claremont: David Philip, 1985, pp. 76-7.

39 Kistner, Wolfram, 'Proclamation and protest: outside the gate', in Villa-Vicencio and de Gruchy, *Resistance and hope*, p. 80.

40 Mtwa, Percy, Ngema, Mbongeni and Simon, Barney, *Woza Albert!*, London: Methuen, 1983, Introduction, no pagination.

41 Swilling, 'Introduction', pp. 8-10.

42 Swilling, 'Introduction' p. 11.

43 Ngema, Mbongeni, *Asinamali!*, and Mtwa, Percy, *Bopha!*, in Ndlovu, *Woza Afrika!*

44 Easthope, Anthony, *British post-structuralism*, London: Routledge, 1988, pp. 48, 56.

45 Schwartz, *The best of company*, p. 106.

46 Mhlophe, Gcina, Vanrenen, Maralin and Mtshali, Thembi, *Have you seen Zandile?*, Johannesburg: Skotaville, 1988.

47 Quoted from an unpublished text of the play very kindly given to me by Mbongeni Ngema.

9

The Shakespeare connection

No study of drama in South Africa can ignore the fact that for most South Africans drama in South Africa means, certainly in the formative years, the study and sometimes the performance of Shakespeare. This is because the Shakespeare text, often the only dramatic work prescribed in school syllabuses, has always featured as a compulsory component in secondary education throughout the country. The effects of this are, however, neither innocent nor haphazard. The way the Shakespeare text has been used over the decades not only in South African secondary education, but by the majority of ruling class participants in theatre, the media and in academic, professional and commercial adult life, has made Shakespeare for many a powerful signifier of conservatism.

In South Africa, as often elsewhere in colonial and post-colonial worlds, Shakespeare has been primarily appropriated by most amongst the English-speaking educated members of the ruling classes as a means of evidencing their affiliations with the imperial and colonial centres. Possession and knowledge of Shakespeare texts becomes evidence of empowerment, enabling these members of the ruling classes to construct themselves both as affiliates of the metropolis and as superior to the subordinate classes. For them, enlightened subjects from these inferior classes, those positively seeking affiliation, may be raised and uplifted by the study of Shakespeare. But the Shakespeare text is also made compulsory in almost all cases in secondary education throughout South Africa, implying that all subordinate as well as ruling class subjects, whether or not they positively seek affiliation, need Shakespeare to be fully educated, indeed fully human. Shakespeare has thus become for members of the educated ruling classes one signifier of 'civilisation', astoundingly that is, it should never be forgotten, in South Africa one signifier for white apartheid 'civilisation'. The web of such a use of Shakespeare spins not only through institutions of education, the media, establishment theatre, public cultural bodies, but even into the thinking of some of the country's large conglomerates of capital.

I Separate but equal Shakespeare

The battle for the future South Africa - being waged in many places - within education is being fought, as it in practice always has been, partly by teachers and lecturers in English in classrooms and lecture halls throughout the country. There, as much as anywhere else, the subject is constructed for and in students being educated in terms of, amongst other things, the literatures chosen for study, the reading strategies encouraged in or denied students, the view - or absence of a view - of their culture imparted to them. The discourses to which they are exposed in this process contribute to the way in which they imagine their own positions within the social order.

This has been well understood by the proponents of apartheid and the advocates of Christian National Education, whose control of education in South Africa since 1948 has had important consequences which continue to operate within educational institutions in South Africa - with, in practice, the relative acquiescence of the vast majority of current English educationists. What might be an important site of contestation still remains firmly within the grasp of those forces concerned to preserve existing relations.

It is important to recall in this context what some aspects of the apartheid system of education actually entail. Nqabeni Mathonsi stresses that 'any discussion of education in South Africa, particularly education available to the black section of the population, must be presented against a background of conditions and attitudes which are not immediately educational'.[1] Dr Verwoerd, a future Prime Minister of South Africa, who asked in one of the House of Assembly debates when he was still Minister of Education, 'what is the use of teaching the Bantu child mathematics when it cannot use it in practice?' and who observed on another occasion that 'the school must equip him (sic) (the Bantu child) to meet the demands which the economic life of South Africa will impose on him (sic)' has been credited with the creation of apartheid education.[2] But the evidence indicates that he was merely formalising a process begun much earlier. In 1936 the Welsh Commission on education, for instance, noted that 'the education of the white child prepares him (sic) for life in a dominant society and the education of the black child for a subordinate society' (p. 47). For South African schoolchildren, as Ellen Kuzwayo has pointed out, the consequences of such a policy were manifold. For example, the system established for white children, 'catered fully for the needs and interests of the school population of that community'.[3] But the opposite applied for blacks. Thus, whereas children coming out of that group of 'industrialists, professionals, competent well-to-do tradesmen, wealthy merchants in different spheres, small and big business men, had their school fees and books paid for by the state, which also provided them with school meals' (p. 9), black families remained responsible for school and book fees, while in the early 1950s the government cancelled the school meals schemes for black schools. The long-standing problems of education for black schoolchildren in South Africa include 'overcrowded classrooms, the low standard of the average teacher, both at primary and high-school levels, and the very poor salaries of black teachers over a very long period' (p. 10).

If Bantu education is designed as Mathonsi argues 'to confine Africans to certain forms of labour...an effective bureaucratic machine employed by the capitalist class for the economic and political exploitation of the working class',[4] so far as black students are concerned, one of the pressing attendant problems within this system, in the study of literature, is the compulsory setting of a Shakespeare text. Almost without exception members of the oppressed classes and groups do not have English as their first language. Furthermore, before 1975, English, treated as a foreign language in black schools, only became the medium of instruction at secondary level; since the end of the 1970s it may become the medium of instruction after four years schooling. When we recall that English is not the home language of the children who come to school and that it is not the medium of communication in the everyday lives of most of these schoolchildren, we may, on this basis alone, ask what educative purpose texts written not merely in English but in sixteenth- and seventeenth-century English from another distant culture, will serve in the relatively early years of their acquaintance with a new language. Moreover, it must be borne in mind that the secondary school pupil in DET schools - schools run by the department concerned with black education (there are eighteen different education departments to deal with what the government structures as the different 'groups' in the country) - has only relatively recently been permitted study, in part of the syllabus, of a few South African selected poems and short stories. We may wonder, then, whether the Shakespeare text, so far as the study of English and of literature is concerned, is indeed used at a point in the education of the child when her or his progress in English may be facilitated. Or does its presence in fact inhibit her or his chances of mastering the language?

There are in fact no indications that the Shakespeare text remains central at so early a stage for sound pedagogic reasons. The conditions in black education - including shortage of classrooms and equipment, together with massive overcrowding - makes conceivable use of the text as a means to improve language skills impossible. Questions in examination papers, which determine to an important degree the way the plays are taught, centre on details of plot and the identification of basic information to the exclusion of all else - a procedure designed to retard rather than develop any critical faculty. Most significant, text books designed for students whose first langauge is not English - immensely lucrative for publishers and editors - lay particular stress upon concepts of 'order' in the plays. Quoting on Ulysses's speech on degree to illustrate, the HAUM edition of *Richard III*, for example, published in 1986, identifies, for the Elizabethan world 'a great chain of being', any break in which will 'upset the order of the universe and [create] chaos'.[5] In the Bankside edition of *Macbeth*, which appeared as recently as 1986, very profitably coinciding with the setting of the play for black matriculation students, a more expanded section on order and hierarchy appears, together with a full-page simple drawing to drive home the concept of ordered submission to 'superior' powers.[6] It emphasises to the schoolchildren of the townships, who, as is well known, are frequently engaged - in adverse conditions - in heroic and protracted struggle, the divinely sanctioned virtues of obedience which it finds celebrated in the play and the 'evil' of a 'break in the chain'. It even goes so far as to draw a parallel:

The connections and interactions between Heaven, Mankind and Nature, are, in principle, much like the inter-relationships and interactions studied today in ecology. Ecology is the study of living organisms and groups of people and their relationships with their environments. This science reveals that when the balance of nature is disturbed a chain-reaction results. The most common example is the effect of pollution on Man and Nature. Shakespeare's Great Chain of Being also suffered a chain-reaction when the order of the linked systems was broken. (p. xi)

Such uses of the Shakespeare text should not be taken necessarily as arguments for the abandonment of Shakespeare. The example of post- independent African countries suggests that the Shakespeare text will still have a place in the syllabus, but the timing of its appearance, and the way it is used must surely change.

II The jewel of the language

At present the setting of Shakespeare in South African schools is the work of government-appointed syllabus committees for the multiple groups into which South African education is divided, black, white, Indian, 'coloured'. A law unto themselves, officials in the multiple Departments of Education are unable to provide a reasoned case or explanation for the compulsory and often sole presence of Shakespeare as instance of dramatic literature in the literature syllabus prescribed for all South African schools. For instance when I approached officials located within the department that deals with 'white' education I found that they are unable to explain the rationale for the continuing presence of the Shakespeare text - referred to by one as the 'jewel of the language' - offering responses such as 'we take the text for granted', 'traditionally it has always been there, ever since the days of the old Cape Matriculation Board' and 'Shakespeare is embedded in the very education system itself'. This acceptance of Shakespeare, however, in a system so deliberately designed to achieve particular results, this lack of any desire amongst the bureaucrats who hold complete power over the syllabus to interrogate the presence of the Shakespeare text, cannot but be telling. It argues awareness on the part of government agents of particular kinds of strategic mobilisations of the past[7] and, especially, a non-South African past.

So far as speakers of English as a first language is concerned, use of the Shakespeare text also falls within a tradition of teaching common not merely to South Africa, and one that has been variously described. Ngugi, for instance notes that pre-independent Kenya's English establishment presented

[European]writers, Shakespeare included, as if they were mindless geniuses whose only consistent quality was a sense of compassion. These writers, who had the sharpest and most penetrating observations on the European bourgeois culture, were often taught as if their only concern was with the universal themes of love, fear, birth and death. Sometimes their greatness was presented as one more English gift to the world alongside the Bible and the needle. William Shakespeare and Jesus Christ had brought light to darkest Africa.[8]

And John Drakakis, in another context, notes 'the deification of the man Shakespeare' who, 'removed thus from human history, becomes for us the "Absolute Subject" whose all-embracing "Word" takes its place alongside the Bible as our guarantee of civilisation and humanity'.[9] In South Africa students have been and still are taught Shakespeare and examined on him in ways that entail the assumption of an idealised past; the focus is upon character and interiority, obsession with the 'timeless' and the transcendental all of which, it may be argued, encourage in students a particular view of the subject and attitudes of withdrawal and submission to existing hierarchies.[10] Issues such as those involving language and power, racism or conditions of material struggle, suggested in the texts, are deliberately avoided in the teaching of undergraduate university students as well as schoolgoers, who lodged within a social order that powerfully exploits language to turn the wrong side of many of the sentences it uses outward, are by such avoidances, further distracted from potential recognition of alternative evidences of the nature of their subjection.

Furthermore the determination of apartheid education in the teaching of literature to choose especially the Shakespeare text and literature mainly from England indicates, amongst many of the other deliberate absences evident in state pedagogic aims, an active uninterest in fostering in pupils awareness of South African literature. Ngugi, writing of that mental universe which colonialism sought in Kenya to dominate in order to ensure its control, recalls a similar attitude in university English departments in pre-independence Kenya.[11]

In South Africa, it is, as I remarked, only recently that the government has allowed relatively minimal encounter, in schools, with a few selected mainly white South African authors. Even at tertiary level, where some universities have radically altered their approach in the last decade or so, others cling to an overwhelming emphasis upon literatures of England and the United States. As is well known, colonialist practice encourages awareness only of the literature of the metropolis as a form of control, convenient as means of distraction and disablement. Such processes of dissociation work to divorce and alienate subordinate peoples especially from their immediate environment.

Hardly any of the plays examined in this book, barring perhaps in most cases one or two Fugard texts, is likely to have featured at secondary level, and very few of them, outside the relatively new drama departments in some universities - which have comparatively small student enrolments - appear within syllabuses at tertiary level. Both in the past and at present, for almost the entire population, from whom the future generation will draw its educationists, professionals and leaders, theatre and drama means almost exclusive focus upon a few selected Shakespeare texts. Yet Njabulo Ndebele stresses that, even at the level of basic language usage:

the role of English in South Africa is a matter the complexity of which goes far beyond the convenience and correctness of its use, for that convenience, and that very correctness, are, in essence, problematic. The problem is that recourse to them is fraught with assumptions. Recourse to them begs fundamental historical, cultural and political questions on the assumption that everyone knows what issues are at stake. But, in fact, we cannot assume the validity of premises that have not themselves been scrutinised carefully.[12]

III Shakespeare the conqueror

In 1985-86, when South Africa was experiencing greater struggle, resistance, and turmoil than at any other time in its history, members of the English establishment, founded the Shakespeare Society of Southern Africa and elected Guy Butler, now Emeritus Professor of English at Rhodes and author of numerous poetry and prose works as well as plays, President. The Society - whose bardolatrous condition is evident in the locution which graces its letterhead, 'he was not of an age but for all time', and in its published description of the hallowed moment when 'a Johannesburg journalist suggested that a South African Shakespeare Society should be formed' (thus winning for himself at a stroke, presumably a touch of bardic immortality)[13] - expresses a reformist intention. It promises, in its annual journal and elsewhere, an enquiry into teaching methods and textbooks but with little awareness of the continuing problems within education as well as within the apartheid social order. Thus Butler himself in a message to his members in the first number of the Society's journal asserts:

Perhaps we need to be reminded that Shakespeare has spread in continents that were never colonised by Britain at all. His steady conquest of Europe in the eighteenth and nineteenth centuries took place without benefit of politics or economics.[14]

He also, in the same message, by means of a patronising version of dreams of a democratic millennium, sidesteps the central problem of the way in which the Shakespeare text is presently put to use within South Africa not only in black schools but in white education as well. A report published in the second and most recent issue of the society's journal recognises more honestly the effects of current practice within the Shakespeare text in South Africa.[15] It notes in its conclusion that 'in many respects the present experience of Shakespeare in the schools is doing little to justify his presence in the curriculum on linguistic, aesthetic, literary or personal grounds', while 'in many cases it is apparent that the kinds of assumptions governing the determination to retain Shakespeare studies in the curriculum are not of an educational nature' (p. 74). But it does this only to propose as solutions 'production of appropriate resource material' (by implication appearing, too, to welcome and sanction the Bankside *Macbeth*), 'local initiatives', the development of 'classroom based teaching approaches', a 'fresh look' (etc., etc.) (pp. 75-6). Moreover, the Society's establishment of an education trust confirms the perpetuation of the assimilationist and colonialist discourse so favoured amongst the South African ruling classes of earlier decades and also, indeed, prominent in Butler's own plays. It declares that 'like many precious things, Shakespeare is not easy to teach, particularly to those who do not have English as a mother tongue. Some of us, who have it as a birthright, feel that we ought to make his work more accessible to others'.[16] Moreover, in his message in the first number of the society's journal, Butler sees fit to point out to the then fiercely contestatory oppressed classes that while their problems may be categorised as 'urgent', concern with Shakespeare is of 'permanent importance' (p. v).

IV Shakespeare's rising shares

On Saturday 29 April 1988, at the Alexander Theatre in Johannesburg, now the home of the government-subsidised Performing Arts Council of the Transvaal, the Shakespeare Society held a premiere of the PACT production of *The winter's tale*, which presented an interesting intersection of state and English establishment interests. The Shakespeare Society of Southern Africa has an all-white executive committee almost every one of whom has strong affiliations either with Rhodes University itself or with the Rhodes-based 1820 Settler Foundation. Giving strong support to the Shakespeare Society, this Foundation is primarily concerned to preserve what it sees as its English heritage. It is responsible for the erection of a monument on one of the hills overlooking Grahamstown, where flags of the four counties from which the settlers originally come still blow in the South African wind, and is responsible too for a festival of drama held annually for the past decade or so at Grahamstown. The event has generated considerable support for the generation of new South African plays, but it remains patronised almost exclusively each year by members of the white middle classes throughout the country able to afford the no small expense involved, bringing considerable revenue to hoteliers, shop-keepers and restaurateurs in Grahamstown itself. The festival is hardly patronised by the township dwellers on the outskirts in an area of the country that remains severely economically depressed and in which a recent figure described the unemployment rate as 70 per cent.

This festival was instituted, amongst others, by a past professor of drama at Rhodes university, who, a member of the executive of the Shakespeare Society and of the executive of the 1820 Settlers Founda-tion, at present heads the English Drama Department of the govern-ment-controlled apartheid South African Television Corporation. He was also at the time of the premiere of *The winter's tale* a director of the Local and Overseas Leisure Corporation, a film and record company which sponsored the premiere for the Shakespeare Society. The Shakes-peare Society itself, although only recently and in turbulent times formed, has nevertheless won major sponsorship from South African capital including the Chairman's Fund of the formidable Anglo-American Corporation, the Standard Bank Group of Companies, and Information Services Management who replaced IBM on their decision to withdraw from South Africa - representatives of whom were present at the premiere. Moreover, as well as the head of the English Drama Department of South African television, a sizeable number of the staff of SATV then currently working on a televised version of the PACT production attended. This galaxy of establishment-oriented dignitaries forming - apart from two black individuals - a totally white audience included also teachers and academics, amongst whom numbered professors of English departments from the Universities of the Witwatersrand, South Africa, the Rand Afrikaans University, Pretoria and Vista (a 'tribal' university recently established on the Witwatersrand). Professor Butler's address to this audience about the society and its aims was met with much applause to complement the tangible monetary support which the society had by then already received. And on the very next morning after the premiere, South African Television screened an account of the event and an interview with Butler, facilities, needless to say that have never been offered to cultural organisations emanating from the oppressed classes.

V Impacting Shakespeare on national screen and stage

Shakespeare, as can be imagined, has never provided a problem in production for either the government-subsidised theatre or for South African Television. Any sense in their productions that the texts may include a clash of discourses or explore the nature of power, reflect the contradictions apparent at a particular historical juncture is absent.[17] *The winter's tale* was chosen for production by PACT because it was currently the matriculation setwork for the white schools under the Transvaal Education Department. Black students for that year, required to study a different setwork, were not of course catered for in PACT's choice of play. But this evidence of bias is perhaps not surprising for a subsidised theatre company which has for nearly three decades operated in complete subservience to those discursive formations in the matter of theatre preferred by the state. The practices of PACT, as I noted in chapter 3, one of four provincial arts councils established in 1963 to replace the National Theatre, may stand here as representative of those in the other three.

PACT published a brochure at the end of its first decade in which it quotes the instructions delivered to it at its inception by the Department of Education Arts and Sciences:

Give our performing artists permanent employment, present operas and ballets, provide music and produce plays - in English and Afrikaans. We want high standards. Our people should no longer have to travel abroad to see the best. The Transvaal's your domain, every corner of it. Similar organisations will cover the other provinces. Here is R121,000.00. And with this shot in the arm the performing arts should flourish!'[18]

It proudly announces in its brochure that at the end of its first decade its subsidies - drawn from taxes paid by all the inhabitants of South Africa - had increased. From the state it now received R600,000.00, while the provincial administration's contribution increased to R677,000.00 and that of various Transvaal municipalities to R130,000.00. No figures are given in PACT's publication after its second decade in 1983, but it was during this period that the organisation took up residence, according to its own publicity 'in one of the most luxurious and comfortable theatres in the world, the State Theatre Pretoria'[19] a building on which literally tens of millions of rands of taxpayers' money has been spent. It is this building in which the cast of *District Six: the musical*, refused to play, despite a booking engagement there, because of what the administration resident in Pretoria - largely responsible too for the building of that theatre - had done to District Six in Cape Town.

PACT describes its aim in its first brochure as:

to present the whole spectrum of dramatic art to the whole of the Transvaal, both in English and Afrikaans...strict attention must also be paid to quality, whether a classic tragedy or a simple farce...and the careers of the actor, the producer and the designer must be made secure.[20]

However, as in the choice of a Shakespeare text to play to audiences comprising largely white matriculation students, so, in every other respect, what this organisation actually practises suggests that it attaches a precise and very narrow meaning to what it proclaims to be its concern for 'the whole spectrum of dramatic art', 'the whole of the Transvaal', the security of the artists who work for it.

So far as the production of South African plays is concerned, PACT over the years, as I noted in chapter 7, has perfected the policy evident in its predecessor, the National Theatre Organisation, of performing a majority of Afrikaans plays whilst choosing North American and European plays instead of South African plays for performance in English. Given PACT's dearth of attention to drama in English, that particularly at the end of the 1960s and from the first half of the 1970s on has emerged within the South African social formation, the preference on the part of this subsidised organisation for European and North American plays, confirms that its continued avoidance is a matter of policy - one which serves to encourage colonial, North American and Eurocentric visions. Its self-advertised interest in 'the whole spectrum of dramatic art' excludes the voices of the dissenting and the oppressed, a policy evident in the other Performing Arts Councils too - except for the production, with equivocal results, by PACT of *Poppie* and the Performing Arts Council of the Cape, CAPAB's productions of Fugard at the beginning of the 1970s. No evidence of the production of any work by a black dramatist in PACT's list of productions up to the 1980s exists. Similarly, in its first decade, roughly 450 artists according to its brochure, worked in PACT productions, with not a single black artist amongst them. This picture remains the same for the second decade, with a minor difference: of about 600 artists six at a rough count are black. This number, at best suggestive of a somewhat hesitant tokenism (including a recent somewhat notorious attempt to absorb Gibson Kente and some work by Peter Sepuma) may have increased very slightly since then, but, needless to say, no permanently-based black directors or administrators of PACT with controlling powers have yet emerged.

It is in this context that PACT's fairly regular choice of a Shakespeare play for production should be seen. Whilst there can be no objection to performances of Shakespeare in South Africa, subsidised theatre chooses Shakespeare and other European and North American texts as part of a state policy which marginalises as much as possible that drama written in English directly engaged with the social formation of which PACT itself is part.

The presence of members of South African Television at the Shakespeare Society première of The winter's tale was, as I remarked, in part probably because they were attempting to film the production for later use. Like PACT itself, perhaps more determinedly, South African Television permits, in its own practices, only dominant discursive formations. And this too includes the expenditure of vast amounts on productions of Shakespeare intended to signify no doubt ruling class affiliation with the best in Europe and North America. The increase in the number of Shakespeare productions on South African television is, furthermore, significant in the context of the Corporation's policy of producing for its audiences a combination of pure entertainment or government controlled information, and nothing more. Divided into 'black' and 'white' channels, television, in its English Drama section, marginalised the existence of the oppressed classes as much as possible throughout the 1980s: besides Shakespeare unimaginative and derivative mysteries, thrillers and comedies, poorly made and with little reference to the South African social order were produced. In such ways English drama on South African Television has remained completely submissive to prevailing discursive formations - so much so that the Chairman of the Publications Control Board once observed that he has no occasion to view the work of South African Television because its code is stricter than that of the Board itself.

VI Free Shakespeare

Such intermeshing of state, media and educationist interests suggests the way in which the Shakespeare text has been and largely at present remains used in South Africa. And with the advent of a Shakespeare

Society, the curious formation, in a continuing state of emergency, of a Shakespeare laager, indicates the extent to which Shakespeare is perceived by agents of the dominant order as not merely harmless, but positively useful in reinforcing or perpetuating or, at the very least, not disturbing apartheid structures. It is worth in this context recalling further Drakakis's account of the emergence of a 'culture industry':

'obedient', as Adorno and Horkheimer observe in relation to the general category, 'to the social hierarchy', deeply implicated in 'that process of cataloguing and classification' which brings culture 'within the sphere of the administration'...the growing affinity of 'business' and cultural pleasure, or to use Adorno's and Horkheimer's term, 'amusement', accords a specific political significance to the latter sphere of activity, which is to 'defend society'.[21]

In the matter of the Shakespeare text, both in education and performance, the urgency, as Njabulo Ndebele argues, of the 'need to alter fundamentally the nature of cultural practice itself',[22] or the appeal of Es'kia Mphahlele that members of the English establishment in this country 'disengage from the oppressive, unimaginative and official structures they are serving'[23] has yet to find an adequate response. It is for the sake of the very text they claim to care so much about that the Establishment Shakespeareans should consider too Ngugi's points in a related situation:

a critic who in real life is suspicious of people fighting for liberation will suspect characters who though only in a novel, are fighting for liberation. A critic who in real life is impatient with all the talk about classes, class struggle, resistance to imperialism, racism and struggles against racism, of reactionary versus revolutionary violence, will be equally impatient when he or she finds the same themes dominant in a work of art.[24]

Notes

1 Mathonsi, N., *Black matriculation results: a mechanism of social control*, Johannesburg: Skotaville, 1988, p. 11. See also, for example, Kallaway, Peter, *Apartheid and education*, Johannesburg: Ravan, 1984; F. F. Auerbach, *The power of prejudice in South African education*, Cape Town: Balkema, 1966; Cornevin, M., *Apartheid: power and historical falsification*, Paris: UNESCO, 1980.
2 Quoted in 'The historical roots of Bantu education', anonymous author, *Africa perspective*, XXIV, 1984, pp. 51-2.
3 Kuzwayo Ellen,*Call me woman*, Johannesburg: Ravan, 1987, p. 9.
4 Mathonsi, *Black matriculation results*, p. 11.
5 *Richard III*, Pretoria: De Jager HAUM, 1986, p. vi.

6 Macbeth, Johannesburg: Hodder and Stoughton, 1987, p. xi.

7 Holderness, Graham, 'Preface: all this'. in Holderness, Graham, ed., The Shakespeare myth, Manchester: Manchester University Press, 1988, p. xvi.

8 Wa Thiong'o, Ngugi, Decolonising the mind: the politics of language in African literature, London: James Curry, 1987, p. 91.

9 Drakakis, John, 'Theatre, ideology and institution: Shakespeare and the roadsweepers', in Holderness, The Shakespeare myth, p. 25.

10 See Orkin, Martin, Shakespeare against apartheid, Johannesburg: Donker, 1987, especially ch.1, ch.5.

11 Wa Thiong'o, Decolonising the mind, pp. 90-1.

12 Ndebele, Njabulo S, 'The English language and social change in South Africa', The English academy review, IV, 1987, p. 4.

13 Noted in the Society's information leaflet and application form.

14 Butler, Guy, 'Editorial', Shakespeare in Southern Africa, I, 1987, p. iv.

15 Lemmer, André, 'Upgrading the study of Shakespeare in Southern African secondary schools: an interim report on the schools' text project', Shakespeare in Southern Africa, II, 1988.

16 From a publicity leaflet distributed at the premiere of The winter's tale, mentioned below, to encourage support for 'The Shakespeare Education Trust' recently established by the Society.

17 See Orkin, Martin, 'Quintessence of dust', Speak, I,3, 1978, pp. 46-7.

18 Cited in Decade, published by the Performing Arts Council Transvaal, no date given, but it is likely to have appeared in 1973. Much of the following information comes from this as well as the brochure Decade II published at the end of PACT's second decade, probably in 1983.

19 See Decade II, unnumbered pages.

20 See Decade, unnumbered pages.

21 Drakakis, 'Theatre, ideology, and institution', p. 26.

22 Ndebele, 'The English language and social change', p. 7.

23 Mphahlele, Eskia, 'Prometheus in chains: The fate of English in South Africa', The English academy review, II, 1984, p. 104.

24 Wa Thiong'o, Decolonising the mind, p. 104.

Look back in anger – March 1990

The emergence of South African drama and particularly plays with dominant or exclusive oppressed class participation in the face of sustained repression – especially the deliberate deprivation in townships of theatre space, absence of subsidies and lack of capital – has been over the decades remarkable, frequently heroic. Towards the end of the 1980s Nadine Gordimer, commenting on the cumulative effects of the continuing process of suppression in the South African social order which culminated finally in the draconian censorship measures accompanying the state of emergency initiated in 1986, argued that state laws:

inhibit and mentally impoverish South Africa... the State of Emergency is the culmination of many laws that have been steadily taking over and extending the functions of censorship for some years, sending out tentacles far beyond the reach of a censorship board... The banning of journalists and the closure of newspapers and journals in order to stifle information and weaken independent thinking is a *general* cultural deprivation from which we are not, in our calling, exempt. On the contrary, our task to express, transform in words, in paint, in film, or on a stage, the lives of the people we belong to and live among in our country cannot be fulfilled while we are kept from knowing what is happening to them in the next town, when our knowledge of vital events is restricted to the bald statement of the numbers killed, when the words of a speaker at a meeting can't be quoted to those of us who were not present, when a photographer is turned away by the police or the army from a street drama that will not be recorded as our real, current history. That is the vast extent of censorship today. It is far more fundamental than anything the Publications Control Board could do.[1]

All the plays discussed in this book have been produced within versions of these processes of suppression, although, with the unbanning of the African National Congress, the Pan African Congress, the South African Communist Party and other organisations, and the partial lifting of state censorship of the media, in early 1990, some change in direction appears at last to be sought by sections within the ruling classes. But the continuing impact of these processes should never be underestimated or forgotten. As late as 1988 they were, for instance, active even within the allegedly non-dissident sectors of ruling-class white education, as the following reported incident shows:

A play staged by pupils of Greenside High School in Johannesburg has been withdrawn from two inter-schools drama competitions because aspects of it were found to be offensive by some members of the community, headmaster Mr Kenneth Milne said today. The cast of 'A Dry White Season' were told by Mr Milne this week that the play would no longer participate in the Director's Cup competition organised by the Transvaal Education Department (TED) or the Repertory Amateur Player's Society (Raps) competition open to both TED and private schools. The play was performed in the first round of the Director's Cup competition on May 17. It incorporates readings from the novels of Andre Brink and Nadine Gordimer, a section in which pupils mime a death in detention, the simultaneous singing of Die Stem [the official anthem of South Africa] and Nkosi Sikelel 'iAfrika [commonly used by the majority as the national anthem of South Africa] and a series of slides showing protests and poverty in the townships. Pupils and parents are under the impression that the TED was instrumental in banning the play. But the director for the TED, Dr P. H. Bredenkamp, said: 'Such matters are left to the direction of the principal and his staff'. Mr Milne said it was a domestic matter. The parent of one of the cast members, Professor John van Zyl of Wits University's School of Dramatic Art, said he was perturbed by the decision. He said judges praised the play but said a TED official said it was too much of a 'protest' play.[2]

Drama has been continually subject, as this book itself is, to processes designed by a state actively engaged, as I remarked at the outset, in the obfuscation of existing relations and processes. In a manner of speaking indeed, in South Africa a very special, crude, even grotesque version of what in other contexts has been referred to as *suture* takes place. The space opened up by theatre on the South African stage, remains one that in certain respects continues to be disabled by the active determination of the state to *ensure* absence, to promote only plays that provide a coherence for the spectator structuring views offering apartheid fixities. The state's 'induced suture' in the dramatic work is such that in a loose sense – in the South African space to which the stage space attempts to relate – its point of origin is, through legislative and hegemonic process deliberately undermined.

Consequently, as I have argued in this book, the practice of and study of drama has been and continues to be difficult where for so long the state has banned scripts or intimidated and persecuted their authors. As I have also noted, the imperial and colonial centres and then the apartheid centre with its control of establishment media, theatre and publication have further seen to it that even where plays, particularly from the subordinate classes, have been performed, they still remain marginalised. Thus, where the student may turn without difficulty to, for example, Fugard's diaries, even now there remains relatively little published information from or about practitioners such as Kente, Mhangwane, Manaka, Maponya, Ngema, Mtwa, Maqina – to say nothing of the existence or availability of published playtexts. The collection published in America *Woza Afrika!* which includes *Gangsters, Children of Asazi, Asinamali!* and *Bopha!* is still not easily obtainable in South Africa. South African theatre remains subject to either openly legislated or hegemonically induced absences and erasures in a multitude of other ways. For instance – barring only a few attempts noted in chapter 7 – master/mistress-servant relationships in their multiple versions have not been scrutinised. Nor have the actual relations of domination and subordination in the ordinary everyday context, understood in terms of particular elements of cruelty and indifference, barbarism or amorality beyond a certain point been explored. Some plays both within South Africa and by a playwright in exile have addressed the South African Defence force's role, but mainly in terms of teenage rites of passage, rather than in terms of the South African government's military adventures and what these signify.[3] No concern as yet has been paid either to the army's role in the townships in the 1980s or to issues raised by the End Conscription Campaign. The imprisonment of children in jails, the fact that policing the townships has been taken over by blacks and vigilantes, producing in parts of the country forms of civil war and bloodshed in which police appear complicit – the state violence this bespeaks – also remains largely absent from the stage. And the role of state agents within government institutions or agents of large corporations, and the role of those countries abroad whose substantial support perpetuates present structures, has not been touched on. To attempt to break these or other silences on the South African stage, it should never be forgotten, still requires acts of courage in spaces potentially full of danger.

If *Sarafina!* ends with the dream of the freeing of Nelson Mandela, this book has been completed in the heady days following not only the actual release of Mandela, Walter Sisulu, Ahmed Kathrada and other prisoners but also President F. W. de Klerk's unbanning of organisations, while, to the disapproval of their respective right and left wings, the Nationalist Government and the African National Congress stand poised for some form of negotiation. South African Television, which until two or so weeks ago, had presented South Africa in programme after programme as a vast game reserve populated by wild life and caring (white) veterinary doctors, or as farms on which South African wine might be endlessly drunk, always of course marginalising or erasing the existence of oppressed classes and groups, now contains lengthy interviews with members of the African National Congress at prime news time and even broadcasts extracts from Nelson Mandela's speeches. At the same time, warring factions in Natal increase their violence upon one another, guns and ammunition are reported in the newspapers as being out of stock in armoury shops, the racist right-wing tries to organise its own resistance, the horror of hit-squads with connections in the police and the defence force is slowly unravelling.

In what must be a hopeful, even thrilling but dangerously unpredictable period, many of the plays discussed in this book still bear witness, as they always will, to that which has for so long blighted this country. But, as important, in their very determination to address directly, represent or fictively interact with the social order from which they come, they provide a glimpse of and prepare for a democratic South Africa – one freer and more able to tolerate both difference and dialogue than the worlds in which they have until now often had to struggle to claim some space. In the strength and courage of their moves towards contestation, dissent and dialogue, lies part of their value, not only as anti-apartheid statements, but as drama.

Notes

1 Gordimer, Nadine, 'Censorship and the artist', *Staffrider*, VII, 2, 1988, pp. 15-16.
2 *The Star*, Friday 27 May 1988, p. 4.
3 See Akerman, Anthony, *Somewhere on the border*, Amsterdam: Thekwini Theatre, 1983.

Index